REAL ESTATE BROKERAGE MANAGEMENT

SECOND EDITION

Bruce Lindeman

Professor of Finance and Real Estate
H. Clyde Buchanan Professor of Real Estate
University of Arkansas at Little Rock

Prentice Hall, Englewood Cliffs, New Jersey 07632

Library of Congress Cataloging-in-Publication Data

Lindeman, Bruce.
    Real estate brokerage management.

    Includes bibliographies and index.
    1. Real estate business—United States—Management.
I. Title.
HD255.L55 1988   333.33'068   87-32847
ISBN 0-13-762469-7

To Patty

Editorial/production supervision
and interior design: **Eleanor Ode Walter**
Cover design: **Ben Santora**
Manufacturing buyer: **Barbara Kittle, Margaret Rizzi**

Printed in the United States of America

10 9 8 7 6 5 4 3 2 1

ISBN 0-13-762469-7

Prentice-Hall International (UK) Limited, *London*
Prentice-Hall of Australia Pty. Limited, *Sydney*
Prentice-Hall Canada Inc., *Toronto*
Prentice-Hall Hispanoamericana, S.A., *Mexico*
Prentice-Hall of India Private Limited, *New Delhi*
Prentice-Hall of Japan, Inc., *Tokyo*
Simon & Schuster Asia Pte. Ltd., *Singapore*
Editora Prentice-Hall do Brasil, Ltda., *Rio de Janeiro*

CONTENTS

PREFACE   vii

Part One   Real Estate Brokerage and Its Business Environment

ONE   INTRODUCTION   1

The Brokerage Business   3
The Management Approach to Real Estate Brokerage   6
The Scope of Our Study   8
Real Estate Principles Background Reading   10

TWO   THE NATURE AND FUNCTION OF REAL ESTATE BROKERAGE   12

Characteristics of the Real Estate Brokerage Business   13
The Brokerage Process   15
The Brokerage and the Law   20
State and Local Legislation   21
Federal Legislation   23
Professionalism   25
Discussion Questions and Projects   29
References   29

THREE   THE LEGAL ENVIRONMENT OF REAL ESTATE BROKERAGE   30

Vulnerability to Legal Action   31
Licensure   32
License Law   33
Broker and Salesperson   37
Infractions of License Law   40
Agency Law   42
General Contract Law   44
Requirements of Valid Contracts   46
Duress, Misrepresentation and Fraud   50

Discharge and Breach of Contract   51
Conclusion   54
Discussion Questions and Projects   54
References   57

Part Two   *Management and Personnel in the Brokerage Business*

FOUR   BROKERAGE MANAGEMENT CONCEPTS   58

Business Functions   59
Organization of Brokerage Firms   62
The Management Function   67
Brokerage Personnel   72
Evaluating Personnel Needs   74
Support Personnel   75
Discussion Questions and Projects   76
References   77

FIVE   EMPLOYMENT AGREEMENTS   78

Independent Contractor   79
Problems with the Independent Contractor Relationship   84
The Salesperson's Contract   86
Support Personnel   93
Discussion Questions and Projects   94
References   95

SIX   PERSONNEL SELECTION   96

Recruitment Sources   97
The Selection Process   100
Support Personnel Selection   111
Termination   113
Discussion Questions and Projects   114
References   115

SEVEN   THE POLICY MANUAL   116

Purpose of the Policy Manual   117
Arrangement of the Manual   118
The Policy Manual and Independent Contractors   119
Revision   119
Example   119
Discussion Questions and Projects   128
References   128

Part Three   *Marketing Management*

EIGHT LISTING MANAGEMENT   129

Contract Form Design   130
Listing Contracts   131
Establishing the Right to the Commission   135
Listing Policy   138
Listing Information   141
Setting Commission Rates   141
Dissolving Listing Contracts   146
Discussion Questions and Projects   147
References   149

NINE   MARKET OPERATIONS   150

Sale Contracts   151
Offers   153
Cooperating with Other Brokerage Firms   158
Franchising   161
Information Services   162
Settlement   163
Defaults   168
Discussion Questions and Projects   172
References   174

TEN COMPENSATION OF SALESPEOPLE   175

Commission Sharing   176
Incentive Plans   180
Company Listings and Referrals   183
Nonmoney Compensation   186
Compensation During Training of New Salespeople   187
Discussion Questions and Projects   188
References   189

ELEVEN   SALES MANAGEMENT   190

Sales Meetings   191
Training   192
Contests and Incentives   193
Marketing Procedure   194
Prospect Management   199
Property Advertising   200
Assisting Buyer Financing   204
Broker Liability   205
Proper Performance   206
Discussion Questions and Projects   207
References   209

Part Four   *The Professional Brokerage*

TWELVE FINANCIAL CONTROL   211

Requirements   212
Some Basic Financial Concepts   212
The Company Dollar and Profits   214
Profit Analysis of the Average Sale   215
Budgeting   215
Identifying Financial Problem Areas   216
Cost Effectiveness of Personnel   217
Insuring the Business   220
Using Borrowed Money   221
Starting Up   222
Startup Example   225
Discussion Questions and Projects   229
References   230

THIRTEEN THE WORKING ENVIRONMENT   231

Locating the Office   232
Office Layout   237
Furnishings and Equipment   241
Computer Facilities   243
Outside the Office   246
Discussion Questions and Projects   248
References   248

FOURTEEN ESTABLISHING AND MARKETING THE SUCCESSFUL
REAL ESTATE BROKERAGE   249

Establishing a New Brokerage Firm   250
Choosing the Market Area and Segment   252
Marketing the New Brokerage   254
Publicity   256
Advertising in Media   258
Brokerage Office Open Houses   259
Mailouts   260
Advertising Cost: The New and the Established Firm   263
Identification of the Firm   263
A Final Word: Philosophy and Policy   266
Discussion Questions and Projects   266
References   267
Appendix: REALTOR® Code of Ethics   268

Index   272

PREFACE

There are tens of thousands of real estate brokerage firms in the United States. Brokerage is one of our most popular small business endeavors; however, since several large firms employing hundreds of people also exist, it is a business which has excellent potential for growth and success.

To most people, real estate brokerage appears to be concerned largely with salesmanship, with success dependent upon the listing and selling capabilities of the sales force. While this is true, it is not the whole truth. Real estate brokerage is a *business,* and to be successful, a brokerage firm has to be properly operated. There may have been a time when selling ability alone was enough, but in today's competitive market the ability to operate a brokerage firm as an efficient business is just as significant as the quality of the service the firm provides. In today's successful brokerage firm, the management personnel (principal brokers, sales managers) spend little or no time on direct listing and selling because the company's organization, control, and finances require their full-time attention. It is this aspect of the real estate brokerage business that this book addresses.

These pages contain little about the mechanics of listing and selling, sales techniques, or negotiating. Rather, we are concerned with the *management* of the business: planning, organization, control and financial well-being. A great many new firms are created every year and most of them eventually fail. While the reasons for failure are many, much of the time it is because of improper management and the confusion, inefficiency, and money troubles that result. Many brokerages that survive do so far below their potential for the same reason.

This book is arranged as a text, but it is not intended for classroom use only; the working broker and sales manager will be able to find it of use and value. Additionally, anyone considering owning and/or operating a real estate brokerage business should be aware of the concepts and ideas contained here, even if a salesperson's license already is held. Approaching the operation of a full-fledged brokerage firm armed only with the skills and knowledge associated with the selling process is a very risky venture. However, since most states require that an individual's broker's license be preceded by a certain period of licensure as a salesperson, we can assume with reasonable safety that someone interested in the independence of a brokerage operation will have acquired some knowledge of the selling process itself. This frees us to concentrate upon the management and organizational aspects of the real estate brokerage business.

ORGANIZATION OF THE BOOK

This book is oriented to the practical application of management techniques and organizational form as they apply to the real estate brokerage business. The specific characteristics and necessities of the brokerage business are given full emphasis, and brokerage-related examples are used throughout the discussion. Every effort has been made to produce a book that will cover all aspects of the management of the real estate brokerage enterprise.

The book incorporates a number of special features: Case experiences are included in most of the chapters; these are real-life incidents and situations that illustrate particular points. While they may have been edited slightly to make them more suitable to the book's direction and tone, the significant aspects of the actual experience they relate has been left intact. Illustrations, graphics, tables, and other material have been chosen to augment the text discussion and should be read and examined along with it. The bibliographic references at the ends of the chapters are intended to provide useful direction to additional reading which will augment or further illuminate points raised in the chapter. Discussion questions, also provided at the ends of the chapters, will direct the reader or student to examine particular topics in further detail.

An entire chapter is devoted to the legal situation of the brokerage firm: contract, agency and licensing law are emphasized. Examination of the hearing records of the real estate commissions and other regulatory licensing agencies of the states will reveal that without exception, the majority of complaints they hear concern improper practice by licensees in these areas. In recent times, the emerging field of consumer advocacy has begun to seek potential paydirt in the area of proper and legal performance by real estate licensees who ignore or are unaware of all of the law under which they operate; see Chapters 3 and 11.

The book is arranged in four parts. Part One, Real Estate Brokerage and Its Business Environment, contains three chapters. They introduce the real estate brokerage business and the business, economic, and legal environments within which it operates. These chapters will provide the fundamental basis upon which the rest of the book rests.

Chapter 1 introduces the study of real estate brokerage and provides a preview of the study pattern of the book and its subject matter. Also included is a brief list of typical books on real estate principles for the reader who has no real estate background. Chapter 2 presents an overview of the real estate brokerage business and its function in our modern society and economy. The brokerage process and its methods are reviewed, and professional approaches to the business are discussed. Chapter 3 is devoted to consideration of the legal framework within which the real estate brokerage business operates. Particular attention is given to licensing laws, agency law, and contract law.

Part Two, Management and Personnel in the Brokerage Business, introduces the concepts of management in a brokerage framework. While the management approach is used throughout the book, after the introductory management chapter the remainder of this part considers the relationships with and control of the brokerage's personnel, particularly the sales force.

Chapter 4 introduces the basic concepts of management that come into play in the brokerage industry. Organization of the firm, patterns of management, and the functions of management are discussed. Once these matters have been presented, attention is given to the initial discussion of personnel selection and management.

Chapter 5 considers the arrangements and contracts that exist between the brokerage firm and its personnel. Particular attention is given to the very important features and requirements of the independent contractor form of employment with respect to sales personnel. Specific discussion of the requirements of the legal agreements between brokerages and salespeople is also included.

Chapter 6 presents the methods and problems of personnel selection by the real estate brokerage firm. Sources of potential salespeople, the recruitment process, the selection process, and the choice of sales personnel are presented.

Chapter 7 is devoted entirely to discussion of the firm's policy manual—the statement of policy and goals each firm should have and make available to its personnel. An example of such a manual is included.

Part Three, Marketing Management, considers the management of the sales activity of the real estate brokerage firm. While this book does not present the "how to's" of successful selling, it is necessary to examine the procedures and controls that management uses to maximize the productivity of its sales force.

Chapter 8 considers the firm's policy with respect to the listing of real estate for sale. The design and use of a proper listing contract form is discussed, followed by consideration of the legal means of assuring the firm's right to a commission upon the sale of listed property. Other important uses of the various kinds of listings, accumulation of information on listed property, and setting the proper commission fee to be charged also are discussed. The chapter concludes with a discussion of the dissolution of listing contracts.

Chapter 9 concerns the firm's policy in the process of selling listed property. The sale contract and its form introduce the discussion, which is followed by consideration of the offer and acceptance procedure. Specific topics of concern in this area are discussed. These include cooperation with other brokerage firms, multiple listing, franchising, information services, and the settlement process. A final word is devoted to the firm's policies with respect to default of contract by buyer, seller, or both.

Chapter 10 considers the compensation of the salesperson. Means and policies of commission sharing are discussed, along with incentive pay plans.

Attention also is given to the use of company referrals and company listings as compensation, and to various other means of nonmonetary support to the salesperson.

Chapter 11 is devoted to sales management. The various procedures of controlling, training, and motivating the sales force are considered. Marketing procedure policy is given considerable attention, as is the use by the firm of property advertising. The chapter also considers finding financing for buyers, broker liability, and proper performance.

Part Four, The Professional Brokerage, focuses on management problems affecting the entire brokerage firm rather than its component parts. We now are treating the firm as a complete, self-contained business, and will investigate the functions of management in the assurance of initial and continued success of the brokerage business enterprise.

Chapter 12 discusses the proper administration of the firm's financial resources and obligations. The concepts of costs, cash flow, the company dollar, financing, and cost control are presented in a framework devoted to their significance in the brokerage business.

Chapter 13 considers the physical space and equipment needs of the firm and its sales force. Office layout, equipment, and location are discussed, along with the needs of the individual salesperson.

Chapter 14 concludes the book. It discusses the problems of establishing a successful brokerage business and considers the important topic of marketing the brokerage firm itself to the public in a competitive business environment.

It is expected that the reader has the knowledge contained in a basic course in the principles of real estate or the reading knowledge contained in any of the well-known and widely used texts for such courses. A serious and conscious effort has been made to eliminate unnecessary material from the discussion. While it is tempting for an author to increase the thickness of a book with frequent rehashes of the same material, irrelevant tables and illustrations and the like, my goal has been to avoid such tactics and concentrate upon a clear and readable presentation of the subject matter.

CHANGES IN THE SECOND EDITION

As I write this, the first edition is in its seventh year. Its acceptance has been most gratifying, and has increased year by year. The real estate brokerage business is not characterized by frequent upheavals and wholesale change. However, over a period of years changes do occur, even though they may be subtle or in degree rather than substance. I have tried to incorporate these changes into this edition. Many users of the book have provided helpful suggestions, and I thank them all. Most of these dealt with detail, another gratifying indication that the first edition hit its target pretty well.

Readers familiar with the first edition will find most of it intact in these pages. To be sure, there has been updating and some rearrangement. A few paragraphs have been deleted; these dealt with matters no longer relevant to the subject. Most of the changes for this edition have been the addition of material on new subjects or the expansion of an existing discussion.

End-of-chapter references have been updated. Chapter 5 now incorporates the clarifying law and rules on independent contractor. Added to Chapter 9 is a discussion of the terms of sale reporting requirements of the Tax Reform Act of 1986 and a section on buyer qualification. Chapter 11 has new sections on assisting buyer financing and the evolving problem of broker liability. Chapter 12 now has a greatly expanded section on insuring the brokerage business. Also, the somewhat confusing and very long Figure 12–1 in the first edition has now become a separate text section; I hope this rearrangement will make it clearer. The discussion of computer usage in Chapter 13 has been expanded and completely updated.

ACKNOWLEDGEMENTS

I would like to thank the following for their help on this book: Eleanor Walter, production editor; Catherine Rossbach, acquisitions editor; and Sharon Pelt, who reviewed this text in an early version. I would also like to thank my wife Patty for her forbearance and patience.

No book is perfect. Therefore, I earnestly solicit comments and suggestions from readers, who can write to me in care of the publisher.

BRUCE LINDEMAN
January, 1988

A SPECIAL NOTE TO READERS

Please note that when you read "he," "his," or "him" in this book, that they are being used in their grammatical sense and refer to women as well as men.

ONE

INTRODUCTION

The Brokerage Business

The Management Approach to Real Estate Brokerage

The Scope of Our Study

Real Estate Principles Background Reading

The real estate brokerage business is one that holds fascination and excitement for many people. It offers the opportunity for considerable independence to rely on one's own capabilities. The business can start as small as one that can be run in the owner's home, but it has the potential to grow to great size. The real estate broker can have a significant impact upon his home community and, as the years pass, can point with pride to a great many highly visible and lasting results of his work.

To someone who is unfamiliar with the real estate business, it looks deceptively easy. After all, doesn't a broker just put a sign in someone's yard, show people around the house a few times, and find a buyer? And doesn't he collect a handsome commission every time he does so? Of course, the experienced real estate salesperson knows there's much more to it than that, but each year several hundred thousand people sit for state real estate licensing examinations so that they may become eligible to join this lucrative business. And each year nearly as many others—people who already have obtained licenses and tried their luck—drop out of the business. Perhaps one licensee in ten manages to make a decent living, but his success attracts thousands of others who attempt it.

Success in the real estate brokerage business demands many qualities. The successful broker must be at ease with people and be able to convince them of his sincerity and reliability. He must have an excellent knowledge of the law, even though he cannot practice law in and of itself. He must be able to manage his personal life to accommodate his chosen work, since the real estate licensee works odd hours for an irregular, commission-based income. He faces a considerable number of business risks that no one else can help him with: He is at the mercy not only of the fluctuations of his local real estate market, but of the financial markets as well. When mortgage money is scarce or when economic conditions shrink the demand for real estate, he must tighten his belt and work harder than ever to get a decent share of the business available. When times are good, he finds that practically everyone else seems to be licensed and competing for business. He usually has no regular salary to fall back on and so must handle his personal finances very carefully. In compensation, he usually can hold onto his job (since he is, in effect, the creator of his job), but in bad times he may find that although he doesn't lose it, the job can just dwindle away unless he works hard.

And of course, as in any business, the successful broker must be an expert in his chosen work. He must know his community, its practices, and its preferences. His customers expect him to be aware of property value trends and neighborhood developments; they feel quite free to ask him practically anything and to get a proper and informative answer. He has to have the psychological instincts to be able to shepherd nervous buyers and sellers whose transactions, to them, are of vital and overriding importance, and he is expected to bring these transactions to successful conclusions that satisfy all parties.

All these things may not be apparent to someone who watches from outside as a competent broker goes about his business. Observers see the "large" commission rates, the FOR SALE and SOLD signs, but not the immense amount of work and experience necessary to get these results. In this book we will examine this work and show some of the things necessary for it to be successful.

THE BROKERAGE BUSINESS

Real estate brokerage encompasses a large number of services. Most observers relate brokerage to selling houses, but all kinds of real estate are handled in the business. Some firms specialize in certain kinds, though it is true that many firms tend to concentrate on *residential sales* (the selling of houses), both new and *resales* (older houses being sold by owner-users rather than builders).

Beyond residential sales, real estate brokers are involved in the sale and rental of all other kinds of properties, each with its own features, problems, and required knowledge. There is a full spectrum of *investment property*, ranging from duplex structures to apartment projects, shopping centers, office parks and buildings, industrial properties and more, from the very small to the very large. Brokers handle *land sales*: from parcels of "raw," undeveloped land to building sites; entire subdivisions; downtown commercial sites; and the assembly of large tracts of land, for a variety of purposes, by combining the purchases of smaller parcels. Some brokers sell entire businesses, as well as the buildings and land they occupy. Others specialize in the sale of farms, recreational properties, and so on.

In addition to sales, brokers handle *real estate leasing*. Some handle only the transaction of leases, but the field of property management can include handling for a property owner all transactions associated with investment property such as maintenance, hiring personnel (janitors, resident managers, etc.), recordkeeping, and more. Many brokers expand their businesses to include the provision of *related services* such as property insurance, mortgage brokering, and investment analysis and advisement. Also, many brokers engage directly in such activities as *land development* and *construction*. Clearly, the real estate brokerage field is considerably more far-reaching and involved than is apparent to the casual observer.

Function of Brokerage

In essence, the real estate broker is hired by the owner of a property to arrange a sale of the property or to arrange for one or more tenants to rent it. The broker signs a *listing contract* with the property owner, in which the terms of the broker's employment are spelled out. Normally, the broker's compensation is in the form of a *commission*: a certain percentage of the sale price or rental value of the property. He is paid when he has done his job. In a sale arrangement, he usually collects his commission at the time title to the property is transferred to the buyer and the sale becomes an accomplished fact. In a rental arrangement, he either collects a certain sum when the lease begins or takes a percentage of each of the tenants' rent payments. Sometimes the commission is arranged so that he does both. (It should be noted that the broker, under the law of many states, actually *earns* the commission before the transaction is consummated, even though he is not paid until then. This point is discussed more thoroughly in Chapter 3.)

The Brokerage Process

Once he has secured a *listing* (signed a listing contract with a property owner), the broker begins marketing the property. He advertises it, contacts potential buyers, and often advises other brokers that the listing exists. As potential buyers appear, he screens or *qualifies* them, determining that they are indeed potentially capable buyers of the particular property. To do so, he examines their needs and their financial situation. If the property is not what they need or if they cannot afford it, there is no point in showing them the listed real estate. However, even though a particular interested buyer turns out not to be a good prospect for a certain property, the broker does not lose interest. Instead, he tries to find the buyer a more suitable purchase. In this manner brokers may show a variety of properties to buyers who originally responded to the marketing of real estate they were not actually qualified to buy.

When a qualified prospect is determined to be interested in a property, the broker arranges to *show* it by taking the prospect to the property and allowing him to see it for himself. In order to describe the property properly and to answer the prospect's questions, the broker has to be intimately acquainted with all its features and drawbacks. Once the showing has occurred, and if the prospect appears to remain interested, the broker begins trying to solicit an *offer*. If an offer is made, the broker takes it to the seller and they discuss it. Sometimes it is accepted, but more often than not it is not entirely satisfactory to the seller and a *counteroffer* is made from the seller to the prospective buyer. The transaction is now in the negotiation stage, and buyer and seller may offer and counteroffer several times before a final arrangement is concluded or it is decided that no common ground exists. In the latter case, the broker tries to find another prospective buyer, and this process continues until the sale is made. At that point, a *contract of sale* will exist between the seller and the buyer; but the broker's job is by no means over.

The contract of sale is an agreement that buyer and seller will actually *transact* the sale at some time in the future; in the meantime they prepare for the transaction. The buyer seeks financing, often with the assistance of the broker. A variety of other activities also must be carried out during this period, including appraisals; surveys; termite inspections; other inspections; preparation of documents such as deeds, mortgages, and the like; and a number of other arrangements. The broker often handles or arranges many of these. Finally, at the *closing,* all papers are signed and all other arrangements are concluded, and the buyer receives a deed from the seller.

Many brokers find it useful to enlist the aid of other brokers in transactions. One broker will arrange with other brokers that if they find buyers for his listings, he will split the commission he earns from the sellers with them. Usually, he also is assured that if he or his staff sell listings of other brokers, they in turn will split their commissions with him. In some areas these arrangements are informal, while in others they are formalized through an arrangement called a *multiple listing service*, or *multilist*.

What we have described are elements of typical brokered transactions, but it should not be inferred that all transaction arrangements are the same for the broker. While brokers usually are employed and paid by owners of properties to be sold or rented, they can also be employed by prospective buyers or tenants to find them suitable quarters. In most states it is legal for a broker to be paid by both parties under certain circumstances, but this commonly occurs only in cases when real estate properties are exchanged rather than sold. Brokers need not accept only commissions as payments; they can contract to receive a flat fee if they wish. They may choose to receive payment in a noncash form, such as a percentage of ownership of the property.

The Broker's Contribution

While many people think of real estate brokerage as essentially a selling exercise, perhaps the most important function of the real estate broker is resolving differences in negotiations and dealing with unexpected events that threaten a transaction. Especially in residential sales, the actual participants in the transaction—buyer and seller—often are inexperienced and not particularly knowledgeable about the alternatives available to them. They are perfectly capable of placing classified ads, putting signs in their yards, and filling out loan applications, and they may even know enough to hire a lawyer or other professional to handle the technical details of the transaction. Many do this, and with some success, to avoid the payment of brokers' commissions. However, it is unlikely that very many can perform these functions with anything like the efficiency and confidence of a professional real estate broker. They waste enormous amounts of time and energy, and many nonbrokered deals fall through because of unanticipated problems.

The broker sells knowledge, expertise, and experience, and this becomes of inestimable value as he assists in arranging well-conceived transactions that foresee the common risks, avoid the common mistakes, and provide satisfaction to all parties. A good broker understands the implications of each deal and explains them thoroughly to the parties involved so that they are fully aware of them and know what to expect. He can tailor each transaction to fulfill everyone's needs, and he should be ready to handle any and all problems that may arise by giving proper, considered advice and by proposing and arranging the necessary solutions. More than anything else, even more than ability as a salesperson, he sells professionalism and experience, and it is this that constitutes by far the most valuable part of his service to his customers.

THE MANAGEMENT APPROACH TO REAL ESTATE BROKERAGE

Real estate brokerage is a business, and for a brokerage business to succeed it must be managed properly. Indeed, the prime cause for business failure in all aspects of commerce is the failure of management to do its job properly. The function of management is to get things done by an organization; most particularly, management should seek the best way of accomplishing the goals and objectives of the firm involved. Management should not be confused with the actual purposeful activity most of the firm's employees engage in; rather, management should see to it that those things get done by the people who are supposed to do them.

The Importance of Management

While it may appear that operating a real estate brokerage means knowing how to list and sell real estate well, that is not by any means true. It is the function of the brokerage firm's *sales force* to be able to list and sell real estate in a profitable manner that fits in with the company's policy. The *management* of the firm has the responsibility of educating and directing the sales force to accomplish this. In a small firm, management may consist of only one person—the broker-owner—and even he may devote a considerable portion of time to listing and selling activities, and may do management only on a part-time basis. Nonetheless, this management is necessary if the firm is to operate efficiently and profitably and if it is to have a good chance to succeed.

Therefore, we must distinguish between management of a brokerage firm and *sales activity,* and in our discussion we will look much harder at the management function than at sales activity. This means that we have no chapters that enumerate the "secrets" of a successful listing or tell how to wangle a reluctant prospect into making an offer. The reasons for this approach are important to understand.

First, management is the key to long-term success. A firm with competent employees but poor management is much less likely to survive than a firm with good management but poor employees. In the first case, management will give the employees the wrong things to do by misreading the market and having employees produce the wrong mix of goods and services for the market. Good employees will probably leave the firm for more secure and more lucrative positions at better managed firms. In the second case, good management can take effective steps to improve the quality of the employees by providing additional training and a more suitable working environment and by replacing poor performers with better ones.

A second reason for emphasizing the management approach is that virtually all individuals seeking to enter the real estate brokerage business must have had at least minimal experience in the selling or leasing aspects of the business. Most states do not permit application for real estate broker licenses unless the applicant has held a salesperson's license for some minimum length of time. Thus, newly licensed brokers are likely to have had some degree of experience doing sales force work, but need not have had any experience at all in the problems associated with properly *managing* a business. Simply because a person has been successful at listing, selling, and/or leasing real estate while in the employ of someone else does not necessarily mean that he will be equally competent and successful when he turns his energies toward managing such a concern.

Finally, we must consider the fact that one can easily fill a good-sized bookcase with literature describing the techniques of successful and profitable listing and selling of all kinds of real estate. However, the search for information on the proper operation of a business whose goals are to do those things is much harder to fulfill. There is a need for this information: The majority of new brokerage firms fail within a very short time. Somehow, the successful salesperson who sets up a business for himself often finds that for some reason the expected profits do not materialize, and at every turn new and unexpected problems arise, problems with no easy solutions.

Organization of the Brokerage

As in any business, a brokerage firm must be managed properly in order to succeed. In any except a one-person operation, some kind of chain of command must be set up. The duties of each person in the organization must be defined so that everyone knows who does what and all the functions of the business are handled efficiently. Brokerage personnel can be classified in three categories, though it must be understood that in many firms, especially smaller ones, an individual may perform functions in more than one category.

Management personnel are in charge of operating the business and seeing to it that everyone else does his job properly. Management determines the goals, objectives, and scope of the firm; hires and fires personnel; and determines their duties. The *sales force* is the group that actually performs the brokerage's main business functions of listing and selling real estate. They are the ones who will produce the company's income. *Support staff* are nonmanagement personnel who perform the nonsales duties that assist the sales personnel. These employees are secretaries, receptionists, accountants, lawyers, and others whose services are necessary to the proper functioning of the brokerage, but who do not engage directly in sales activity or management.

Sales personnel and management personnel in the real estate brokerage business are required to be licensed by the states in which they live and work in order to be able to carry out their jobs legally. The states have two types of licenses, those for *brokers* and those for *salespersons*. The exact nomenclature for these licenses varies slightly from state to state, but each type of license has essentially the same attributes nationwide.

A *broker's license* entitles the holder to establish an independent brokerage business. A *salesperson's license* entitles the holder to engage in the real estate business, but only under the supervision and responsibility of a licensed broker. Although state licensing laws do not specifically refer to it in this way, it might be thought that the salesperson is a sort of apprentice, qualified to engage in some selling activity but not yet considered qualified to act fully on his own and assume full responsibility for what he does.

The broker's license is issued directly to the broker. The salesperson's license actually is issued to the broker who will *hold* that license, and for whom the salesperson will work. Therefore, a licensed salesperson can work for only a single broker, and that broker assumes legal responsibility for everything the salesperson does in the course of business.

The broker has the opportunity to set up his own business, while the salesperson represents someone else's brokerage firm. A licensed broker with his own business is required to fulfill certain requirements in the organization of the firm. He must establish certain trust accounts for the handling of other people's money, and he is responsible for seeing to it that all transactions handled by his firm are properly done. He must also make sure that unlicensed employees do not engage in any sales activity and that his licensed salespeople do business properly and within the law. All this requires careful supervision, since it is dictated by law and especially since the sales force by its very nature operates independently. The broker can rarely be physically present every time a salesperson solicits a listing, solicits an offer, or shows a property.

THE SCOPE OF OUR STUDY

Real estate brokerage firms come in all sizes. The vast majority are very small: a broker-owner operating alone or with a few associated salespeople. At the other end of the scale are large concerns with several branch offices and salespeople numbering in the hundreds. Indeed, especially in California, real estate brokerage firms exist that have over 100 branch offices and well over 1,000 salespeople. Our concern here will be the small to medium sized residential firm (under 100 salespeople) that is so typical of the industry nationwide. Much of what we will discuss will be applicable to the much larger firm, since such organizations usually are composed of several branches that tend to operate in a quasi-independent manner and could be treated, in some ways, as separate firms. However, since small and medium sized firms are characteristic of the majority of the nation's brokerage businesses, and since this book is most likely to be read by persons who are interested in starting out in the brokerage field or are in the earlier stages of the development of a firm, that is where we will concentrate our attention.

Our objective will be to examine the management techniques and practices that apply to small and medium sized residential firms. We will consider the problems associated with setting up a firm and getting it under way. We will look very hard at personnel practices—selection, training, and retaining of good people—since a topnotch sales force is a key element in success. We will examine organizational patterns that contribute to the most efficient operation of the sales force. We will consider the marketing problems the firm faces, particularly with regard to marketing the firm's services. We will study the management practices necessary for the continued successful operation of the firm: the establishment of management policy, goals, and objectives; financial controls and planning; dealing with legal liability; and operating in a competitive environment. It is important, therefore, that we understand at the outset that our objective is to study real estate brokerage as a *business*, and not as a personal endeavor. We will not spend a great amount of time examining how an individual becomes a better salesperson or a more effective procurer of listings; rather, we will examine the real estate brokerage firm as a business and describe the techniques and management skills necessary to make it thrive in today's economic and social environment.

An important feature of this text are the *Case Studies*, the first of which appears at the end of this chapter. Taken from actual experiences (with names changed), they illustrate features of the brokerage business.

Previous Preparation

We will have to make certain assumptions about the background of the reader, particularly since real estate is a complex field that we cannot hope to describe in detail in just this single volume. While it is likely that many readers may already be licensed salespersons and so may have had some practical experience in the field, we do not assume that every reader has such a history. Most states require some sort of educational background in real estate principles and practices for salesperson licensees, and we will assume that the reader, whether licensed or not, has at least the minimum educational background required by most licensing laws. That would be the equivalent of a single introductory college level course in real estate, though we emphasize that this equivalent need not actually have been obtained at a college or university. In most states, excellent private schools, business schools, and specialized real estate schools offer such courses. Further, for the purposes of this book, a reading knowledge of any good text in real estate principles and practices ought to be sufficient. A list of some texts is provided at the end of this chapter. The reader with no background at all in real estate will be well advised to purchase one of the books and try to read it through before going on to the remainder of this book.

Readers will find some overlap between this book and those suggested for prior reading. There are several reasons for this. First, there are some topics included in an introductory course or text that we must examine in greater detail. Second, some repetition of introductory material will be necessary to provide a more logical and sensible discussion here. Further, it will be necessary to repeat some introductory material in order to present it in the context of the brokerage business, rather than from the general viewpoint.

REAL ESTATE PRINCIPLES BACKGROUND READING

As mentioned earlier in this chapter, we assume that the reader has a basic knowledge of real estate principles and practices. Those who do not have this background, or who would like to refine what they have, can refer to the following list of basic real estate principles texts. It should be emphasized that this list is *not* comprehensive. *Any* fairly comprehensive real estate principles text will suffice to provide the background necessary to get the most out of this book.

Note that no editions or dates are given for these books. All are popular and all might be expected to be updated into new editions frequently. The reader should search for the latest edition available.

- Bruce Harwood, *Real Estate Principles* (Reston, VA: Reston Publishing Company).
- Alfred A. Ring and Jerome Dasso, *Real Estate Principles and Practices* (Englewood Cliffs, NJ: Prentice Hall).
- Maurice Unger and George R. Karvel, *Real Estate Principles and Practices* (Cincinnati, OH: South-Western Publishing Company).
- Bruce Lindeman and Jack P. Friedman, *Barron's How To Pass Real Estate Licensing Examinations, Salesman and Broker* (Woodbury, NY: Barron's Educational Series).

Case Studies

PREPARING FOR SUCCESS IN THE REAL ESTATE BROKERAGE BUSINESS

1. Robert V. had been a part-time real estate salesperson for a number of years. He had been making two or three sales a year, working occasional weekends, holidays and vacations. Once a year or so he secured a successful listing, usually because he happened to be in the right place at the right time. His brokerage firm paid him about half of the commission revenues he brought in.

One day he wondered why he continued to work for someone else: "Why shouldn't I get my own brokerage license? That way, I would get to keep the entire share of the commission, and I would make almost twice as much money for the same work!" So he took a couple of courses, applied to take the broker's license examination and, on the third try, passed it.

He set up an "office" in his basement recreation room, printed up some business cards and waited for the business to roll in. It didn't. Potential buyers had come to him or been referred to him because of his association with his previous firm, and now he managed to obtain only an occasional prospect referred to him by someone he had previously done business with. Even then, he found it difficult to get the larger firms in town to cooperate with him on the sales of their listings. He got no listings at all himself; potential sellers went elsewhere as soon as they learned that his was a one-man operation.

At the end of a year he discovered that he had worked harder and made less money than he had before. Unhappily, he closed down his business and went back to work as a salesman for another firm. He never understood exactly what had happened. He knew that he was competent at selling real estate, and that considering the time he was able to put in, he did well as a salesman for another firm. But as an independent broker he just had not made it.

2. Louise J. had been a highly successful full-time salesperson for one of the town's major firms for nearly twenty years. She was very active in local and state industry groups and was well-known and highly regarded by her peers in the business. For several years before she finally started her own business, others had suggested such a move to her. Even her own broker admitted that, although he would be very unhappy to lose her, he knew that she had what it took to operate her own successful business.

Louise knew that, too. But she also had learned that a real estate brokerage business involves a lot more than the ability to sell and list property if it is to succeed. She discussed the business with her own broker and sales manager, and made a point of getting all the information she could from the managers of the other respected firms in her city. Initially she decided that while she loved real estate and the brokerage business, she did not have the neccesary management knowledge and experience. She enrolled at the local university on a part-time basis and took several courses in management and accounting. She attended a number of seminars related to the management of the real estate business. When her sales manager went on vacation, she asked her broker to appoint her to fill in for him. That experience taught her more about the nature of the business, and that she worked well with people and enjoyed the administrative duties. She consulted with bankers to determine how much money she would need to start a business, and how easily she would be able to secure the necessary funds.

Finally she felt she was ready. She breezed through the licensing examination and set up her firm. She was realistic enough to realize that it would take her some time to get it going at the level she desired, and she made sure she had the resources to last her until it did. Several good salespeople expressed interest in affiliating with her, and she was able to assemble a good sales force of seven people at the very beginning. Her new business was prospering well before the deadline she had set for herself.

TWO

THE NATURE
AND FUNCTION
OF REAL ESTATE
BROKERAGE

Characteristics of the Real Estate Brokerage Business

The Brokerage Process

The Brokerage and the Law

State and Local Legislation

Federal Legislation

Professionalism

In a very few words, real estate brokerage can be described as a business devoted to providing the service of finding buyers or renters for real estate properties. It is a complex business, however, and a more thorough description is necessary for our purposes. Real estate is a varied commodity. While most observers see real estate brokerage as essentially the selling of peoples' houses for an apparently lucrative fee, few are aware of the complexities involved in even that limited enterprise. Real estate does not sell itself; each transaction is different, with its own set of problems to be solved. Buyers must be matched to properties, and a considerable amount of additional facilitative service usually is provided by the broker. He advertises, screens buyers, negotiates the final transaction to everyone's satisfaction, and usually is responsible for *closing* the transaction—seeing to it that all papers are properly drawn and recorded and that all monies are properly paid to those entitled to receive them.

CHARACTERISTICS OF THE REAL ESTATE BROKERAGE BUSINESS

Real estate brokerage is a competitive and highly localized business. It is not difficult for a conscientious and dedicated person to acquire a sales or brokerage license, although most states require applicants for broker's licenses to have spent a certain length of time as licensed salespersons. New brokerages are constantly being formed, and within the business competent salespersons are in great demand and so have frequent opportunities to leave one firm to work for another. Therefore, the successful brokerage must not only be able to get its share of the listing and selling business, but must also be organized to retain productive salespersons.

Ease of Entry

Real estate brokerage is one of the most popular small businesses in the United States. One reason is that it is deceptively easy to enter. The cash investment can be quite small: a few hundred dollars for license exam courses, examinations, license fees, and some signs and business cards. The family car and a desk in the corner of a bedroom can function as an office. One may even be extravagant and install a separate "business" telephone in the home.

The big stumbling block, if there is one, is that most states require that one hold a real estate salesperson's license for a certain minimum time before one is allowed to apply for the broker's license. Even so, few states require more than that the sales license be "active" for that time: Usually the person does not have to show any actual business experience while the sales license was held.

Of course, the trick is not entering the business, it is *staying* in the business. It helps to start out by entering the business the right way, with the right experience. This, and the requirements for staying in the real estate brokerage business successfully, is what this book is all about.

The Local Character of Real Estate Brokerage

Brokerage firms tend to list and sell properties located in their own immediate vicinities, neighborhoods, towns, or cities. In large cities, firms frequently specialize in partial areas, and rarely if ever engage in any activity outside familiar geographic confines. The reason is that a successful brokerage has to have an intimate knowledge of the real estate market it operates in, and the larger the market area, the more difficult it is to keep abreast of. In addition, so long as brokers actively *show* properties to interested buyers, they are limited in their geographic scope by the time and effort it takes to make a trip to a given location for a showing. For certain kinds of real estate, the market area the broker must consider is much larger. Very expensive investment property such as shopping centers, major office buildings and complexes, and the like fall into this category, along with all kinds of specialty properties such as hunting preserves, vacation estates, and some large farming operations.

Competition and Cooperation

Within the brokerage business, the individual firm both *competes against* and *cooperates with* other firms. On the one hand, a firm competes against others to list properties and to find buyers for listed properties. At the same time, in most localities it is common practice for brokerage firms to allow other firms to find buyers for their listings.

Usually there is a conventional industrywide pattern by which such cooperating brokers share the selling commission, and a broker who finds a buyer for another's listing knows that the listing broker will pay him a certain portion of the commission when he is paid by the seller. Most states have laws or rules and regulations that govern the manner in which brokers must respect one another's listings. This recognizes the fact that cooperative selling often occurs. Many localities have an arrangement within the brokerage industry that formalizes such cooperative action. Usually it is called a *multiple listing* or *multilist* program, which is an organization composed of member brokers who have agreed to share some or all of their listings. The multilist agreement spells out the procedures for listing properties eligible for multilist and the manner in which selling commissions are split between selling and listing brokers.

The Brokerage Firm and Its Markets

The real estate brokerage is a firm that deals largely in services. That is, it produces no goods, but instead offers to the public the ability of its sales force to bring about and fulfill real estate transactions. Since it is a business that assists sales, it may be said to operate in two separate markets. First, it offers its services to potential buyers, sellers, lessors, and lessees of real estate. In this market it seeks its customers and competes with other, similar firms. Second, it operates directly in the market for real estate itself when its services are used. The first market we can refer to as the *brokerage market*; the second is the *real estate market*.

We must always keep clear the distinction between these two markets. In the brokerage market, the firm sells or markets *itself* in the form of the services it can provide to others who want to operate in the real estate market. We often refer to the firm as marketing property in the real estate market, but it must be remembered that in its real estate market operations, the brokerage is selling and/or buying on behalf of someone else, and it is these others who, properly speaking, do the actual buying, selling, and renting. However, if they use the services of a brokerage firm, they normally expect considerable assistance and expert advice from the brokerage in return for the fees they pay. Therefore, the competent brokerage firm must maintain a continuously updated and accurate knowledge of the forces at work in the real estate markets in which they operate.

Since most real estate sales involve the use of borrowed money in the form of mortgage or other loans, it is essential that the broker be aware of the trends in a third market: the *money market*. Although the broker may offer a wide range and variety of services in a single transaction, often one of the most significant is to assist in arranging the financing the buyer needs in order to complete a transaction negotiated by the broker. Indeed, in times of tight money, the broker who knows where the mortgage money can be found, or who has had the foresight to make early arrangements with lenders to keep funds flowing to customers, will have a formidable competitive edge over those who have not paid the necessary attention to this crucial market. Since the broker is usually neither lender nor borrower in mortgage transactions, and generally is not agent for either party, we do not consider him an active operator in this market. Nevertheless, we must understand the vital importance of knowing the financing markets to the success of the brokerage business.

THE BROKERAGE PROCESS

The brokerage business is dominated by contractual arangements; indeed it may be said that the broker's stock in trade is his ability to arrange advantageous contracts for his customers. Generally he is hired by a property owner to find a buyer or a tenant for the real estate. The broker is usually paid in the form of a *commission* when he succeeds; the commission is based on the proceeds secured by the owner as a result of the transaction negotiated with the assistance of the broker.

Since the broker usually is employed by the property owner, it must always be remembered that he has a legal obligation to look out for the owner's best interests. This means that the broker cannot do anything that would be thought of as opposed to the owner's interests. Potential buyers often assume that when they contact a broker to show them property, the broker is working for them and will advise them and look out for *their* interests, when in fact he is only acting as the agent for the potential seller.

The next chapter, in its discussion of licensing and agency law, elaborates on these points. However, it should be pointed out that what we are discussing here is the *usual* way of doing things in the brokerage business. This is not to say that less familiar ways of operating do not exist. A broker can be hired by a buyer to find him suitable property; in such a case, the broker is in fact the buyer's agent and has the responsibility to look out for his interests alone. Furthermore, no law requires that a broker work only on commission: He may choose to accept a flat fee for his work and be paid the same amount regardless of the eventual proceeds to his employer. However, in the large majority of broker-assisted transactions, particularly in the residential brokerage field, the broker is employed by the property owner and is paid a commission based on the dollar price that the property sells for. Unless specifically directed otherwise, the reader should assume this kind of arrangement to be the case throughout the discussion in this book.

The reader will note that our discussion of the brokerage process (summarized in Figure 2–1) tends to devote itself to the residential sales element of the brokerage business. One reason for this is that such transactions are probably more familiar to readers. Also, a huge proportion of brokerage activity is devoted to sales of houses. Finally, much of the essence of brokerage activity can be explained in the context of a firm specializing in residential sales; nonresidential sales tend to be more complicated, and require more sophisticated approaches. However, since our basic discussion is devoted to the study of the proper management of a real estate brokerage business, most basic principles developed will be applicable to any kind of brokerage firm, regardless of its specialty.

Listing

Before a brokerage firm can sell property, it must obtain *listings*—agreements with potential sellers that they will pay the brokerage a commission for selling their real estate. A new firm may start out by trying to sell the listings obtained by other brokers, through cooperative deals or multilist, but a successful firm must also be able to establish its own listing program.

Soliciting listings is done in many ways. Salespersons can use their own contacts and word of mouth, and should keep files of all past customers to use for references and potential contacts to lead them to future business. The firm's reputation will secure listings from people attracted by advertising and references from satisfied customers. Although it may seem boring and unexciting, many salespeople find considerable success through *canvassing*: door-to-door, telephone, and other forms of contacting large numbers of people in order to find the few who may want to do business. Advertisements for already listed properties and open house showings may attract potential sellers, and another good source of listings is people to whom one has just sold property—now they may have to sell their current home or other property in order to move into the property they have just bought.

Another excellent source is the FSBO—the "For Sale by Owner" property that the seller is trying to get rid of without the services of a broker. Once the salesperson has found someone who may be interested in listing property with him, he has the task of convincing the potential seller first of all to list, and

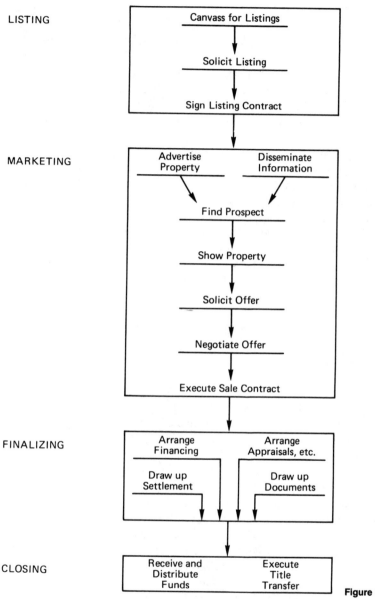

Figure 2-1. The Brokerage Process.

then to list with him. While charm and talents of persuasion may be useful, he is much more likely to get the listing if he can show plenty of proof that he and his firm are professional and capable of doing the job quickly and to the seller's benefit.

When a potential seller is ready to list the property, a contractual arrangement between the broker and the seller, the *listing contract,* is made. This contract, as well as subsequent ones in the transaction, may actually have been negotiated by a salesperson; however, legally the contract is between the broker and the seller, and all contracts negotiated by sales staff are the legal responsibility of the broker. Our discussion concerning the broker can sometimes be construed to include the entire sales staff where appropriate, but remember that legal responsibility for the accuracy and proper handling of these contracts rests ultimately with the broker. The brokerage firm therefore must have within its organization the proper means of controlling and supervising the drawing up of such contracts.

Many states require that the listing contract be written. Some permit verbal listings, but a professional broker should insist that all listings taken by his firm be in writing no matter what local law may permit. Listings are the source of the firm's livelihood, and they should be treated with proper respect and not left to the inaccurate memories of the parties involved.

Typically, the listing contract will describe the property to be sold and all details of the expected transaction, including the seller's asking price and other sale terms he desires (Will he allow a loan assumption, a VA guaranteed or FHA insured sale? Does he plan to take certain fixtures with him?), the length of time that the listing contract will be in effect, and the amount of the commission and the manner in which it will be paid. Listing contracts can have many other provisions as well; they are discussed in much greater detail in Chapter 8.

Marketing the Property

Once the listing contract is signed, the broker begins to solicit potential buyers. He usually places a For Sale sign on the property (but note that some communities have ordinances forbidding the use of such signs), advertises the property, and makes other brokers aware of the listing. Prospective buyers are shown the property.

One of the major services rendered by the broker to the seller is the *qualifying* of *prospects*, or potential buyers. Qualification of prospects consists of weeding out those for whom it is likely that the property is unsuitable, so as to assure a good chance that someone who is shown the property will be interested in buying it. This saves a lot of time and energy that might otherwise be devoted to selling efforts that are doomed from the start, for buyers may have a great many reasons why a given property is unsuitable. The most important reason is price: They can't afford the house, or they can afford more. Prospects also seek particular neighborhoods or kinds of neighborhoods, particular styles of homes, and particular features. The experienced broker interviews prospects to determine just what would be suitable for them. As he shows them various properties, he listens to their comments and uses the information he gains to refine his perception of their needs. Often prospects themselves do not really know what it is that they will be happiest with, and the skilled broker often finds that by showing them the right property he does them a useful service, in addition to selling his employer's property. Generally, an owner trying to sell property by himself has no opportunity to qualify buyers, and he often misses out on a chance to sell to someone who would have bought had a professional broker been involved.

When the broker has solicited an offer, he takes it to the owner for his reaction. At this point the broker can offer very useful advice concerning the advisability of accepting, declining, or countering the offer. *Countering* is the process of turning down an offer to offer the potential buyer a counterproposal that will be more suitable to the seller. Here the broker's knowledge of the market and of the particular situations of the parties involved is critical. If he does his job well, he not only arranges a transaction that benefits all parties, but also manages to convince all concerned of that fact.

The Sale Contract

Once an offer is accepted, a *contract of sale* exists. This contract gives certain rights and responsibilities to both buyer and seller. The property has not yet actually changed hands (that happens when the deed is given by seller to buyer), but both parties are obligated to have it do so at some time in the future. The contract of sale spells out the terms and conditions under which the sale will take place. It is rare that the parties involved will have the experience or knowledge to anticipate all possible problems and solve them at the outset within the contract.

Here is an area where the broker's expertise can make the difference between a clean, mutually beneficial transaction and one that results in one headache after another and perhaps cannot be resolved. The objective of any sale contract should be to arrange a transaction that all parties can live with comfortably and that all are capable of going through with. The broker, with his experience, knows where the potential pitfalls are and can explain them at the very beginning, when there is ample time to anticipate them. He can suggest solutions at a time when no one is under pressure to act. Furthermore, if unanticipated difficulties arise later, the broker can make suggestions and arrangements that will facilitate the solution.

The *terms of sale* are, after the sale price itself, the most important parts of the contract of sale. These include all *contingencies:* conditions or performance that have to be satisfied before the transaction can occur. The most important contingency and the one most frequently encountered is financing. Buyer and seller agree that if the buyer cannot find suitable mortgage financing, the deal will be called off. Other common contingencies include the requirement that the buyer be able to sell his own house within a certain length of time and that the seller make certain repairs or changes. Of course, a great many other contingencies may become a part of a particular deal, depending upon the circumstances. The role of the broker looms large here in assuring not only that the right conditions are included, but also, in the interest of a clean, smooth deal, that the improper or inconsequential conditions one party may desire be excluded.

Finalizing the Transaction

Once buyer and seller have agreed to transact, the broker begins preparation for the transaction itself. Often he will find it advisable to "shepherd" the buyer through the loan application process and to make sure that all paperwork is being expedited properly. He is responsible for seeing to it that all necessary documents are drawn up (deeds, mortgages, etc.) and that both buyer and seller meet all the special conditions specified in the contract. Finally, at the *closing*, when the transfer of the property ownership actually takes place, the broker has to make sure that all payments are properly made by everyone concerned; that all documents are recorded, if necessary, and delivered to the proper recipients; and that everyone signs and understands everything that has happened.

The Broker's Services

Clearly, the broker has a lot to do, even in the simplest of sale transactions. By employing a competent broker, the seller can go about his daily business while the broker handles all the work of arranging and concluding the sale. The preceding description concerned a simple sale of a home by one person to another; imagine the additional complexity involved in more involved transactions. Sales of commercial or other rental properties require financial analyses to be made before serious buyers will consider the property. Arrangements concerning existing leases, handling of rent money during the transaction period, and detailed breakdowns of income and expenses must be made. Many deals involve purchase and/or sale by more than one party, adding complexity to the transaction. Successful brokerage, then, requires much more than merely finding sellers willing to list and buyers willing to buy.

THE BROKERAGE AND THE LAW

The real estate brokerage firm operates in a situation in which legal requirements and arrangements are a constant factor. Brokers and salespeople are licensed by all the states. They are legal agents and so are covered by agency law. They draw up contracts and so must have a knowledge of the basics of contract law and detailed familiarity with the particular contracts they use. Each of these contracts is discussed in subsequent chapters; the following chapter provides a general coverage of license, agency, and contract law. Here we will discuss briefly some other elements of state, local, and federal laws the broker should be familiar with.

It must be emphasized that the possession of a real estate license does not entitle its holder to practice law. Most states allow brokers and salespeople to assist in the preparation of sales and listing contracts that they use, but complicated or confusing questions always should be referred to a competent attorney. Legal advice should never be given by licensees.

STATE AND LOCAL LEGISLATION

States and localities throughout the country have passed a large variety of laws that in one way or another affect real estate marketing practices. Most of these occur at the local level, although some states have adopted significant legislation, other than licensing law, that may apply statewide. In these pages, some of the more significant examples will be covered.

Land Use Regulation

Land use regulation has been in existence since early in this century. It usually is applied at the local level, although in most states the actual authority to develop and enforce these regulations had to be given to local government by the states. Furthermore, some states have statewide land use statutes, although only Hawaii controls and implements nearly all land use planning entirely at the state level.

The most obvious example of this kind of legislation is *zoning* and *building code* regulation. These laws specify minimum standards of construction and development and, in the case of zoning, prohibit certain uses of land in specific areas. Usually laws or ordinances are passed that are sweeping in nature, designating the entire geographical area under consideration as various kinds of development zones. Then what usually follows is a long series of *variances* from the law that are granted to petitioners who convince the responsible authorities that their building or development plans will not significantly affect surrounding area growth and development and will be of advantage to the community. These variances apply to specific parcels of property, and by requiring that variances be granted before land use that does not conform to the ordinance or law is undertaken, the authorities manage to retain some kind of control over the manner in which development takes place.

Since prohibiting or permitting certain kinds of uses for a given parcel of land can materially affect its usefulness and consequently its market value, licensees should be aware of these restrictions and their effects. Furthermore, since it usually is possible, to some degree, to obtain the necessary permissions and variances to put land to more profitable use than current zoning and other restrictions dictate, licensees should be aware of the possibilities when they deal in properties that might be so affected. In fact, a few firms in the country actually specialize in such properties, and part of their service includes going through and orchestrating the steps necessary to obtain the required permissions. Frequently a buyer will make an offer on a piece of property subject to proper rezoning. In such cases the licensee must make certain that the sale contract contains the proper language to explain this contingency fully.

Sign Ordinances

For various reasons, some localities have passed ordinances that restrict or prohibit the use by real estate brokerage firms of the familiar FOR SALE signs. The constitutional legality of these laws is often challenged, and in some cases the laws have been overturned, although it is generally legally accepted that ordinances and statutes properly drawn can have this effect. The reasoning behind such laws varies from purely aesthetic ("the signs are ugly and mar the appearance of neighborhoods") to attempts to prevent panic selling in changing neighborhoods.

Some sign ordinances merely restrict the size or appearance of FOR SALE signs without actually prohibiting their use. They may also restrict the length of time that a sign may be in place and the length of time that a SOLD sign may stand. They may permit FOR SALE signs but prohibit SOLD signs. Many local laws, in the interest of safety, prohibit such signs from being installed within a certain distance of roadways or sidewalks. All licensees should be fully aware of any sign restrictions that may be in effect in the areas in which they operate and abide by them accordingly.

Implied Warranty

It is an ancient precept of law that the buyer must assure himself of the quality, quantity, and usefulness of goods that he buys and that the seller is under no obligation to reveal any information of this nature unless he is asked. In modern law this precept is gradually being changed, and in the past decade or two considerable legislation at all levels has been passed that requires sellers of goods to recognize that the buyer may *infer* that certain warranties and guarantees exist even if he has not bargained for them. One area in which states in particular have been very active has been that of real estate. Here we are concerned with the *physical* quality of the real estate, rather than the "quality" of title.

There is an enormous variation in treatment of this matter from state to state, and some still adhere to the doctrine that the buyer is still totally responsible. But be warned that the trend is turning very strongly to favor the buyer. Licensees should make special efforts to keep up to date in this area, because the changes are occurring rapidly and in many states each session of the legislature makes alterations.

This matter is important to the real estate broker because he is the seller's agent and the law is frequently interpreted to allow the broker as well as the seller to be held liable for violations of implied warranty. When this is the case, it is absolutely necessary for the broker to be certain of the physical condition of property sold and to insure that all necessary legal notifications of this condition have been made to the buyer, preferably in writing as part of the sale contract.

FEDERAL LEGISLATION

It would take a book ten times the size of this one just to give marginally adequate coverage of all the federal laws, rules, and regulations that might be of concern to a real estate brokerage business. We can consider only a few here. Some affect the everyday pattern of doing business, and others will affect business only occasionally. We will attempt to deal with these in order of importance to the brokerage firm.

Fair Housing

Title VIII of the Civil Rights Act of 1968 and subsequent refinements made it illegal to discriminate in the sale of housing with respect to race, sex, creed, color, or national origin. There are exceptions to the law, the major one being that an owner selling the property unassisted may be exempt from all or part of the law. The effect, then, is that the law covers mainly brokerage practices, and almost all enforcement attempts and suits have been aimed directly at real estate brokerage firms for alleged violations of the law.

Violation of this law can be assumed from the actions of a brokerage firm, and not just from specifically published or elucidated policies. Several firms have been successfully prosecuted and sued not because they specifically refused to show certain people houses in certain areas, but simply because their practice appeared to be to take some people to certain areas and others to different ones, apparently based on racial characteristics.

All brokerages should display the poster illustrated in Figure 2–2, which is a statement that the firm abides by fair housing laws and also explains those laws briefly. State license laws also contain provisions that make this kind of discrimination in selling practice a specific violation of license law.

Credit and Lending

A number of recent federal laws aim at preventing discrimination and unfair practices in the allocation of credit. While brokerage firms themselves are rarely lenders as well, they work closely with lenders in order to facilitate mortgage loans for buyers. Since borrowed money is so important to successful real estate sales, brokers should be aware of the regulations that surround this industry. They then will be prepared to answer some of the questions prospective buyers are likely to ask with respect to the availability of loans.

Regulation Z   *Regulation Z* of the Federal Reserve System implements the Truth in Lending Act of 1969, which requires lenders to disclose certain facts and charges surrounding loans and lending policies. A particular requirement is that interest rates be stated as an *annual percentage rate* (usually abbreviated APR) in order to make comparison of terms from one loan to another easier and more standardized.

Brokers should always use the APR term and its methods of calculation

Figure 2-2. Fair Housing Poster.

in advertisements that state the interest rate available on loans to be used for purchase of a property, whether the loan is to be assumed or negotiated as a new loan. A significant consideration is that the APR should take into account variations from the face rate of interest that may be caused by the use of loan discounts, points, or other charges by the lender that have the effect of materially altering the *net* rate of interest he receives.

The Equal Credit Opportunity Act of 1974 and 1976 amendments prohibit certain practices that have the effect of favoring certain people for credit while denying it to others—discrimination purely on the basis of race, creed, color, national origin, sex, or marital status. The major effect of this legislation has been to restrict practices which made it difficult for women to obtain loans.

The practice had been to pay scant attention to income provided by a working wife when calculating the ability of a couple to pay a loan (on the theory that the wife could become pregnant or for other reasons choose not to work in the future); similarly, the incomes of single or divorced women often made little impression because they might remarry and quit working. To a lesser extent, the elderly were discriminated against because they might die or retire before a loan was fully paid. The effect of the legislation was to make this kind of discrimination largely illegal.

Land Sales

Certain land sales are regulated by the Interstate Land Sales Full Disclosure Act of 1968, which was passed in response to complaints about selling practices associated largely with interstate sales of land in developments in certain Sunbelt and resort areas. The law requires considerable disclosure to be provided to prospective buyers of land in affected subdivisions. This information and the answers to a number of specified questions required by the U.S. Department of Housing and Urban Development (HUD) is contained in a handout called the HUD Report, which must be given to all prospects.

These regulations usually do not cover most subdivisions in which brokers may operate, unless a substantial number of sales are made to out-of-state buyers. If there is doubt as to whether or not compliance with these regulations is required, efforts should be made to ascertain whether it is or is not necessary. A broker involved in sales practices that violate this law can be prosecuted and held liable for damages.

RESPA

The Real Estate Settlement Procedures Act of 1974 (RESPA) was designed to assure that buyers received, at settlement, the proper information as to the disposition of the monies involved and the charges assessed against them. A particular function of the law is to assure full disclosure of the itemized costs involved. Costs must be disclosed in advance, a uniform settlement statement must be used (see Chapter 9), and a booklet prepared by HUD must be given to all applicants for loans secured by real estate. There are some exceptions to this law, but its provisions generally apply to all normal sources of third-party loans except for totally private arrangements among friends, relatives, and so forth.

While the prime responsibility for abiding by the law rests with the lenders themselves, brokers whose service includes handling of closings and settlements should make certain that proper procedures are followed even though they are not directly responsible for the actual lending of the money.

PROFESSIONALISM

Some people feel that the word "professional" can only be used to describe someone who practices a job that requires a high level of education and very specialized knowledge and skills and is greatly recognized and respected by everyone. These jobs might include medicine, the law, the ministry, and the like. It is evident that the real estate brokerage field is not viewed by the public in this same hallowed light. However, if we define a professional as one who is talented and knowledgeable in his work, is respected by those who deal with him as a competent and reliable person, and takes considerable pride in doing a good job every time he has the opportunity to practice his chosen work, then we certainly can consider professionalism as something all real estate brokers and licensees should strive for.

The professional real estate broker is most easily noticeable for pride in his work, competence, desire for recognition for his chosen field, and continuing efforts to improve his abilities. This book will assume that the brokerage business should be peopled by this kind of professional and will discuss the brokerage business in this light.

Several organizations exist whose purpose is to promote professionalism in the brokerage field and recognition by the public of the service, high qualification, and ability of its members. The most prominent of these is the National Association of REALTORS® and the many organizations affiliated with it in various ways. These include, among others, the American Institute of Real Estate Appraisers, the Institute of Real Estate Management, the REALTORS® National Marketing Institute, and state associations in all fifty states. These organizations speak for their members on a variety of public issues of interest to them, provide many kinds of training programs and classroom sessions designed to improve their skills, and provide professional designations to members who meet the rigorous sets of standards that identify them as being recognized by their peers as highly competent professionals.

All members of REALTORS® organizations must meet certain qualifications, including proper licensure and recommendation by other members. They are also required to subscribe to and conform to the REALTORS® Code of Ethics, which is presented in the appendix to this book. Its concern is with the sound, ethical business practice that will make the REALTOR® member a valued and recognized contributor to the welfare of his community, state, and nation.

The reader should note that the word REALTOR® is a federally registered identifying term. It cannot be used by anyone who is not a member of a board of REALTORS® that is affiliated with the National Association of REALTORS®. It is improper to refer to a real estate broker as a REALTOR® unless he is such a member, although many uninformed members of the public do just that. Most successful, ethical, and respected real estate brokers and their associates are members of their local board of REALTORS®: they find that the recognition and the contributions to their profession are well worth it. The term REALTOR® should always be written as it appears in these pages: in capital letters and using the registered trademark (®) sign.

Membership in a REALTORS® organization is highly advantageous to any ethical real estate broker and the members of his firm. In addition to its concern for proper recognition of the real estate business and the wide variety of educational opportunities in the real estate field that the organization offers, it is the best available source of continuing information likely to be of interest to real estate brokerage professionals. Its magazine, *Real Estate Today*, publishes articles on matters of interest, and other newsletters and publications are made available that can keep the real estate professional informed and supplied with useful ideas.

The National Association of REALTORS® is a large organization. In the mid-1980s there were about 1,800 local Boards of REALTORS® with a total membership of about 750,000. These numbers are growing every year, not only as the real estate brokerage industry expands, but also as more and more licensees recognize the obvious advantages of membership and as the business as a whole strives for higher and higher standards of professional excellence.

DISCUSSION QUESTIONS AND PROJECTS

1. Approximately how many brokerage firms exist in your local area? How many of these would be classified as large? Small? Does it appear that a relatively few firms seem to have a large part of the total business among them? Why or why not?

2. Does there appear to be evidence in your area that "fair housing" has worked? Are some areas predominately white and others mostly black? If so, is this due to prejudice or to other factors? If other factors are important, what are they?

3. Describe the essentials of the process a brokerage firm goes through as it handles a transaction from beginning to end.

4. Of the procedures you described in the answer to (3), which are the most interesting to you? Why? Which seem the least interesting? Why?

5. From newspaper articles and other sources, try to find out how effective the zoning process in your area has been. What are its objectives? Can you point out any parts of your city or town where these procedures have failed to work as hoped? What caused the failure?

6. Find out from your state REALTORS® association what fraction of the state's brokerage firms belong to the organization. What kinds of services does it offer?

7. Interview three or four brokers whose firms are REALTOR® members. Find out from them what they consider to be the major advantages of membership.

A Case Study

NATIONAL BROKERAGE FIRMS

Although real estate brokerage firms are localized by nature, there has been a trend during the 1970s and 1980s toward national identification of "chains" of realty firms. Foremost among these are the national "franchise" firms. While these companies have a national image, the individual member "offices" actually remain separate, locally owned and operated entities. They are owned by the people who run them, and affiliate with the national franchise organization.

Franchisor firms offer name identification, national advertising, media advertising and other features of nationally-oriented businesses which are well beyond the means of local small businesses to afford. Also, these companies often provide training services, information networks, referral exchanges and other facilities which are useful to many real estate brokerage firms.

There have been attempts by other national firms, especially stockbrokerages and other investment houses, to establish their own chains of company-owned and -controlled realty office systems. Many of these have encountered serious problems. First, state license laws make it very difficult for real estate brokerage companies to be controlled in a nationally centralized manner. Second, many of these companies have discovered that in spite of their success in marketing in other investment areas, they often turn out to be lacking the experience and knowledge to operate a successful realty business. As a result, many originally ambitious plans for such nationwide chains have been abandoned or severely scaled down. Those which survive have relatively few branches, and tend to concentrate on "big-ticket" investment properties. They compete very little in the residential, owner occupied real estate area which is the mainstay of most local real estate brokerage firms.

In spite of the national identification or even ownership by a single national firm, the main objective of most individual real estate brokerage offices or firms will continue to be to offer locally-oriented service, particularly among those which specialize in home sales. The nationally-oriented image may become important as an advertising tool and to establish a broad-based identity for the individual brokerage firms. However, the actual services rendered will remain very local in nature.

However, unless and until state licensing laws change in philosophy, it is unlikely that a true nationwide chain of centrally controlled real estate brokerage offices can be formed. The focus of license laws is on the locally owned brokerage which operates exclusively within the state. Since there is almost no reciprocity among the states with respect to real estate licenses, a broker who desires to operate in more than one state must be licensed separately by each state in which he desires to do business. Thus, a national organization will have to meet license requirements in as many states in which it operates, and so will many of the management people in such a firm.

Many states do not allow a licensed firm to be owned or controlled by an out-of-state entity. Therefore, there will be some aspects of the business in which a national organization could not have a single company-wide policy or company-wide control because it would be difficult or impossible to structure it to conform with the laws of all the states in which it does business. The end result would have to be a loosely-knit outfit, very similiar to today's franchised realty firms, in which most of the significant control would be concentrated at the level of the company's "branch" offices. This would defeat the purpose and the alleged advantages of a nationwide company.

A Case Study

EDUCATION AND THE REAL ESTATE PROFESSIONAL

For decades, one important objective of the real estate brokerage business has been to increase the professional image of licensees as well as to increase their professional knowledge and capacity. A key element in this process has been the growing requirement in state licensing laws for certain educational standards for licensees.

Educational accomplishment as a prerequisite to licensure has been common for a long time. By the 1970s almost all states required at least a minimal real estate education experience for anyone applying for a salesperson's license. Most states require additional education for broker's license applicants. Also, all states require at least the equivalent of a high school education, and some are requiring some college-level general education as well. Overall educational requirements still vary greatly among the states, from a minimum of 24 to 30 clock hours of real estate education for salesperson's license applicants in some states, to 300 or more clock hours of specialized real estate education for broker's license applicants in some others. Most states also specify the content of the required real estate education, as well as the length of time required.

A trend which has emerged in recent years has been the additional requirement of *continuing* education for those who already have real estate licenses. In the growing number of states with this provision in their license law, the education requirement does not stop once a person is licensed. In order to retain the license, the licensee must satisfactorily complete an additional specified amount of real estate education every year or two. Some states which do not require continuing education do offer series ot seminars which licensees are encouraged to take on a voluntary basis.

Other requirements which extend beyond those mentioned also are under consideration. One is to require periodic re-examination for licensees. Another is the designation of additional license categories. An example would be different licenses for residential, commercial, investment, appraisal, etc.

One thing is certain: As time passes the general nationwide trend will be to require more and more education and other evidence of competence from real estate licensees. While some may object, most professionally-oriented real estate people applaud this trend and, indeed, are among the prime movers in bringing it about in their respective states. The end result will be a continually improving population of real estate professionals to serve the nation's real estate brokerage needs.

REFERENCES

ATTEBERRY, WILLIAM L., KARL G. PEARSON, AND MICHAEL P. LITKA, *Real Estate Law*, ch. 20. New York, NY: John Wiley & Sons, 1984.

BORDESSA, RONALD, "Rhetoric vs. Reality in Real Estate Brokerage," *Real Estate Review*, Winter 1979, pp. 46-52.

CASE, FRED E, "Why Some Brokerage Firms are Successful," *Real Estate Review*, Fall 1979, pp. 102-105.

KRANTZ, JERRY, "The Residential Real Estate Market," in *The McGraw-Hill Real Estate Handbook*, ed. Robert Irwin, ch. 10. New York, NY: McGraw-Hill Book Company, 1984.

KRATOVIL, ROBERT, AND RAYMOND J. WERNER, *Real Estate Law* (8th ed.), ch. 38. Englewood Cliffs, NJ: Prentice Hall, 1983.

NATIONAL ASSOCIATION OF REALTORS®, *Interpretations of the Code of Ethics* (8th ed.). Chicago, IL: National Association of REALTORS®, 1983.

PHILLIPS, BARBARA, "Getting Started in Real Estate," in *The McGraw-Hill Real Estate Handbook*, ed. Robert Irwin, ch. 31. New York, NY: McGraw-Hill Book company, 1984.

PIVAR, WILLIAM H., *Real Estate Ethics*. Chicago, IL: Real Estate Education Company, 1979.

THREE

THE LEGAL ENVIRONMENT OF REAL ESTATE BROKERAGE

Vulnerability to Legal Action

Licensure

License Law

Broker and Salesperson

Infractions of License Law

Agency Law

General Contract Law

Requirements of Valid Contracts

Duress, Misrepresentation, and Fraud

Discharge and Breach of Contracts

Conclusion

The real estate brokerage business is covered by a large body of law. *Licensing law* establishes standards in each state that real estate salespeople must meet. *Agency law* describes the responsibilities of the brokerage's function as an agent for its customers. *Contract law* covers much of the business activity of the brokerage firm. Other laws deal with specific factors of the business and business practice.

The intelligent broker cannot hope to function efficiently without a thorough understanding of his legal position and the legal framework that governs him. This need is becoming more and more important every day; the broker's customers and clients cannot any longer be expected to take whatever he dishes out to them without protest. Dissatisfied customers in all areas of business are discovering very rapidly that the law is often on their side, and that they have recourse to a great many legal remedies. In nearly every state, the branch of state government that supervises and enforces real estate licensing law is becoming much more vigorous in seeking out and punishing violators of the law.

To the ethical broker, this trend is welcome, for it rids the profession of undesirable members, and helps to create in the public mind a better and more favorable attitude to brokerage. Any professional likes to take pride in his work and to be proud of his membership in his chosen profession. The real estate business is one in which the public's attitude toward the entire profession is easily affected by the poor behavior and performance of a few of its members.

VULNERABILITY TO LEGAL ACTION

This is the age of the consumer. To the business operator, however, it is more important to recognize that this is the age of the consumer's *lawyer*. There is no question that our legal system and its interpretations are undergoing a profound transformation in favor of the consumer, the buyer and user of products. It used to be, so it is thought, that the rule of *caveat emptor*—let the buyer beware— prevailed in purchase situations. Actually, buyers have long had many legal rights and expectations, but in recent years they appear to have become more aware of their rights, and all levels of government have been busy passing new laws defining more strictly just what these rights are and just what responsibilities sellers have.

In the past few years the news has featured stories of spectacular awards to consumers in cases where sellers of products and services have been held responsible for damages suffered by their customers. Faulty gasoline tanks on automobiles, disintegrating power lawn mowers, and dubious insurance selling practices are among the many cases that have been brought to public attention. It may not seem that this consumer attitude has spread into the real estate business, but it has, and it will spread further. Every year, in every state, licensed brokers and salespeople are required to pay large sums in damages, and even lose their licenses, their businesses, and their livelihoods because of improper practice of their profession.

Of course, cases arise where the broker's improper performance leads customers into unfortunate situations, and in such cases the broker usually can be held legally liable for damages to the injured parties and may be in jeopardy of having his license suspended or revoked as well. But even the blameless broker may find himself defending his actions in court; irate customers may try to make him the scapegoat. Sometimes they can find an attorney who is willing to take their money to press a spurious case; sometimes they do not tell their attorneys the true facts.

Regardless of whether or not a suit against him has merit, the broker will incur some expense defending against it, and it is one of the characteristics of the business that such things will happen. They cannot be avoided, but the broker who keeps up with the law, and who understands how it affects his business, can keep these unhappy events to a minimum. And, of course, by doing so he also eliminates the risk that he will be assessed substantial damage judgments or lose his license, because he will be assured that he is always working within the law.

Further discussion of broker liability can be found in Chapter 11.

LICENSURE

Every state requires that real estate brokers and salespersons be licensed. There are two categories of licensees: brokers and salespersons. The salesperson may function in the brokerage business only if his license has been issued to a licensed broker: He is under the supervision of a broker in his work, and the broker is legally responsible for what his licensed salespeople do in the course of business. Whereas all states refer to the primary license of the independent operator as a real estate broker's license, the salesperson's nomenclature differs among the states: most call it a *salesman's license*, but such terms as *salesperson* or *associate broker* also are encountered.

Qualifications

The applicant for a license must meet a number of qualifications. Nearly all states require a minimum general education, such as the equivalent of a high school education, and most have minimum age requirements. Applicants generally must be able to show that they are of good character. Those who have been convicted of certain crimes, for example, may be disqualified. Some states will run credit checks and other investigations to substantiate the applicant's worthiness. Most states require a minimum level of educational attainment in the real estate area for one or both licenses, and the majority of states will not allow an applicant for a broker's license to take the qualifying examination until he has served at least a minimum amount of time as a licensed salesperson.

Licensing Examination

Every state has a qualifying examination the applicant must pass before he can be issued a license. The examination concentrates upon knowledge of the features of the real estate business, the brokerage business, ethics, contract law, real estate contracts, real estate mathematics and, especially, license law and real estate practices of the state giving the examination. Examinations vary from state to state, although there are two national examinations, one or the other being used, at least in part, in about forty states. In other states, the examination is prepared by or for the arm of state government that supervises and regulates real estate licensing.

Variations among States

Real estate licensure is regulated entirely at the state level; there are practically no federal laws or regulations that influence real estate licensure as such. However, the broker should be aware that a lot of other federal law affects him, even though it may not be directly related to licensing. Examples are fair housing laws, truth-in-lending laws, tax laws, environmental protection laws, land use regulation laws, laws and regulations affecting federally supported financing such as FHA, VA, etc., and a maze of other laws and regulations as well.

Since licensure is a state operation, we will find variations in the laws of the fifty states. Most of these are in details, while the general thrust of all of these laws remains the same from state to state. The reader should contact his state's real estate licensing authority for information about its law and regulations, and should examine it for details of its nature and enforcement. Variation occurs most often in such areas as administration of examinations, qualifications for licensure, fees charged for licenses and examinations, and the like. The following discussions, therefore, will have to be general in nature, and will concentrate (except where indicated) on those aspects of licensing law that are generally uniform among the states.

LICENSE LAW

This is not the place to engage in an elaborate discussion of license law, because license applicants are required to study their state's license law carefully if they hope to pass the examinations. Readers of this book either already have studied their state's law, or will have to do so in order to be licensed to put this book's information to use in business. And, as we have mentioned, it is wise for any person in the real estate brokerage field to have a thorough knowledge of state laws and practices.

License laws originated early in this century as a means of controlling what at that time appeared to be widespread abuses and improper practices in the real estate business. Today, their purpose is to protect the public by assuring that real estate salespeople will have met certain minimum standards of ability and knowledge and by providing a set of rules, laws, and regulations governing the business. Licensing standards vary from state to state, but there is a strong nationwide trend under way at present to make the qualifications for licensure increasingly rigorous.

For example, many states require that newly licensed real estate brokers will have to have taken and passed a course of study equivalent to as many as 200 or more clock hours of classroom work in the various areas of real estate. In addition, many states require some amount of *continuing education* of licensees in order to keep the license once it is earned. The amount, quality, and subject matter will vary among the states, but as time passes it can be expected that these requirements will become more rigorous and will spread to additional states.

Licensure and Exemption

Usually, anyone who sells, rents, buys, or leases real estate belonging to others, and who does so for pay, must hold a license before he can engage in *any* aspect of the business. This goes so far as to render illegal the actions of someone who *intends* to seek a license but who, before it is issued, begins to line up people with whom he will do business once he is licensed. Several exceptions to the law are provided for.

Attorneys may be exempted from licensure since they are presumed to be expert in law anyway, and they are licensed and regulated by other branches of state government, usually even more rigorously than real estate salespeople. One who has an owner's power of attorney to act for him may be exempted, though most states will not permit someone to circumvent the law by getting powers of attorney on a regular basis. Trustees, executors, government employees acting in the course of their duties (for example, employees of the state highway department who conduct negotiations for the purchase by the state of highway right-of-way land), and some others who are acting in special capacities are also exempted. Resident managers of apartment projects may not have to be licensed, even though they sign leases and sometimes negotiate on behalf of the owner. Generally, no one has to be licensed to sell real estate that he owns himself; however, some states restrict even this privilege by requiring licenses for owners of large subdivisions if they wish to sell them on a lot-by-lot basis. These latter provisions, which are fairly new in license law, were a response to customer complaints involving speculative subdivisions and, more particularly, rapid increases in the growth of sales of undeveloped land lots accompanied by overenthusiastic sales efforts.

In some states, an employee of a real estate owner may sell that owner's real estate while unlicensed, provided that it is part of the employee's full time job with that owner, and that the employee sells real estate for no one else but that owner. A provision like this would allow a homebuilding company to hire an unlicensed sales force, provided that they were employed only by that company. But other states specifically require that such employees be licensed.

Administration of License Law

The majority of states have a *real estate commission* that administers the real estate license law. In those that do not have a separate real estate commission, the law is administered by another branch of state government such as the department of state or a department or branch that is set up to handle most or all professional licenses the state issues.

Real estate commissions usually are made up of appointed members who have the responsibility of administering the law. Most often they are required to be members of the real estate business and to hold licenses issued by the state. Many states also require that commission members from other walks of life, such as a consumer representative, be included. Generally the commission will have a staff that handles its day-to-day business, since it is rare that the commissioners themselves hold their positions on an exclusive, full-time basis. Staff members are concerned with handling the paperwork, administering the examinations, and arranging for commission business such as hearings, examination reviews, and the like.

In states that have no commissions, staffs handle much of the work in the same way as described above; however, they may be concerned with more than real estate licensure. In these states there may or may not be representation of the real estate brokerage business in a decision-making capacity similar to the commissioners in other states. Most states require their real estate commissions, departments, or divisions, if they have them, to be self-supporting from the fees and other charges they collect. Fees are charged for license examination (sometimes an additional fee is charged for application as well), and for the licenses themselves. The brokerage license fee is usually higher than that for salespersons. Fees also are charged for administrative matters such as changes of address or transfers of salespersons to different brokers.

Financial Responsibility

Most states require that the licensee have some sort of financial responsibility to protect the public in case he causes loss to someone. Some require that he post a bond wronged customers can claim against. Many states have instituted what usually is called a *Real Estate Recovery Fund*. These are funds set up and administered by the state government, and aggrieved parties may claim against them if they can provide proper proof that a licensee has caused them loss. The fund is supplied by assessments against all active licensees in the state.

The exact manner and requirements of these assessments vary from state to state, but the effect is to provide a fund of money, supplied by the brokerage industry itself, against which claims can be made. The exact nature of the fund, and the manner in which monies are paid in and claimed against usually is somewhat complex. The interested reader should consult his own state's law to determine if such a fund exists in his state, and how it operates.

Violation and Penalties

In most states, violating the license law is a misdemeanor, and the penalty is a fine or imprisonment. A violation would include any infraction of license law by a licensee (in which case the licensee could also be subject to suspension or revocation of his license), as well as any activity by an unlicensed person for which the law requires licensure (in which case the unlicensed person may jeopardize his eligibility to be issued a license in the future).

If there is reason to believe that a licensee has violated the law, a hearing will be held. The licensee will be notified of the charges against him and will have an opportunity to defend himself against them in the hearing. He is usually allowed to have an attorney present, but in most states hearings do not follow the rigid rules of courtroom procedure and so tend to be more informal in that sense. As a result of the hearing, a decision can be made as to whether or not the licensee's license will be suspended for a period of time or revoked outright.

Of course if it is decided that the licensee is blameless, no action against him will result. Actual prosecution for the criminal offense of violating the law or license regulations generally is up to the state's prosecuting attorney or other similiar official. Even though a licensee has suffered the loss of his license, he still is subject to possible criminal penalties if he is prosecuted successfully. In addition, he suffers a third jeopardy: Those who have suffered because of his actions may sue him in a civil case to recover damages.

Generally, decisions made in license law violation hearings may be appealed by the licensee to the regular court system. It frequently happens that a license is suspended or revoked, and the licensee is required to fulfill certain conditions in order to get it back. A frequent condition is that the former licensee must retake the licensing examination. Sometimes brokers who are found in violation of license law are prohibited from holding broker's licenses for a period of time during which they are allowed to apply for salesperson's licenses and work, once again, under the supervision of another broker. A decision may require that the former licensee take and pass courses in certain areas of the real estate field before he can apply for reinstatement of his license.

License Valid Only in Issuing State

Every state requires that in order for anyone to operate as a real estate broker or salesperson in any way within the state, the person must hold a duly issued license from that state. Unlike driver's licenses, therefore, real estate licenses usually are valid for use only within the state that issues them. Thus, a broker who wishes to do business in more than one state must secure licenses from each of the states in which he wishes to operate. To allow for this, most states will issue nonresident licenses to nonresidents of the state.

Normally, the nonresident applicant must fulfill at least the same requirements—except residence location—that are required of a resident licensee, including coming to an examination site in that state to take the licensing examination. A few states do not issue nonresident licenses: To operate in those states a resident broker of another state usually is required to operate in cooperation with a resident broker of that state. In most states, any kind of real estate brokerage activity by nonresidents requires licensure, even the act of selling out-of-state property by mail to residents of the state.

A few states have a limited form of reciprocity with neighboring states, particularly with regard to large metropolitan areas that overlap state boundaries. However, even this is the exception rather than the rule. About the only other form of reciprocity exists among some of the states that use the same "national" licensing examination: Some will allow licensees from other states using the same examination to take only the state laws and practices portion of the licensing examination, since they have already passed the general portion of the examination in another state.

BROKER AND SALESPERSON

As we have seen, license law requires anyone engaging in certain real estate selling activities for pay to be licensed; the license law will have a long section in which all these activities are spelled out in detail. Every state provides for two types of licenses, that of the *broker* and that of the *salesperson*.

Broker

A *broker* is a licensee who is permitted to act independently. He may operate his own business and has certain responsibilities and duties outlined in the law: He must prepare (and take responsibility for the preparation of) certain documents, such as sale contracts and leases, and must arrange the settlement of transactions in which he is the agent. The law, or some other source, will have a long list of rules and regulations that govern the conduct of the broker with respect to his clients and customers and the other licensees with whom he may operate.

The broker generally is considered by the law to be legally responsible for anything that is done by his business and his employees. This responsibility extends to anything done in the course of business by licensees whose licenses the broker holds. Most states require that if a brokerage firm has more than one office, a licensed broker or salesperson with a certain amount of experience must be in charge of each branch, and salespeople's licenses must be held and displayed at only one branch office per salesperson, although they usually would be allowed to operate out of other branches as well. The broker, in addition, takes all responsibility for trust monies coming into the possession of the firm.

Salesperson

The *salesperson*, regardless of what he may be called in the laws and definitions of the various states, is allowed most of the activity permitted to the broker, with certain exceptions. Generally, he cannot conduct closings, unless the broker supervises; he cannot handle trust monies, except to transport them directly to his broker; he cannot act as an independent entity. His license is held by a broker, and he is considered to be an employee of that broker. Normally, the brokerage's advertisements must feature the name of the broker, although the salesperson who is involved may have his own name and telephone number included. Everything he does, he does in the name of the broker, for as we have seen the broker takes the legal responsibility for the salesperson's actions in business.

The sales license may be likened to an apprenticeship, although no state law refers to it as such. However, the gist of the law is to imply that the salesperson is an apprentice: The law usually states that he must be under the constant supervision of a broker, and most states will not allow anyone to apply for a broker's license without having spent a certain length of time as a licensed salesperson.

Commission Payments

License law regards the salesperson as hired by, and the responsibility of, one broker and one broker only. Normally, a salesperson may be paid commission money by *only* his own broker. In the case of cooperative sales, where a salesperson finds a buyer for property listed by a broker other than his own, the seller of that property will pay the entire commission to the *listing* brokerage. That brokerage firm then pays an agreed upon share of the commission to the *selling* brokerage. Then each broker individually pays the proper portion of his share of the commission to his own salesperson involved in the deal.

The exact nature of the manner in which a broker shares commissions with his salespeople depends upon the arrangements between broker and salesperson. It is not determined by the license law. In fact, the actual commission arrangement between the property owner and the broker is always a matter of negotiation. License law does not specify any commission schedule. Also, in the last decade or so, even suggested commission schedules drawn up by local organizations of brokers have come under fire from the Antitrust Division of the U.S. Department of Justice. Therefore, recent revisions in license law often mention that actual commission rates are a matter of negotiation in each transaction.

Handling Money

A real estate broker frequently comes into possession of money rightfully belonging to others: He is custodian of the money, but it is not his. The sources of such money are earnest money payments, rents the broker collects, and a wide variety of other collections he makes. At settlement, the broker is required to disburse all the money involved in the transaction to the parties entitled to it.

A considerable portion of license law rules and regulations is devoted to discussion of the manner in which the broker handles this money. Normally, he is required to set up at least one special bank account into which all of this money is deposited, and from which he withdraws the money when it is time to disburse. Some states call this a *trust account*, and the broker is regarded in the state law as a *trustee*. In other states it is called an *escrow account*, and the broker is regarded as the *escrow agent*. But whatever the nomenclature, the intent of the law is the same: The broker is entrusted with money belonging to others and has to take special steps to ensure that the money is not jeopardized. The broker must keep scrupulous records of these accounts, the money that goes into them (and from whom it came and why), and the money that is disbursed (to whom and why).

License law enforcement agencies are extremely sensitive on this matter because improper handling of trust (or escrow) monies is a frequent subject of license law violation hearings. In most of these cases there is no malicious intent on the part of the offending broker, only ignorance or sloppy recordkeeping. However, this is small consolation to the broker who finds himself without his license or his business because his records were not kept properly.

It is not enough that the broker himself knows where the money came from or where it went. It is not enough that no money ever actually got lost or misappropriated or even mishandled. The states have rigorous laws and regulations concerning the recordkeeping itself, and if they are not followed scrupulously and to the letter, the broker is in violation of the law and can rarely expect to find sympathy when he is called upon to explain his lapse.

Generally, the license laws and regulations will explain in some detail just how the records are to be kept; also, the state's license law enforcement agency will provide detailed instructions to brokers concerning the exact method of keeping the records, and brokers are expected to be fully aware of them and to abide by them. This is particularly important because the state's inspectors have the right to enter any brokerage office in the state whenever they please and demand to see the trust account records, and they do it, too. The reasons are obvious: The handling of money is the most delicate and sensitive of the broker's duties, and a licensing agency will be very careful to assure that it is done properly by all.

The account the broker keeps this money in is a special type of account that identifies the money as being in the custody of the broker, but not actually his own. This is critically important: If the broker should go bankrupt or have a judgment entered against him, his trust accounts are immune from claim, since they do not represent any assets of his own. Thus, the owners of the money are protected from changes in the broker's personal or business financial position.

Because of this protection, one specific rule must be followed to the letter. First, the broker must *never* put any of his own money into the trust accounts. (Some states allow him to keep a minimum balance of his own personal funds for the specific purpose of avoiding or reducing service charges banks impose.) Second, he must *never* keep trust money anywhere but in such accounts. Any violation of these rules is considered *commingling*; that is, the broker is keeping his own money and trust monies together, and that is the cardinal sin of trusteeship or escrow agency. Further, he usually is required to deposit all trust monies coming into his possession into such an account as soon as possible: Many states allow him only until the close of the business day following the receipt of the money. Therefore, salespersons who collect such money are required to give the money to the broker as soon as possible. Some brokers even give the salespeople deposit slips to the account to use for the proper deposit of these funds to avoid the time delay of bringing them back to the office. Other brokers insist on having the trust monies delivered to them by salespeople immediately so that the broker can personally supervise their proper handling.

INFRACTIONS OF LICENSE LAW

License laws and the accompanying rules and regulations contain lists of specific offenses that are defined as violations of the law. These lists should not be interpreted as being exclusive in that they are the *only* possible infractions; the laws are full of phraseology allowing much broader interpretation. Frequently a catchall category is written in to include "any other behavior or practice which constitutes unethical, fraudulent or dishonest dealing." This kind of definition would enable inclusion of just about anything that might be considered detrimental to the licensing purpose.

Following is a list of specific business practices usually included as particular infractions of the law. It should be noted that the law can be violated in many other ways, also, such as by acting while unlicensed, improperly paying licensing fees, improper responses to requests to appear at hearings, and so on.

Mishandling Trust Monies

1. Commingling trust monies with personal funds.
2. Not remitting trust monies to a trust account within a reasonable time.
3. Salesperson not remitting trust monies to the broker quickly.
4. Accepting noncash payments on behalf of a principal without the principal's knowledge and agreement. (This is a particularly knotty problem: It is required that trust monies be in the form of cash or check; if they are in any other form, such as a postdated check, a note, etc., then they cannot be deposited immediately and so are not money in hand. If a broker submits an offer in which, say, the earnest money is in such a form, the broker's employer must know of it, and approve.)

Misrepresentation and Fraud

1. False advertising.
2. Intentionally misleading someone.
3. Acting for more than one party to a transaction without the knowledge *and* permission of all affected parties.
4. Using trademarks or other identification of a firm or organization (such as REALTORS®) of which one is not a member.
5. Not identifying oneself as a licensee in a transaction to which one is also a party (this often is not necessary if the licensee does not share in any way in the commission).
6. Taking kickbacks, referral fees, placement fees, commissions, and the like without the employer's knowledge. An exception would be taking referral fees or commissions from financing companies, since the act of getting financing for a buyer cannot be thought of as damaging to a seller.

7. Guaranteeing future profits. Most state license laws or regulations forbid the licensee to promise a potential buyer that he will prosper in any particular financial way.

8. Pretending to represent owners by whom one is not actually employed.

9. Failing to identify the broker in all advertising. Many states specifically prohibit "blind ads," which are advertisements by brokerage firms but which appear to have been placed by individuals.

Improper Business Practice

1. Salesperson pretending to be a broker, or pretending to be employed by a broker other than the one he actually works for.

2. Offering property on terms other than those specifically authorized by the broker's employer.

3. Failing to submit *all* offers to the broker's employer. The broker is usually hired to solicit offers; even silly or ridiculous offers must be submitted to the broker's employer for his consideration. This must also be done when the employer already is considering other offers. Only after the employer has accepted an offer, and so created a sale contract, may offers be withheld. However, a broker may be instructed by the employer to turn down offers below a certain price, or lacking some other requirement of the seller's, but these instructions must be specific.

4. Attempting to thwart another broker's exclusive listing. When a broker has an exclusive agency or exclusive right-to-sell listing, the law requires that any other broker who comes across an offer on the listed property must submit it to the listing broker and may not deal directly with the owner. Also, it is generally illegal for a broker to attempt to convince an owner to fire his current broker and hire him instead. This provision often goes so far as to prohibit contact with owners who have listings that are about to expire; the competing broker must wait until the listing has expired before contacting the owner.

5. Inducing someone to break a contract.

6. Accepting a net listing. (Some states prohibit net listings, but in states where they are allowed this practice would not be a violation. See Chapter 8 for description of net listings.)

7. Failing to put an expiration date in a listing.

8. Putting the brokerage's sign on listed property without the owner's permission. In most states, the creation of a listing between an owner and a broker does *not* automatically give the broker the right to post his sign: This must be agreed to specifically.

9. Blockbusting or discrimination. Blockbusting is the practice of soliciting listings by pointing out that "undesirables" (i.e., persons of another race, creed, color, national origin) are moving into the neighborhood, and the owner would be advised to get out while the getting's good. Discrimination refers to any action denying the right to buy or sell to someone for the same reasons.

Failure to Impart Required Information

1. Failing to leave copies of relevant contracts with all parties involved.

2. Failing to deliver a closing statement to all parties entitled to one.

3. Failing to inform all parties of relevant closing costs.

4. Failing to impart any other required information. Various states have differing

requirements here. Some have none; others may require disclosure of any significant structural defects, liens against the property, and so on. The broker should check his own state law to see what the requirements are in his jurisdiction. Sometimes local law will have influence in this area as well.

Improper Handling of Commissions

1. Paying a commission to an unlicensed person. Many states allow a broker to pay a small referral fee to unlicensed persons, but generally this is limited to referral only, and the unlicensed person may not have engaged in any other aspect of effecting the listing and/or sale except to refer the broker to a possible client or customer.
2. Paying a commission to a licensee not in the broker's employ.
3. Salesperson receiving a commission payment from someone other than his employing broker. License law is very specific about (2) and (3). A broker may share a commission with another licensed broker with whom he has cooperated on a deal. However, in no other case may he share commissions with anyone other than the licensees who work for him.
4. Collecting a higher commission from an employer than agreed upon, unless the employer agrees with the new arrangement.

Other

1. Being convicted of certain crimes.
2. Making false statements on license applications.
3. Violating any part of license law.
4. Any other evidence of incompetence, unworthiness, dishonesty, and the like.

It should be pointed out that not all of these provisions may be found in the law of each state, and that each state is likely to have additional provisions not listed here.

AGENCY LAW

In addition to abiding by his state's specific laws governing real estate licensees, a broker is legally an *agent*, and comes under that broad category of the legal system called *agency law*. Whereas brokerage and licensing law generally is well codified and conveniently described, agency law has its roots in history and has developed over the years as a part of the common law as well as specifically legislated and codified law. Many aspects of agency law are included within licensing law, but it is wise to have some basic knowledge of the generalities of agency law itself, since it affects the broker just as much as any other law he must abide by.

An *agent* is employed by his *principal* (usually the property owner in the case of the real estate broker). The broker's function is to deal with third parties (prospective buyers or tenants) on behalf of his principal.

A *general agent* has broad powers, including the right to commit his principal in business and financial transactions. A real estate broker, however, is a *special agent* because his agency powers are quite limited. Essentially they include little more than publicizing and presenting the principal's property to prospects, and soliciting offers from them. The broker normally cannot *commit* his principal to anything; it is the principal who decides how to respond to offers. In some instances a principal will grant a broker additional agency powers, but these are special arrangements that are not typical of the business as a whole.

The principal may even refuse to deal with anyone the broker brings to him, although he still may be liable to pay the broker a commission. This is because the broker has been hired to solicit offers. The existence of a listing is not construed by the law as an offer to sell, but merely as a *solicitation* of offers to buy. Even though an offer may agree specifically with all the conditions the owner spelled out in the listing, the owner is not legally compelled to accept the offer. But this refers only to any responsibility he may have to someone who makes him an offer.

His contract with the broker is another matter entirely. If a broker has brought someone to make a *bona fide* (genuine and in good faith) offer that exactly meets or exceeds the conditions put in the listing by the owner, then the broker has done exactly what he was hired to do: to solicit an offer meeting certain conditions. Therefore, the broker normally would be considered to have earned his commission. Even if the owner refuses to accept the offer, he must pay the broker the agreed upon commission.

Duties of the Parties

The agent is an employee of the principal, and must follow his principal's intructions implicitly. Furthermore, he has a duty to act in his employer's best interests, even when doing so means that he cannot act in his own favor. More specifically, agency law requires that the agent abide by the following obligations to his principal:

He must *obey* his principal's instructions. (Except, of course, when he is instructed to do something illegal.)

He must be *loyal* to his principal's interests.

He must act in *good faith.*

He is expected to be able to use his own *professional judgment, skill,* and *ability* in his actions. This is particularly so in the case of licensed agents such as real estate brokers, because they are assumed to have met certain standards by virtue of qualifying for licensing.

He must be able to *account* for all money belonging to others that comes into his possession. Real estate brokers often collect rents, earnest money payments, and other money on behalf of parties other than their principals; by doing so they also develop responsibility to these other parties for the proper handling of their money.

He must perform his duties *in person.* Normally, this would mean that he could not delegate his duties to anyone else unless the principal approved of the arrangement. Because of the nature of the real estate brokerage business and the establishment of the broker-salesperson relationship by all state licensing laws, a real estate broker has the implied right to delegate his funtion to duly licensed salespersons and brokers in his employ.

He must keep his principal *fully informed* as to developments affecting their relationship. In the case of a real estate broker, he should report all offers made on the principal's property, as well as all other information he acquires that may affect the principal's property, price, etc.

The principal also has responsibilities to the agent. He must *compensate* the agent for his services and reimburse expenses the agent makes on his behalf. However, selling expenses, such as advertising, are paid by the agent out of the commission the principal pays him. The principal also should make the agent fully aware of his duties and inform him about anything that will affect his performance.

The fact that the broker as agent is responsible to his employer and must remain loyal to him creates some significant problems in the proper conduct of the brokerage business. Most important, it must be remembered that in most transactions, *there is no such thing as the buyer's agent.*[1] All agents involved usually will be paid by sharing in the commission that the seller will pay; therefore they *all* are the seller's agent. In brokerage practice, it is certainly prevalent that buyers themselves assume that the agents they work with are working for them.

Even among brokers and in license law, it is considered unethical practice for a broker to bypass another agent in order to deal with that agent's *client*. In brokerage terminology, a client is a potential buyer to whom a broker is showing property in an effort to make a sale. Certainly, clients are absolutely necessary to the operation of the business, but all agents must be especially careful to make sure that nothing they do while they work with a client could be thought of as detrimental to the interests of a seller, since under the law the agents are working for the seller and must protect *his* interests, and not the buyer's.

GENERAL CONTRACT LAW

The average American has a little familiarity with contracts: usually enough to inspire fear, but not understanding. A wide belief is that contracts must be filled with obscure, legalistic language and a lot of fine print, and that only someone with a lot of training can hope to be able to write them and interpret them properly. This really is not so, because all the law requires of a contract is that it clearly state what it is supposed to. At the present time, there is an admirable trend under way to simplify the language in contracts, making it easier for them to be understood by laymen.

The real estate broker will find his work to involve a great many contracts, with which he must be totally familiar and comfortable. He has to be able

---

[1]We are not saying that buyers *never* employ agents; sometimes they do. However, in most transactions, especially in residential sales, the agent is employed exclusively by the seller, and the buyer pays no commission or other agent's fees.

to explain them to the people he works with and, in most states, he takes the responsibility for actually drawing up many contracts that will affect the actions and responsibilities of others. Therefore, it is imperative that he understand their nature. But one word of warning: A real estate broker is *not* an attorney. He may not give legal advice. In any discussion of contracts he should make a point of emphasizing that he is not practicing law and that any significant questions concerning contracts must be referred to a qualified attorney.

Nature of Contracts

A contract is an agreement between two or more *parties*, in which each promises to do, or is shown to have done, something *benefiting* the others. Benefit can take many forms; one is the payment of money, although contracts involving no money can be perfectly valid. Since each party must benefit, contracts must involve *exchanges* of benefits. Jones gives up something to Smith, in return for which Smith gives up something to Jones. One example is a purchase: A gives up money to B and B gives up the thing A is buying. A valid contract without involving money might be swapping a car for a lawn mower. Two people could agree that neither will build ugly structures on their land where the other could see them.

While there are other requirements that must be met, the critical test of the validity of a contract is whether or not the parties can be shown to benefit from it. So, if you and I sign an agreement which says simply that I will give you my automobile next Tuesday, we do not have a contract because no benefit *to me* appears in it. However, if our agreement says that I will give you my car next Tuesday in return for some benefit to me from you (money, your car, etc.), then a contract could exist.

Enforcement of Contracts

A valid contract has the *force of law* among the parties to it. It is as if they had agreed to enact a law among themselves and promised to abide by it. However, when someone violates the provisions of a contract, the law will do nothing about the dispute until one of the injured parties petitions the court to intervene. At that point, the law requires the affected parties to appear and to present their arguments. Then the court (a judge or jury) makes a decision as to what is to be done, and by whom. (This description, of course, is somewhat simplified; resolving a contract dispute in court often consumes a lot of time and expense. Many violated contracts never reach court because the offended parties do not want to bother with it.) All parties to contracts have the inherent right to request the court to render judgment if they feel that other parties to the agreement are not living up to it.

Generally, one who brings a contract to court has two remedies available. First, he can ask that the court require *specific performance* of the offending party. This means he wants the court to order the other party to live up to the agreement. By the time a contract dispute reaches court, it often is too late for mere performance to do any (or enough) good. In such a case, the injured party may seek *damages*, claiming that he had suffered a loss due to the other party's violation of the contract, and asking that the court order the violator to make the loss good.

Once the court has reached a decision, parties to the dispute are *required by law* to abide by it. If they do not, they are in contempt of court and can be fined or jailed; thus every contract carries the threat of court action against violation, backed up by potentially severe penalties.

REQUIREMENTS OF VALID CONTRACTS

A contract cannot be considered by a court unless it is *valid*. Some kinds of contracts may have additional requirements for validity, but all must show the following:

1. Mutual agreement
2. Consideration
3. Legally competent parties
4. A legal purpose
5. Legal form

Mutual Agreement

Mutual agreement (often referred to as "offer and acceptance," "reality of consent," "mutual assent," "meeting of the minds," and similar phrases) means that all parties recognize that an offer has been made and has been accepted by the others. All agree to the nature of the requirements made of each. Generally, the parties will agree to do, or not to do, some thing or things in return for some kind of obligation from the others.

Provided that the other essentials of a contract are present, once an offer has been accepted, a contract exists. The parties' actions creating the contract must be intentional and deliberate. Generally their signatures to a written contract are evidence of this, provided that no fraud, misrepresentation, duress, or mistake occurred. However, many kinds of contracts need not be written; in such cases the testimony of the affected parties provides the evidence that an agreement exists.

Consideration

Consideration refers to the benefit received by the parties. It can take many forms; all that must be shown is that each party received something of use to him and that he was willing to oblige himself in some way in order to get it. Payment of money is always consideration, as is the transfer of ownership of anything that can be shown to have a market value. In addition, some transfers of *rights* are consideration also; as an example, a lease transfers rights to use property, but not ownership of the property. Some further examples are:

1. X pays $50,000 to Y. Y transfers ownership of his house to X.
2. X pays Y $300 per month. Y gives X the right to use an office for each month for which X pays.
3. X agrees not to hang his laundry outside where Y and Z can see it.
   Y agrees not to hang his laundry outside where X and Z can see it.
   Z agrees not to hang his laundry outside where X and Y can see it.
4. R agrees to try to find a buyer for S's house. S agrees to pay R a commission of 8% of the sale price if R finds a suitable buyer.
5. J agrees to pay K $80,000 in 30 days, at which time K will transfer ownership of a certain building now owned by K.
6. A transfers ownership of his house to B. B transfers to A the ownership of his parking lot, four albums of rare stamps, two sets of dishes, and a mongrel dog.
7. M transfers to his son (M, Jr.) the ownership of a building in return for the "love and affection" which M, Jr. has given to M in the past.
8. L lends Q $10,000. Q gives L the right to have Q's house sold if Q defaults on his debt to L.

All of these include legal consideration. Some involve money, but in 3 and 6, no money changes hands. In most, the consideration involves the parties performing some act; in 3, however, the parties agree *not* to do something. Numbers 2, 3, and 8 include the exchange of rights; 4 includes the exchange of services, and the others involve the exchange of ownership of things.

All of the examples are real estate contracts: 2 is a *lease*, 3 is a *restrictive covenant*, 4 is a *listing*, 5 is a *contract of sale*; 8 is a *mortgage*, and 1, 6, and 7 are *deeds*.

Good and Valuable Consideration   In all except 7 we have *valuable consideration*, which is anything that would be of value to practically everyone and thus could be sold for money. Money itself is valuable, as is ownership of things, receipt of someone's services, receipt of various kinds of rights, and so on. However, things like friendship, love, and affection are not valuable consideration because their worth is entirely subjective: You may set a very high value upon the love you receive from your spouse, but to most of the rest of us it is valueless since we don't even know him or her. Also, someone's affection is not a transferable benefit, in that it can't be sold. Friendship and love are of value to the one who receives them, and if he agrees to transfer benefit in return for them he can be held to his bargain. However, these are called *good consideration* to distinguish them from marketable valuable consideration.

The law does not require that *equal* consideration accrue to all parties, only that some consideration exist. There is only one exception: The courts will not enforce a contract requiring only the simultaneous exchange of different sums of money.

Competent Parties

Competent parties are persons whom the law allows to enter into contractual arrangements. Not all *legal persons* are human. Corporations, partnerships, trusts and some other organizations are legal persons, and can be parties to contracts: One can contract to purchase an automobile from XYZ Auto Sales, Inc., although the firm is not a living being. Furthermore, not all people are *competent* to contract; some are legally unable to, and many others may do so only under carefully defined circumstances.

Nonhuman Parties   Usually the law requires each party to a contract to ascertain the other's legal competence. While the law places few restrictions upon the contracting ability of corporations and some other organizations, they may operate under self-imposed restrictions. A corporation's charter can permit or forbid it to enter certain kinds of contractual agreements, and it may require that some or all of the permitted functions be carried out in certain ways. A person contracting with an organization must assure himself that it may engage in such a contract, and that the contract is executed and carried out consistent with its limitations and prescribed methods.

People   Among people, there are two important categories of incompetent parties—infants and insane persons—and several lesser ones, such as drunkards, convicts, and others.

INFANTS   *Infants* (or *minors*) are people who have not yet attained the age of majority, which is eighteen to twenty-one in various states. While one may doubt that a hulking seventeen-year-old football star could be incompetent at anything, the law says he is. One who is immature, foolish, or naive in business judgment can be considered by the law to be quite capable of assuming responsibility for his actions providing he has attained the age of majority. Minors are not prohibited from contracting, so no law is broken if a minor signs a contract.

However, the minor can *void* the contract later on, if he wishes, while adult parties to the contract do not have that privilege. The minor may not void (or disaffirm) only part of the contract; he must abandon it entirely. If he agrees to buy property from an adult, he has the right to void the agreement anytime before it is carried out. The adult, however, must honor the contract unless and until the minor actually disaffirms it. However, the minor cannot, for example, disaffirm the part of the contract that specifies that he must pay for the property while at the same time requiring the adult to transfer it to him anyway; he must abandon the *entire* contract. Furthermore, if he disaffirms it after the adult party has provided him some benefit under it, he may have to pay for what he had already received by the time he decided to void the contract.

The whole idea behind legal incompetence is a matter of *protection*. We know that people can be too young to make binding commitments requiring mature judgment. Some age has to be chosen to represent the limit of protection, and that is why each state has an age of majority. Once a person attains this age he loses the protection of legal infancy, but he is given a reasonable time beyond the attainment of majority to decide whether or not he will disaffirm any contracts he had entered into as a minor.

INSANE PERSONS *Insane persons* are another important category of legal incompetence. Unlike infancy, insanity is a state that can come and go. One who is sane can become insane, and one who is insane can be cured and become sane again. Also, a person under severe stress or other temporary disturbance can become so disoriented that the law may extend the protection of incompetence to him during that episode.

Legal protection of an insane person takes two forms. If he has had a guardian appointed by the court, then all contracts he enters into are *void*: He has no capacity to contract at all. If he has no guardian, his contracts usually are voidable, like those of minors. He has the choice to require that his bargains with others be carried out or to disaffirm them.

OTHER INCOMPETENCY Certain *other forms of incapacity* earn one the legal protection of incompetency. Contracts made by a person who is severely intoxicated with alcohol or is under the dominating influence of drugs known to affect judgment might later be considered voidable. Felon prisoners usually have no right to contract; this situation is described by the rather grim term of *civilly dead*. Usually when the sentence has been served, and sometimes at the time parole is secured, most rights are restored.

Necessaries Not all contracts by incompetents are voidable; generally courts will enforce contracts for *necessaries*, which are such things as food, clothing, shelter, and sometimes others such as contracts for employment or education. Here again the law extends protection, acknowledging that in today's world some contracts are so important that they take precedence over other protection. A known incompetent may be at a serious disadvantage if his personal circumstances *require* him to contract, so the law allows some incompetents what amounts to a limited competency. For things that are necessary to them, they are allowed to create binding contracts that they cannot disaffirm and that a court can enforce against them. This gives other competent parties the protection *they* seek in any contractual arrangement, and removes any reluctance they may have to deal with an incompetent.

Lawful Purpose

A contract requiring any of its parties to violate the law is usually void. However, if the contract's basic purpose can be saved, a court will uphold the contract but strike out that part requiring an illegal act. As an example, the Federal Open Housing Act of 1968 declared illegal certain deed covenants that required some home buyers to agree that they would resell only to people of particular racial or cultural backgrounds. Many deeds to homes contained such clauses, but their prohibition had no effect upon the main purpose of the deeds, which was to transfer title to realty in return for consideraton. However, if someone had created a special separate contract *only* for the purpose of restricting the racial or cultural background of purchasers of certain real estate, then that entire contract would have been voided by the enactment of the law. If this kind of agreement came into being after the law was passed, then it would be void from the beginning and would *never* be a contract.

Legal Form

Some contracts are required to follow a certain form or be drawn in a certain manner. For example, deeds and contracts of sale require that legal descriptions of the property be included; without them they are invalid. However, much of the wordy, archaic language that frequently appears in contracts is *not* required by any law and appears only by tradition.

Statute of Frauds   For most real estate contracts, there is one critical requirement with respect to form: In most states, all real estate contracts—except leases of one year or less—*must be written*. Each state has a law called the *Statute of Frauds*, which requires that all contracts of certain types be written if legal enforcement is to be possible. Included are all contracts in which land or an interest in land is sold and contracts that cannot be performed within one year. This latter category would include lease contracts extending more than one year.

A listing contract is a contract of *employment*, which is a category not usually covered by the Statute of Frauds. However, many states, in their real estate licensing laws, require or imply that listings must be in writing.

The definition of "land or an interest in land" is very specific and quite broad. It includes future interests, so in addition to deeds, contracts of sale must be written. It includes partial interests, so mortgages must be written. It includes improvements to land and attachments to it, so contracts involving purchase of buildings or growing plants must be written, even if the actual land beneath them is not part of the transaction. However, once an attachment to land is severed from it (such as trees being cut down or crops being reaped) it becomes personal property and is no longer subject to that part of the Statute of Frauds covering realty. This law usually covers much more than just realty contracts, so it is quite possible that many other nonrealty contracts can also be required by law to be written.

DURESS, MISREPRESENTATION, AND FRAUD

All parties to a valid contract must have entered into it willingly and without having been misled about significant matters. Thus, a person who points a gun at someone else to force him to sign a contract cannot expect much sympathy from the courts. Nor could he if he had misled (deliberately or unintentionally) others so that they agreed to contracts based on false information. The former situation is *duress*; the latter is either *misrepresentation* or *fraud*.

Duress

Duress can take many forms. When circumstances force someone to do something against his will he could say duress exists, but the law does not always see it that way. Duress caused by one who benefits under the contract usually will be recognized by the court; this would include forcing someone's assent by threatening him illegally. If duress is caused by one's *own* actions, the court is reluctant to recognize it. If you buy a new house and thereby become desperate to sell your own home, that is pretty much your own fault. If you create your own duress, you usually have to suffer with it.

Misrepresentation and Fraud

Misrepresentation is loosely defined as *unintentional* giving of false information, whereas fraud is *deliberate*. There is another difference, too: Fraud is a *crime* as well as a civil wrong. A victim of either fraud or misrepresentation is entitled to compensation for what he was misled into losing. Fraud victims may also receive *punitive* damages, which is a form of extra payment required of the culprit, as a kind of punishment. Finally, the perpetrator of a fraud may be prosecuted in criminal court and may end up being convicted, fined, and/or imprisoned.

Proving Misrepresentation or Fraud   A victim must prove three things to show that misrepresentation or fraud exists: (a) that the incorrect information was relevant to the contract he is disputing—that is, it was *material*; (b) that it was *reasonable for him to rely upon* this false information; and (c) that this *reliance led him to suffer some loss* as a result.

Some Information Must Be Divulged   For some kinds of contracts, the law requires that certain information be provided by at least some of the parties. If it is not, then misrepresentation or fraud may exist. For example, most licensing laws require that brokers inform other parties if they are acting as principals in the contract as well as agents. Also, most states require a broker to disclose which party he is acting for, especially if more than one party to a transaction is paying him a commission.

DISCHARGE AND BREACH OF CONTRACT

Contractual arrangements can be terminated in two general ways. *Discharge* of a contract occurs when no one is required to perform under it any longer. *Breach of contract* occurs when one party makes performance impossible, even when other parties are willing, by refusing to do his part or by otherwise preventing discharge of the contract.

Discharge

Most often discharge occurs by *performance*: this means that everyone has done what was promised to do and nothing more is required of anyone. Other forms of discharge involve agreement to terminate a contract, for one reason or another, before it would have been discharged by performance. Sometimes the parties may decide to terminate one agreement by substituting another one for it. Discharge can also occur when the parties simply agree to abandon the contract without substituting anyone or any other for it. It is advisable that any agreement discharging a contract for reasons other than performance or limitation be in writing. Under some situations (particularly when some, but not all parties have performed or begun to perform under the contract), an agreement discharging an existing contract *must* be in writing.

Statute of Limitations The law limits the time in which a contracting party may take a dispute to court for settlement. This law is the *Statute of Limitations*, and it varies from state to state not only in the length of time allowed, but also with respect to types of contracts, which are allowed various lengths of time for challenge. Once the time limit has expired, a dispute will not be heard in court unless it can be shown that extraordinary circumstances prevented a more timely filing. Therefore, once the time limit has expired, a contract can be said to have been discharged, since legal remedy is no longer available.

Breach

Breach occurs when a party violates a contract's provisions. Often this action can be considered serious enough to terminate the contract by making it impossible, or very disadvantageous, for the other parties to continue the arrangement. The injured parties must seek remedy from the courts, unless they and the violating party or parties can come to some agreement discharging the contract. If breach is successfully proved, the injured parties are entitled to a *judgment* for damages or for specific performance. A judgment is a ruling by the court that the offending party must perform some act, and if he does not he is in contempt of court and various sanctions are available.

There are several ways of proving breach. Failing to perform completely as specified in a contract is breach; so is a declaration by the offending party that he does not intend to fulfill his obligations under the contract. It is also a breach if a party makes it impossible, by his actions, for one or more of the other parties to the contract to perform their duties. One important attribute of a breach is that it terminates the obligations of other parties to continue to perform under the contract; one who has breached a contract cannot have that agreement held good against other parties.

Following are some common forms of breach that occur in real estate contracts brokers often deal with.

Listing Contracts *Breach by broker* includes (a) failing to advertise and market the property as specified; (b) misrepresenting the buyer's capacity to perform; and (c) subverting the agency responsibility by acting to the benefit of buyer against the principal's interest.

Breach by principal includes (a) failing to pay a commission earned by the broker; (b) failing to allow the broker to market, show, and sell the property as specified; and (c) misrepresenting pertinent facts about the property to the broker.

Sale Contracts *Breach by seller* includes (a) failure to provide the deed when the buyer has performed and tendered payment as specified in the contract; and (b) failure to perform to other specifications of the contract (i.e., provide termite bond, abstract, etc.).

Breach by buyer includes (a) failure to conclude the transaction when the seller performs and tenders deed; and (b) failure to perform under other specifications (i.e., make good faith efforts to acquire financing, etc.).

Injustice

The courts will not enforce a contract if it appears that by doing so it will aid an obvious injustice. This does not mean that someone can get out of a bad bargain on this basis, but only that the court will not enforce the contract if, in its judgment, there is a gross injustice involved. As an example, if Jones freely agrees to buy Smith's property for $50,000 and later discovers that is is worth only $40,000, he cannot claim injustice if he cannot show that Smith or his agent misled him into paying the higher price. Suppose, however, that Green and Brown *orally* agree that Green will buy land from Brown. After paying for the land, Green builds a house on it. At that point Brown goes to court saying that since the purchase agreement was oral and not written it has no validity, and Green must vacate, thus allowing Brown to take over the house and land at no cost to him. Here the court will award title to Green even though no written sale agreement exists and no written deed exists. First, there is a principle of law that recognizes such transactions when the buyer "substantially improves" the property. Second, if Brown had engineered the whole scheme specifically in order to take advantage of Green, the court would be legalizing a fraud by recognizing Brown's continued claim to the title.

Outside Circumstances

Contracts can be terminated by events outside the specific terms of the agreement. New legislation may invalidate all or part of a contract. The death of a party can void some contracts; so can illness or injury to the point that the party affected cannot properly discharge his obligations. If the subject matter of the contract is destroyed (such as a house burning down while it is listed with a broker for sale) the contract usually is terminated. Finally, under the doctrine of *reality of consent*, a contract that is the result of a genuine mistake can be void. For example, if a seller has two properties for sale, one on 21 Street and the other on 31 Street, and a buyer makes an offer on one and the seller thinks he is accepting an offer on the other, there is no contract because, in actuality, the parties have not agreed to anything. Regardless of what may be written down and signed, no genuine meeting of the minds has occurred, and so no contract exists.

CONCLUSION

The broker operates under a number of bodies of law; most important are license law and agency law. In order to conduct his business properly, it is essential that a broker and his employee licensees be fully aware of the provisions of these laws as they apply in their states and localities. A broker's license is the key to his livelihood; it is imperative that he avoid violations that will jeopardize his license. Many violations also will subject him to judgments for damages; he can lose much of his accumulated wealth as well as his business.

Many brokers violate the law unknowingly because they are ignorant of it; however, that is no defense in court or at a hearing. No ethical broker would knowingly engage in fraud or deceptive practices or other kinds of improper dealing—not if he values his reputation. In the brokerage business, a broker's reputation is his most useful business asset. But even if he is dealing honestly and straightforwardly he may still violate various provisions of the law. Although some may seem unreasonable at first glance (actually, upon further investigation their significance usually becomes apparent), they are nonetheless part of the law and must be observed. There is no point in becoming a sadder but wiser person when it is too late, not when a comparatively small effort devoted to understanding the laws governing one's conduct is all that is necessary to avoid trouble. This is all the more important because in this day and age dissatisfied customers are becoming more and more likely to take legal action against businesses and businesspeople they feel have treated them unjustly.

DISCUSSION QUESTIONS AND PROJECTS

1. From the agency in your state that regulates and licenses real estate brokers and salespeople (Real Estate Commission, Licensing Agency, Real Estate Department, etc.), secure a copy of your state's licensing law and review it thoroughly.
2. From the same source, find out how many people apply to take real estate licensing examinations each year, how many pass, and how many appear to remain in the business on a career basis.
3. From the same source, find out the most common violations for which complaints are received and hearings held concerning real estate licensees.
4. What are the penalties in your state for violation of license law?
5. Describe the legal differences between a broker and a salesperson.

6. What are the procedures that your state law requires a broker to follow in the handling of trust (escrow) monies?

7. Describe a situation in your experience in which a real estate licensee violated agency law. What would have been the proper procedure? Did anyone suffer from his actions?

8. Describe three situations in which you think a real estate licensee would be tempted to violate license or agency law. Why are they tempting? What would be the proper procedure to follow in each instance?

9. If a contract is breached, what are the remedies the injured party should seek? Does it make sense to take every dispute to court? Why or why not?

10. What should a salesperson do to make sure that all parties to contracts that he negotiates are competent?

11. Give three examples of misrepresentation or fraud in a real estate transaction. How could they have been avoided?

12. Find out exactly what contracts in your state are required by its Statute of Frauds (or similar legislation) to be in writing. Given this information, can you think of any situations in which verbal contracts would be enforceable in your state in situations a real estate brokerage might encounter?

13. Using one of the contract forms presented on pages 132 and 154 of this text, analyze it to make sure that all the required parts of an enforceable contract are present.

Case Studies

LICENSE LAW

1. Elwood R. was a licensed real estate salesperson; his license was held by licensed broker James G. Elwood's wife became ill with cancer. After hospitalization and surgery she was cured, but the cost of her treatment came to more than $20,000. Since she was employed by a firm which provided medical benefits as part of its fringe benefits package, Elwood had not included her in the medical insurance policy he had on himself. However, it turned out that her employer had made an error in his insurance coverage and in actuality, Mrs. R. had not been covered. She and Elwood were liable for the full extent of her medical bills.

The result for them was financial disaster. Elwood tried to make ends meet, but he was unable to do so, and eventually he did something illegal. He negotiated a contract of sale involving Mr. and Mrs. L., who paid a $1000 earnest money payment toward the purchase of a house. However, without their knowledge, Elwood altered the contract to read that the deposit was $100, and pocketed the other $900. Naturally, he intended to pay it back somehow before the transaction closed, but he wasn't able to. When Mr. and Mrs. L. found out what had happened, they went to James G., Elwood's broker, and demanded that he refund the $900. He refused to do so, saying that he had had no knowledge of what had happened, and that he was not responsible for his salesperson's criminal activity. Mr. and Mrs. L. appealed to the State Real Estate Commission.

The Commission held a hearing at which the facts were presented. They pointed out to Broker G. that license law specifically stated that he was responsible for *all* activity by his sales force in the course of business, and required him to refund the $900. They also revoked Broker G.'s license, as well as Elwood's.

2. Jane R. and Ben M. passed the broker's license examination and set up a real estate brokerage business in May of 1988. Shortly afterward they secured a listing on a large tract of land offered at $300,000, with a 10% selling commission. In August they negotiated a full-price sale of the land. Naturally they were pleased; when the deal closed they would get a commission of $30,000. However, they overlooked one thing. The buyer had given them an earnest money check for $25,000, but had dated the check October 15, 1988, which was the contracted date of closing. He explained that he did not have the ready cash, but by the closing date he would be able to make it good.

Brokers R. and M. did not disclose that the earnest money deposit was a postdated check; they simply wrote into the contract that a check for $25,000 had been received. They put it into their office safe, but their seller naturally assumed it had been deposited and cleared. Of course, the obvious happened. On the closing date the buyer did not show up and attempts to contact him were fruitless. The brokers deposited the earnest money check; however, it was returned unpaid because of insufficient funds.

The seller demanded his share of the forfeited earnest money. When the brokers told him what had happened, he sued them for his share and complained to the State Real Estate Commission. The court awarded the seller a judgment for $15,000, plus court costs. The Real Estate Commission revoked the brokers' licenses.

If the brokers had notified the seller that the deposit was in the form of a postdated check, and if he had accepted the offer on that basis, they would have been blameless. By concealing that fact, they lost their licenses, their business, and several thousand dollars.

A Case Study

INCOMPETENCY

Broker Marion C. showed a lovely new home to prospect Janis P. Janis decided that she wanted to buy it, and offered $125,000 for it. The builder accepted the offer, and Janis's earnest money check for $25,000 was deposited. Five days later, Janis drove up in her new Cadillac and discussed some alterations she wanted to have done. The builder agreed to do them, but asked that $20,000 of the earnest money be paid to him to provide the funds he needed to make the changes. This was agreeable to Janis, who signed an agreement instructing Broker C. to release $20,000 of her deposit to the builder and acknowledging that if she defaulted on the deal, her entire earnest money deposit would be forfeit. Broker C. and the builder further agreed, in a separate contract, that if Janis defaulted, Broker C. would keep the remaining $5,000 of the deposit, and would relist the property for sale.

The work began immediately, and for several days Janis would appear at the construction site to observe the work. At all times she was expensively dressed. One day she said that she had to return to her home in South Carolina to make final arrangements to move to her new home, but she would return in three weeks to close the deal as scheduled and move into her new home.

Ten days after she left, her earnest money check, which had been drawn on a small bank in the same state where she bought her new home, was returned to Broker C. for insufficient funds. The broker called the bank. He was told that they were sorry that it had taken so long to return the check, but that they had been a bit shorthanded. Further investigation by Broker C. revealed that in South Carolina Janis had been undergoing treatment for severe psychosis and a year before had been declared legally incompetent by the courts. When she had returned there, her family had committted her to a mental hospital for treatment.

Broker C. then contacted the builder to get back the $20,000. Legally, the earnest money had been the builder's all along, and Broker C. was only holding it in trust; therefore, he was liable to make good the bad check. However, the building business was poor, and he was in the process of filing bankruptcy. The best Broker C. could do was to secure a lien on the unsold property; however, her lien was low in priority and no payment ever was made.

Naturally, she was upset. By abiding scrupulously by the law (by handling trust monies as instructed by the people it belonged to) she had lost $20,000. As soon as the $25,000 check was returned, she had to make good the deficiency in her trust account; $5000 of the deficiency was due to her anyway, so her net loss was $20,000. She complained to the real estate commission that the law required her, in effect, to take the risk that a deposited check would clear. They were sympathetic but could say only they would look into the matter, and possibly suggest revisions in the law that would lessen brokers' risks in the future.

Marion C. is philosophical about the experience. "If I tried to check the competency of everyone I do business with, I wouldn't have time for anything else. If you run a business you take some chances, and things like this will happen. I'm having my lawyers look into the possibility of rewriting my contracts so that I don't have to pay money out of my trust account until checks have cleared, but we have to make sure that it's legal for me to do that.

"Luck runs good and bad. I lost a lot on this deal, but I've had other deals that were so smooth that I've made large commissions with what seems like only a few hours work. I suppose it all evens out."

REFERENCES

ATTEBERRY, WILLIAM L., KARL G. PEARSON, AND MICHAEL P. LITKA, *Real Estate Law*, ch. 10. New York, NY: John Wiley & Sons, 1984.

FISHER, FREDERICK J., *Broker Beware: Selling Real Estate Within the Law*, ch. 1-3. Reston, VA: Reston Publishing Company, Inc., 1981.

GOLDSTEIN, PAUL, *Real Estate Transactions*. St. Paul, MN: Foundation Press, 1985.

HARWOOD, BRUCE, *Real Estate Principles* (4th ed.), ch. 17, 18. Englewood Cliffs, NJ: Prentice Hall, 1986.

HENSZEY, BENJAMIN, "Broker's Liability: Cause for Concern," *Real Estate Review*, Fall 1978, pp. 57-60.

KRATOVIL, ROBERT, AND RAYMOND J. WERNER, *Real Estate Law* (8th ed.), ch. 10. Englewood Cliffs, NJ: Prentice Hall, 1983.

NATIONAL ASSOCIATION OF REAL ESTATE LICENSE LAW OFFICIALS, *Guide to Examinations and Careers in Real Estate*, ch. 4. Reston, VA: Reston Publishing Company, Inc., 1979.

ORDWAY, O. NICHOLAS, "Agency Role of Real Estate Brokers," in *The McGraw-Hill Real Estate Handbook*, ed. Robert Irwin, ch. 21. New York, NY: McGraw-Hill Book Company, 1984.

RING, ALFRED A., AND JEROME DASSO. *Real Estate Principles and Practices* (10th ed.), ch. 7-9. Englewood Cliffs, NJ: Prentice Hall, 1985.

SHENKEL, WILLIAM M., *Marketing Real Estate* (2nd ed.), ch. 15. Englewood Cliffs, NJ: Prentice Hall, 1985.

TOSH, DENNIS S., "Real Estate License Law," in *The McGraw-Hill Real Estate Handbook*, ed. Robert Irwin, ch. 20. New York, NY: McGraw-Hill Book Company, 1984.

FOUR

BROKERAGE MANAGEMENT CONCEPTS

Business Functions

Organization of Brokerage Firms

The Management Function

Brokerage Personnel

Evaluating Personnel Needs

Support Personnel

Let us compare a business organization to the human body. Both are designed to perform certain functions. The body is controlled by the brain and to a lesser extent by the nervous system; its other parts perform their functions and keep it alive. The vital organs (heart, digestive system, etc.) keep the body healthy and consume the food and oxygen it needs, process them, and dispose of the unusable parts. The senses (sight, hearing, touch, smell, taste) relate it to its environment and take account of its surroundings so that it may react to them. The rest of the body (limbs, parts of the brain) perform its functions, which can be many and varied. They include physical activities such as walking, hitting a baseball, and writing a letter, or mental activities such as reading and analyzing material, composing music, and speaking. All the parts operate together smoothly and in excellent coordination, so long as the body is kept healthy and properly stimulated.

BUSINESS FUNCTIONS

Now let us consider the business organziation. We will find that the analogy with the body is a very apt one. *Management* is the brain of the organization; it directs and motivates the organization to fulfill the objectives it has set. Lines of communication link management with line and suppport functions, just as the nervous system links the brain and the rest of the body.

The *line functions* are those parts of the organization that actually perform the actions necessary to achieve its objectives; in a real estate brokerage operation these would be the activities of the sales force in securing listings and making sales. *Support functions* are those necessary to keep the business operating smoothly; these include secretarial services, receptionists, data processing, and the like. Also *specialized support functions* are necessary. These might be legal counsel, accounting assistance, and similar professional assistance that can be contracted on a part time, as-needed basis from outside the firm, although larger brokerages often will have such specialists employed full time in their support staff.

We ought not to give the impression that everyone in a firm should be a specialist; actually, personnel may perform a variety of functions that may be classified among the ones we have listed. Just as the brain both controls and directs the body as well as performing some of its objectives, and just as the senses can be used both to sense the environment and to direct it to some extent, a given individual in a brokerage firm can perform a variety of tasks. In a small brokerage, the broker-owner may perform most of the management functions as well as being an active member of the sales staff performing line functions. Sales personnel may perform service functions by typing their own contracts, doing their own filing, or doing floor duty that includes answering telephones and receiving visitors. Nonetheless, the differences among the functions of the organization need to be distinguished, even though we realize that they may not necessarily be performed exclusively by certain members of the firm.

Organization

The human body is put together in a certain way to be as efficient as possible in the total performance of its functions, while at the same time keeping itself alive and healthy. A business must be organized not only to achieve its objectives, but also to remain a viable entity. When the body performs poorly it sickens; if the condition is not corrected it may limp along for some time, but it will not perform at its best. If the condition is serious enough, the damage can become so severe that the body will die. When a business performs poorly it also can become "sick," and if the condition lingers and worsens, the firm can "die" by going bankrupt or by being closed down and abandoned.

The purpose of organization is to arrange the business functions so that personnel, and the firm, can perform most efficiently. Organization also allows information to be gathered and processed so that the firm, and its objectives, can be altered and rearranged to reflect changing conditions. Finally, organization allows the management function to direct the business properly. The organizational pattern defines the functions that are to be performed and arranges them so that they complement one another by establishing lines of communication and control. Control is administered by management and communicated through the organization to line and service personnel. It serves the dual purpose of communicating the firm's objectives throughout its system, while at the same time directing the firm's activities so that the objectives may be accomplished.

Management

The purpose of management is to direct and control the organization. *Managerial talent* is the ability to accomplish this effectively. It should be pointed out that managerial talent is not the same as *technical talent*, which is the ability to perform the actual line and support functions. Management personnel need managerial skills, not technical skills, because they must direct and control and need not actually perform technically. Of course, in small organizations the same person may do both, and sometimes it is useful that a managerial person have a good knowledge of technical activity, but it is not always necessary. Managerial ability, however, is essential. If it is missing, the organization is likely to fail since only luck and chance will be available to keep it going, and these cannot be trusted to operate for very long.

While some business failures can be attributed to bad luck or other outside influences, most are the direct result of poor management. Management controls the firm and directs the activities of the line and support personnel. Even if these people are highly skilled and competent technically, they cannot keep the firm going indefinitely if the management is telling them to do the wrong things. On the other hand, competent management does have the option to replace poorly functioning line and support personnel, and to see to it that remaining personnel have the training and motivation to do their work properly.

Line and Support Functions

In a real estate brokerage, line personnel are the *sales force*. These are the people who secure the firm's listings and effect its sales. In larger or specialized firms, these personnel may also list rentals, negotiate leases, and perform similar functions. In essence, the line functions of the brokerage are those that result directly in *revenue*; that is, they are the services the firm provides to the outside world and for which it is paid.

The technical talent that the sales force needs is the ability to convince sellers and landlords to list their properties with the brokerage and the ability to achieve the results desired by these customers: sales and leases. Management must provide the sales force with direction, support, and incentive. *Direction* comes in the form of training, job analysis and description, and management policy. *Support* includes the provision of work space, contract forms, resolution of conflicts, and the availability of assistance from support personnel. *Incentive* includes pay as well as recognition and other acknowledgment of skill and ability.

Support personnel are secretaries, receptionists, and other employees who are not directly involved in the sales process, as well as personnel who handle paperwork for closings, arrange or carry out repairs and other functions in property management, and the like. Additional support functions may be performed by people who are contracted by the firm but are not actually a regular part of its organization. For example, all real estate brokerages ought to have at least one competent contract attorney available for consultation, even if it means paying a retainer fee. Accounting assistance and other specialized legal assistance also should be available.

The particular tasks and functions of the support staff are defined by management, and these people report to management unless they have been specifically assigned to the sales staff. For example, a managing broker will need secretarial assistance; he may also hire secretarial help that he specifically directs is to be available to the sales staff. However, the sales staff will rarely hire their own help, relying upon management to provide it for them if it is to be available at all.

Distribution of Functions in the Real Estate Brokerage

While we can be very specific about the nature of the various functions within a business and can categorize them into management, line, and support functions, we must realize that in many organizations we cannot be so specific about the people themselves. People can and do perform several functions, although generally the larger the firm, the more specialized the particular functions of each individual. In the very smallest real estate brokerage—one broker-owner with no sales or support staff—we will find one person performing all the functions.

In small firms of fewer than eight or ten members, we can find a fairly distinct differentiation between management personnel and the others, but it is less clear with respect to line and support activity. Generally, the broker-owner will perform all necessary management functions, although these may be fairly limited. Sales staff, however, may perform a number of support functions, since the firm is so small that it may not find it economically feasible to hire full time support staff. Sales personnel, then, may do their own filing, type their own contract forms, type their own letters, place their own ads and do a number of other support activities as well—all but those requiring professionals such as lawyers, and, perhaps, accountants. In the small firm, it is also likely that the broker-owner does a lot of sales staff work as well. If secretarial or other support staff are hired, their main responsibility probably will be to the broker-owner, and they will be available to the sales force only if they have spare time.

Real estate brokerage is the kind of business where line personnel—the sales force—have a considerable amount of responsibility that may appear to be that of management. They do much of their work away from the office, where supervision is impossible, and they must be relied upon to perform this work adequately and properly. In smaller firms, they will have quite a lot of responsibility, because the broker-owner will have to spend much of his own time in sales work in order to earn an adequate living from the business and so will be limited in the managerial supervision and control that he can maintain.

Larger firms will be more specific in their definition of duties. They can afford to hire support staff. Management will do relatively little sales work because the demands of managing a large organization will require a full time commitment if the firm is to succeed and survive. Individual staff members in the large brokerage are more likely to have the opportunity to specialize in their specific areas of work, and support staff will have more rigidly defined responsibilities.

ORGANIZATION OF BROKERAGE FIRMS

Any group of people assembled to perform some specific group purpose requires organization, as well as management. If *management* can be defined as the exercise of control over a group of people, then *organization* can be considered to be the structure of relationships that allows this control to be communicated and exercised within the group. It is the organizational pattern that defines the various jobs to be peformed and delineates the controls over each position.

Organization Patterns

Nearly all organizations are *hierarchical*; that is, control is communicated and exercised down a pattern of succeeding layers of operation. Each layer usually is composed of a larger number of people or positions than the one above; each reports to and is supervised by a member of the group immediately above it. If all this sounds very authoritarian and rigid, it usually is. While our American society is democratic, a business must be operated with authority and contol.

Organizational patterns usually can be shown graphically by using organization charts; these are the familiar pyramid-shaped drawings (Figures 4–1, 4–2) showing the organizational lines of communication and control. At the

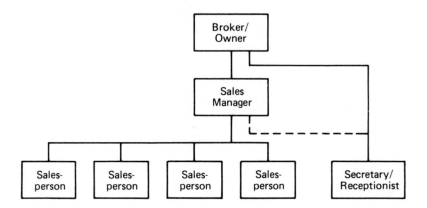

Figure 4-1. Organization of a Small Brokerage.

Figure 4-2. Organization of a Large Residential Brokerage.

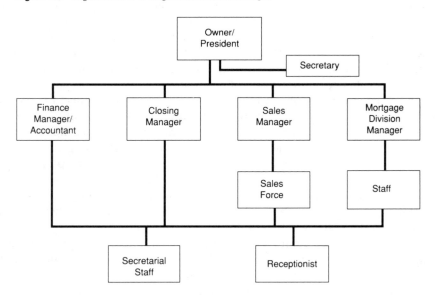

top of the pyramid usually will be found one person—the president, chairman of the board, or the like. This individual is the one charged with the ultimate responsibility for whatever takes place in the organization. In a small firm, he may indeed be the only one giving any significant orders, and his responsibilities on paper are the same as those he directly exercises.

As an organization grows, it becomes impossible for a single individual to be aware of everything that is going on, and to be directly in charge of all of it. At this point, some of the direct responsibility for running things is *delegated* to subordinates. These subordinate managers handle the day-to-day management of the particular parts of the firm they have been given responsibility for, but they report to the top person and relay to their own subordinates whatever decisions he may make. It is an axiom of management science that a given individual cannot adequately supervise more than a certain number of subordinates. The actual number may vary with respect to the capabilities of the person involved and the kind of work he is overseeing, but most authorities agree that, in principle, the maximum number of people a manager can directly supervise with greatest efficiency and productivity is surprisingly small: in most typical business environments this number is as few as three or four and very rarely as many as ten or more.

Management and Sales Activity

In the real estate business, it is likely that a sales manager or owner-broker can supervise a relatively large number of sales personnel since these happen to act fairly independently in their functions and so are required to do a lot of self-supervision. Nonetheless, a broker-owner who also does a considerable amount of sales work must realize that his capacity for supervision is very limited, particularly since he will not be available to his sales force for consultation or assistance during the times that he is conducting his own business away from the office. Ths same would apply to a sales manager who is an active salesperson as well; his capacity to direct and control also will be limited to the free time he can find between his appointments and other work.

Therefore, a broker who decides to appoint one of his sales staff members as his sales manager to free up the broker's own time ought to realize that in order for his new manager to have any reasonable effect at all, he must be freed from some of his sales duties. If he is not, then he is a manager in name only, since he will still have to do just as much selling as before to keep his income up. Often a sales manager will receive an *override* of a small part of the commissions brought into the brokerage by the sales staff he is supervising, but many individuals may look upon that extra income as icing on the cake and will continue to sell and list as much as before unless steps are taken to prevent it.

The essential point, then, is that management requires time, and the manager should be compensated for the exercise of his management skills, not just for whatever work he can do on the side. This also means that the expense of good management is one of the costs of doing business efficiently, and it cannot be avoided. If a brokerage firm is organized so that management activity is not adequately provided for either in compensation to those responsible for it or in the time needed to exercise it properly, then management will not be very good and the firm eventually will suffer and certainly will not reach anything like its true potential.

Brokerage Organization

Figures 4–1 and 4–2 show typical organizational charts for small and medium sized real estate brokerage firms. These patterns, of course, are not the only ones that could apply to a given real estate firm, but they provide useful examples for discussion.

Small Firm   The organization of the small brokerage is very simple. The broker-owner is the boss, and the sales force reports to him. We have also given him a secretary-receptionist whose primary function is to work for him. While charts such as these are suppposed to clarify and explain relationships within firms, this chart doesn't tell us much because there isn't much to tell, the organization is so simple.

Large Firm   Figure 4–2 shows the more complex organization of a large residential brokerage firm. Here we have a president of the firm who has managers and a personal secretary who report directly to him. The sales manager is in charge of the sales force, and the mortgage division manager is in charge of the firm's mortgage brokerage business. Both will have large numbers of people working directly under them. The accountant and the closing manager head smaller divisions; indeed, they may be divisions composed of themselves and no one else at all. Some management theorists might not even consider these two to be management at all, but that would be splitting hairs for our purposes here.

The sales and mortgage divisions of the firm are line functions; the rest are support functions. Note that a secretarial staff and receptionist are included; they are not part of any one division but are available to all. The receptionist, especially, will report directly to *everyone*, although the nature of the job limits this to delivering messages and putting through calls.

In this organization there are two levels of management: the president and the four managers who report to him. The division of management authority in the second level is an illustration of *departmentalization*. Each manager is responsible for an important *part* of the firm's activities, but not for *all*. In the small firm, the broker-owner may handle all these functions himself. In the large firm, these responsibilities are too great for one person, so the top manager delegates some or all of them to the others, who report directly to him. The managers handle the day-to-day activities, but matters of policy and other important decisions are made or approved by the president.

Different firms will organize in different ways; the illustrations given here are just examples. Some jobs may be divided among two or more managers, and others may be combined under one person. Some also may be held by the president. If the sales force is very large, a sales manager may have one or more assistant sales managers who report to him and who in turn have a certain portion of the sales force report to them.

Note that at each level, the people filling the slots report to the person above them, but rarely to each other. This does not mean that they keep wholly to themselves or that they do not cooperate or interact; however, they have no specific authority over one another. If one feels that the other ought to be doing something, he does not have the authority to require such action unless he can convince the president that it is necessary. It will follow, then, that the actual direction to take a specific action will come from the president, under his own authority.

Looking at it from the bottom, we find that the members of the sales force report to their sales manager. He in turn reports to his manager. In a large firm there may be a superior sales manager who reports to the president, while in a smaller firm the sales manager may report to the president directly. In any case, there is a certain organizational "insulation" between the top person and the people who actually perform the line functions. This has both advantages and disadvantages. Top management's time is freed for the more important activities of directing and planning with respect to the entire organization, but at the same time intimacy is lost because top management is estranged from the line activity people who will be required to carry out the firm's functions and achieve its goals. Ideally, however, the organization has both, in that the middle management people (sales managers, etc.) are able to perform the function of motivating the sales staff to do the work required while at the same time giving upper management an accurate picture of their needs and personal objectives.

Communication in the Organization

While direction and control should be exercised from the top downward in the organization, communication absolutely must flow both ways. Management cannot make reasonable and realistic decisions without a full awareness of the abilities, desires, and mood of subordinate personnel. All kinds of information is communicated by subordinates to their managers. Some of it can be dealt with by the manager, especially in the area of day-to-day problem solving. But he must sift through all the information he gets in order to determine what should be communicated by him to higher levels, what can be ignored, and what provides him with information he himself needs in order to perform his managerial function properly.

Relatively little information is communicated unless it is asked for, since people rarely feel proper about taking their manager's time just to engage in casual conversation. Therefore, an essential qualification of a good manager is the ability to discern the information he needs from his subordinates, and then to encourage them to make it available to him. Many managers deliberately ask for more information that they think they may need, theorizing that they can always cull out the useless. Also, by encouraging communication they may receive useful information they might not have thought to ask for specifically.

THE MANAGEMENT FUNCTION

The function of management can be described in a very few words: plan, organize, activate, and control. Planning provides the goals and objectives. Organization provides the structure of relationships and activities needed to accomplish the goals. Activation is the actual process of getting the performance needed from the members of the organization. Control leads to the results of the entire activity which, it is hoped, are the desired results.

Management cannot occur in a vacuum; it requires three essential inputs. These are information, resources, and money. *Information* gives the manager the knowledge necessary to perform functions realistically. *Resources* are what the organiazation uses to accomplish things; these include human resources (the talents and abilities of the people available to the firm) as well as physical resources (paper, pencils, offices and equipment, cars). *Money* is the lubricant that makes it all work, that makes it possible to gather the information and acquire the necessary resources.

The preceding paragraphs make it look pretty simple, but it is not. We cannot expect, in today's world, that a manager can plan, acquire information and resources, organize them, activate them, and then find that they operate smoothly and indefinitely like some efficient machine. Conditions change all the time, and since the prime resource in a brokerage firm is the human one, we cannot expect consistency day in and day out from the people involved. Management is an ongoing process, and the need for it never diminishes. Some organizations appear to work like well-oiled machines, but this is deceiving: The most efficiently run firms are those in which the management talent is the best and works the hardest. Therefore, let us examine these bare bones of the management function in greater detail.

Planning

Planning determines the firm's goals and objectives, as well as some of the continuing development that is needed to achieve them. General goals might be to provide the best and most ethical brokerage service available. Specific objectives could be sell X dollars worth of real estate next year, to show a certain level of profit, to expand to a certain size, and to acquire a certain proportion of the market in a certain area within a certain time. General goals and objectives can be very long term, rather like the ideals that must be lived up to continuously. But specific goals and objectives change all the time, because they are meant to be achieved within a relatively short time, and realistic management should alter them over time as conditions dictate.

It is essential that all goals be realistic ones. It makes no sense at all for a small firm composed of a single full-time broker and a couple of part-time salespeople to set a goal of, say, $10 million of sales and listings in the next year when few firms several times as large can accomplish such a feat. Therefore the manager must have the information at hand to determine what is reasonable or not.

General goals are not so much of a problem, since they tend to be vague to begin with. For example, it is desirable to set a goal of offering ethical and appreciated service, but it is difficult to measure this sort of accomplishment. We might consider the number of complaints from clients and customers as one measure, and could consider management's own evaluation of the techniques and attitudes of salespersons as another. Such a goal is a reasonable one, and its major effect upon the operation of the firm would be to generate concern about the performance of existing sales force members, and to set high standards for the employment of new salespeople.

Information

Specific goals will need considerable input of information and analysis of resources if they are to be at all useful. Required information will concern factors both inside and outside the firm. Outside conditions such as the current state of the real estate market, the projected state of the local economy, and the competitive situation the firm finds itself in within the brokerage business are obvious examples; they set the realistic limits of what the firm can expect to do within its market environment. From this information the potential goals can be formed. Opportunities for expansion, taking advantage of poor performance by competitors, and opportunities provided by an expanding economy can be identified. At this point, however, only *potential* has been noted; this is the maximum accomplishment that outside conditions may be expected to make available to an individual firm.

Examination of information about the firm itself provides the analysis needed to translate the potential goals into objectives that are reasonable given the firm's own resources, talents, and abilities. A firm with a relatively unimpressive sales force cannot expect to achieve as much as one whose salespeople all are highly motivated for success. Analysis of one's own people is not necessarily easy, especially if they are good friends or close relatives; emotional attachment often gets in the way of objective examination. But a decent inventory of the firm's total assemblage of skills and abilities is absolutely necessary for proper planning, because the plans and goals must be within the capacity of the group to achieve them.

Given proper assembly and use of information and sensible analysis of the resources available, specific plans that are proper for a given organization can be made. This kind of analysis can yield all sorts of useful plans, some relatively small and some quite fundamental. For example, analysis of the company's own resources probably will reveal weak points, and plans should be made to overcome them. These may require improvement of skills or activity by existing members or hiring of new members to provide the needed abilities. Other plans might be to achieve certain sales levels or other overall goals within a certain time.

Goals and objectives should not stand alone; they should be accompanied by management plans designed to achieve them. Necessary action should be outlined and anticipated, and steps should be formulated and taken to get them under way. Obviously, the actions necessary to achieve the goals should be within the capacity of the firm to perform them; once again analysis of the firm's resources comes into play. Goals that are outside the ability of the firm to achieve are unreasonable, no matter how attractive they may be. Actual action plans can be relatively modest or quite sweeping depending upon the needs. The more sweeping they are, and the more they dictate fundamental changes, the more carefully they should be analyzed and formulated before they become company policy.

Activation—The Job Description

Accomplishment of objectives requires action. Action, to be efficient, must occur in a proper organizational framework so that all the necessary activity can be properly related and integrated. Then the specific forms of action themselves must be described so that those responsible for them will know what to do. Finally, management must exercise the proper control to see to it that everyone is doing what he is supposed to. Organization has been discussed earlier in this chapter, and control will be considered in the next section.

Activation requires the definition and description of the jobs to be done in order to accomplish goals. Most firms find the use of job descriptions a valuable tool in this process, since they can provide documented illustrations of the duties and responsibilities of particular positions. Frequently, especially in large bureaucratic organizations, they are vague and almost impossible to pin down, full of words like "coordinate," "supervise," "administer," and other language that is easy to use in a meaningless fashion. For example, someone hired for a position where he is supposed to "coordinate supervisory administration of department functions" might end up doing practically anything and will have no idea of exactly what to do until someone explains it to him in English.

Job descriptions should be specific, to the point, and above all understandable. They should describe the following: (a) exactly what work is to be done, (b) whom the person occupying the job should report to, (c) who reports to the person occupying the job, (d) specific skills and qualifications necessary, and (e) if necessary, what the person occupying the job is *not* supposed to do. The description need not define salary, since the employment contract will do that, but it is usually good practice to make the job description itself part of the employment contract. Job descriptions serve two functions: They tell each person what he is supposed to be doing, and they tell management who is supposed to be doing what.

In the brokerage business, job descriptions need not be very complex, since the jobs to be peformed are relatively familiar and specific. A secretary's job description will spell out the particular kinds of work expected, whom to take orders from, whom to supervise and the skills (shorthand, typing, etc.) that are required. A sales manager's description is more difficult, since he is in management and one function of management is to do whatever is necessary. However, the job description cannot be that vague. It should describe the specific duties, such as supervision, hiring, and firing of sales personnel. It should indicate the kinds of information that the sales manager should make available to the sales force (distributing listing information, financing information, etc.) and perhaps the forum that should be used, such as weekly sales meetings. The specific relationships between the sales manager and his superiors and between him and other department heads should be described. Figure 4–3 shows a sample job description for a sales manager in a brokerage firm.

Although the job description is useful to the employee as a guide, its greatest usefulness is to management as a planning and control tool. As the organization develops, competent management will always be aware of the tasks to be performed and the best way to allocate them within the structure of the firm. These tasks are logically and reasonably collected into specific jobs and defined in the job descriptions for those jobs. This will assure management that the organizational structure provides for all the necessary tasks in a sensible manner. The job descriptions then can be used as tools for finding the right personnel to fit each position. Prospective employees can examine them to find if they represent the kind of work desired, while the descriptions will be used by management as the criteria for hiring and assignment decisions.

All this assumes that the organization is being created from scratch; more often than not, these management techniques will be applied to one that already exists. In such cases, it might be wise to make up two sets of organization schemes and jobs descriptions. The first will reflect the resources available to the firm in its current members. The second will take the form of a specific planning goal, something to be achieved over time. This may require retraining of some people currently employed, replacement of some, and hiring of others as the firm slowly transforms itself into the more efficient form that is desired.

Control

Control is the management function that involves supervision of assigned activity to assure that it is being done properly and is consistent with the established objectives. Essentially this involves the exercise of authority to make basic decisions and to enforce them. It requires management that is capable of honest evaluation of performance and has the ability to leave alone someone whose performance is satisfactory. Control is so fundamental a factor of management that it is discussed in its various forms throughout this text, so specific analysis will not be provided here. As the various facets of the brokerage business are considered in later pages, the applicable control techniques and objectives will be incorporated into the discussion. However, two particular elements of managerial control that are significant in the real estate brokerage business deserve special mention and will be considered in Chapters 5 and 7, respectively. The first of these is the independent contractor relationship; the second is the policy manual.

D DOVER REALTY COMPANY

1776 Twelfth Street, Waltham, Xxxxx 12345   (908) 555-4321

JOB DESCRIPTION: RESIDENTIAL SALES MANAGER

QUALIFICATIONS: Licensed broker, at least one year's successful sales experience, proven managerial ability.

AUTHORITY: All residential sales personnel report to the sales manager. The sales manager reports to the President of the company.

DUTIES: Following policy manual procedures whenever applicable,

(a) Assign floor duty

(b) Assign open houses

(c) Supervise system of keeping track of all sales associates whereabouts.

(d) Directly supervise all contracting activities of beginning sales associates.

(e) Resolve disputes among sales associates. Refer unusual problems to the President of the Company.

(f) Interview all prospective new sales associates; hire with approval of President of the Company.

(g) Keep records of productivity of sales associates. Report these monthly at executive meeting. Terminate associates with approval of the President.

(h) Conduct weekly sales meeting.

(i) Distribute all information on new listings (Company, MLS, Co-op) to sales associates.

(j) Attend weekly executive meetings.

(k) Follow directives of President of the Company only. All disputes with other department heads should be referred to the President.

(l) When in doubt, seek consultation with President of the company. Nobody can be expected to know everything, but a good manager will not keep referring the same kinds of problems over and over again to the President once a determination has been made about dealing with them.

(m) Assume all responsiblities also outlined in policy manual. Policy manual directives and procedures should be used in all situations where they will apply.

Figure 4-3. Sample Job Description for Residential Sales Manager.

BROKERAGE PERSONNEL

Proper selection, training and supervision of employees is essential to the long-term success of any business, including real estate brokerage. The selection process should recruit personnel who will fit into the firm and into its pattern of business performance, its goals, and objectives. Training programs are necessary not only to keep experienced personnel up to date on the techniques of the business and the information they need to be effective, but also to prepare new entrants into the business for successful performance. Supervision assures that all are doing the right jobs and are doing them correctly, and that the manner in which they do their jobs is consistent with the firm's methods, image, and goals.

Real estate brokerage personnel can be conveniently divided into two groups, the sales force and nonsales staff. Here we are including such people as sales managers and principal brokers in the sales force, since it is very rare that they can succeed in such positions without the kind of knowledge of sales that can only come from considerable personal experience. The means of selecting, hiring, and managing the two groups is quite different and will be discussed separately.

Characteristics

The real estate brokerage business is a service business, and so is very people-oriented. This means that the behavior, attitude, appearance, and personality of the employee is critical to success. While an assembly line worker might get away with being slovenly, unpleasant, and abrasive, a real estate salesperson cannot. Sales personnel also require certain types of personalities: They must enjoy real estate dealings, of course, but they must also like dealing with people, be understanding and patient, and have the ability to express themselves well and to inspire confidence in those they deal with. Considering that they will be shepherding people through the most important business and financial dealings of their lives, salespeople must be able to inspire optimism, soothe worries, and convince customers that they are doing the right thing.

While a great many people are attracted to the real estate sales career, relatively few of them will have all that it takes to be able to make a successful vocation out of it. Therefore, it is essential that the brokerage firm have at its disposal the means to determine just who these people are and to tell at the outset which applicants will succeed and which may not.

Transience

However, there are a number of problems common to the management of both types of personnel that can be mentioned at the outset. First, many real estate brokerage firms are plagued by *transience*. This refers to personnel who do not remain on the job very long, and who thus necessitate frequent replacement and training of new people. The ideal employee is one who takes the job, learns to do it well and reliably, and stays in the job indefinitely. The objective of management ought to be to have every employee fit this model, since it reduces personnel management effort and costs to a minimum and leads to great efficiency in the firm's operation. This can be accomplished in several ways: by hiring employees who appear likely to remain with the firm and who show the ability to do the job well, by using procedures that maximize employee satisfaction, and by paying well.

Compensation

A second problem is that of compensation. Employees must be paid, and desirable ones must be paid enough to keep them on the job, if at all possible. At the same time, the firm must not pay so much that it loses money. Compensation, however, often can take forms other than money. Recognition, appreciation, and a desirable work environment are examples of nonmoney compensation, and often these can make the difference when money alone cannot. Successful salespeople, especially, tend to be relatively emotional, up-and-down types for whom the right words or actions at the right time can have a profound effect.

Environment

Work environment and working conditions themselves are matters of extreme importance. While management and control is necessary, it should not be so impersonal or harsh that employee dissatisfaction results. Part of the problem can be solved through communication. If employees are aware of the purposes of controls and the need for them, they will be more likely to accept them, particularly if they can be made to feel that to some extent they have had a voice in their formulation.

It is particularly important that judgments about employee performance be made using *relevant* criteria. It is easy to fault someone for being late to work, taking long lunch hours, using too many paper clips. These are things that are easily measured but often tell very little about the actual worth of an employee. So far as is practicable, the firm should measure performance by results. A salesperson who regularly makes the Million Dollar Sales Club should be allowed a considerable amount of leeway in the manner in which he does his job—so long as it does not defy the firm's ethics or principles—because the company makes its money from his performance and not from his attachment to minor and often unnecessary patterns of behavior. A firm that is known for its result-oriented attitude is more likely to attract good producers than is one that seems to rate its people according to relatively inconsequential standards.

Favoritism

A final problem is that of favoritism. Here we refer to management's apparent preference for some staff members over others, without communicating a valid and comprehensible reason for it. It is natural for management to bend over backwards to make life easy for star producers; they are the company's bread and butter. But other staff must be made to know, first, that the favors enjoyed by the preferred few are *earned* and *justifiable*, and even more important, that *all* staff members can enjoy these preferences by earning them. A final important point here is that less successful staff members should not have to feel that there are any obstacles to their own accomplishment of superior status, and that the attainment of it by others will not in any way interfere with the same attainment by themselves.

EVALUATING PERSONNEL NEEDS

Any good business management will constantly evaluate the effectiveness of its personnel, always seeking to improve their productivity and the mix of people working in the organization. This naturally will lead to situations in which additional employees or salespeople will be seen as desirable. Sometimes these needs will be fairly obvious: the sales manager submits his resignation, so the firm must find another. At other times the needs may be felt but may be less specifically defined: Business is good, and the firm ought to have some more talented salespeople because it is felt that the firm can do extra business with them available as associates. Or the firm's management may have to expand into new areas of business, and so new jobs within the firm are created and people are needed to fill them. Essentially, then, the business will have positions to be filled because of replacement, growth, or expansion.

Replacement hiring occurs when a member of the staff resigns or is promoted or assigned to a different position within the firm, and the position becomes vacant. *Growth* is the result of the firm doing more and more business in its particular areas of specialty. As a firm grows, new positions must be created because more and more people will be needed to handle the larger volume of business. *Expansion* is the result of a decision by the firm to enter a new area of business. Jobs are created in entirely new divisions of the company. These jobs are unlike any that may have existed in the company until that time since they involve business that is new to the firm.

In the real estate brokerage business, growth would occur when a firm that specializes in residential sales finds that it is getting more and more listings and that its reputation is securing more and more business. Growth also can occur when the real estate market itself flourishes; there is more business for everybody, and firms in the business find that there is more for all of them to do. Growth also can be sought by the company as a goal in itself. In such cases, rather than expanding the sales staff in order to be able to handle an increasing volume of business, a firm may expand its sales staff so that the new members will actively seek and bring in the new business that the company wants.

Expansion is a somewhat different matter. Here the firm decides to add a new type of business. A residential firm may decide to enter the area of commercial sales or to take up property management. It may add a mortgage lending office or a property insurance branch. All of these may require the use of personnel who are capable of kinds of work that until this time have been unnecessary in this firm.

Whatever the source of the personnel need, once it has been identified and the desired qualifications of the new staff members have been outlined, the firm is able to begin active recruitment. It knows what it wants; it knows the abilities, talents, and skills desired; and it is able now to identify those people who may be best qualified to meet these objectives. The next step is to plan a recruitment program to find the person or people needed. This includes knowing where to look, how to attract the right person, and how to convince him that his best opportunity is with this particular company.

SUPPORT PERSONNEL

Support personnel in a real estate brokerage concern are those who are not directly involved in sales and listing work. They fall into a number of categories, and many of them will have jobs that might also be found in almost any other kind of business. A brokerage firm will need secretaries, receptionists, file and recordkeeping personnel, and accounting and legal assistance. Also, specialized to the real estate business, will be people involved in handling closings, writing advertisements for listed property, and drawing up contracts and other paperwork associated with the business. A real estate firm may wish to use the services of an advertising agent, a real estate appraiser, a property management firm, handymen, specialized repair people, painters, printers, and others.

All of these can be employed on a full-time, part-time or when-needed basis. Full time usually refers to the traditional eight hours per day, five days a week, although in the brokerage business this arrangement often is modified because of the large amount of weekend work. Part-time help generally works a fairly limited schedule, such as during regular busy periods. When-needed help usually is restricted to outsiders who are employed for specific jobs whenever it is necessary.

The manner in which the employment for support positions is handled will vary considerably from firm to firm. A small firm may have no full-time support personnel at all, and a "bare bones" operation may try to get by with no support personnel at all, relying upon the licensees in the sales force to take care of all support activity as well. However, the employment of a secretary-receptionist will usually be of value to even a very small firm, in that it will free the sales staff to concentrate on selling activity and to be wherever they may be most useful at all times. A secretary-receptionist is the first support employee to be hired by a growing firm; such a person has the typing skills to prepare much of the paperwork that otherwise will consume valuable sales force time, and can be in the office at all times, freeing the salespeople from most office duties.

Depending upon the nature of the job, varying degrees of training will be needed. At the very least, the new employee will have to meet and get to know the people he or she will be working with, but there is also the need to know exactly what is to be done. If someone of longer standing in the office is assigned to conduct this training, that person should be required to make sure that the training process is effective. Often, new employees are tossed into the office and left pretty much to sink or swim. At the very least, a few minutes' advance thought should be given to the kinds of information the new employee will need and a successful effort made to provide it.

Of course, the degree to which this training process is necessary varies with the nature of the particular job, but it should not be ignored. The ideal employee is one who knows what to do and how to do it, and the sooner that is accomplished the more quickly the entire office can return to its normal efficient routine. An employee who continually must ask someone else for advice or assistance is disruptive to the entire office, and it is rare that this cannot be avoided with only a little advance planning and effort.

DISCUSSION QUESTIONS AND PROJECTS

1. Find a local brokerage firm that will let you develop an organization chart of the firm. Analyze your results.
2. Describe the difference between line and support functions, in the real estate brokerage business.
3. Since one of the functions of management is planning, what kinds of plans do you think managers of a real estate brokerage concern should make? Why?
4. Why is communication an important function of the management process?
5. Write a job description for a real estate salesperson.
6. Write a job description for a secretary-receptionist who is the only support service member of a small brokerage firm.
7. Examine the organization and control patterns of a small brokerage firm in your area. How do you think it could improve? What serious problems (if any) presently exist?

A Case Study

PLANNING

The real estate brokerage business since about 1970 has seemed like a gigantic roller-coaster ride. Fluctuations in the economy in general and in interest rates in particular have made it a feast-famine business. The first serious downturn came in 1969–1970, after over two decades of general prosperity and growth in the business. Many brokerage firms were caught by surprise by the shrinking markets that many of them were experiencing for the first time.

It happened again in 1973–74, only worse. A few firms which had survived the earlier crisis made contingency plans to cope with a repeat, but most managers apparently assumed that this would never happen again: once more they were faced with unpleasant consequences. Both times a lot of firms went out of business, and a number of brokers and salespeople left the field entirely.

Experience is a good teacher. After the 1974 recession, brokerage firms began acting as if other poor markets would occur again. This meant that they had to be prepared to deal with them when they arose, and one of the best ways of preparing was to get better at predicting when they would occur. Many brokerage managers began to study the economy more carefully and, in particular, the rate of inflation and its effect upon interest rates. Slowly rising inflation in 1977 and 1978 suggested that another bad market could be on the way. Well-prepared firms put off heavy financial commitments that might leave them vulnerable to a bad downturn, and concentrated on building staffs of skilled sales people who could be expected to weather a bad market more successfully.

By 1979 rising interest rates made it clear that tough times were on the way again. In the early 1980s interest rates were at unprecedented heights, so high that most potential buyers stayed away from the market. The real estate brokerage business fell off considerably; in some areas it dwindled almost to nothing. Although interest rates began to fall in 1982, it was not until 1985 that they fell far enough to spark a significant increase in home buying. During that time, huge numbers of licensees left the business. By the time good times returned, only the best, most accomplished, and professional licensees remained.

REFERENCES

FISHER, FREDERICK J., *Broker Beware: Selling Real Estate Within the Law*, ch. 8. Reston, VA: Reston Publishing Company, Inc.

GOLDSTEIN, PAUL, *Real Estate Transactions*. St. Paul, MN: Foundation Press, 1985.

HALL INSTITUTE OF REAL ESTATE, *Managing a Real Estate Tecm*, ch. 3-5, appendix E. Hinsdale, IL: The Dryden Press, 1980.

PHILLIPS, BARBARA, "Office Management for Brokers," in *The McGraw-Hill Real Estate Handbook*, ed. Robert Irwin, ch. 33. New York, NY: McGraw-Hill Book Company, 1984.

Real Estate Office Management: People Functions Systems, ch. 1-6, 22. Chicago, IL: REALTORS® National Marketing Institute, 1975.

Real Estate Sales Handbook (9th ed.), ch. 4. Chicago, IL: REALTORS® National Marketing Institute, 1983.

SHENKEL, WILLIAM M., *Marketing Real Estate* (2nd ed.), ch. 4. Englewood Cliffs, NJ: Prentice Hall, 1985.

FIVE

EMPLOYMENT AGREEMENTS

Independent Contractor

Problems with the Independent Contractor Relationship

The Salesperson's Contract

Support Personnel

As in any business, a professionally operated brokerage firm will have many kinds of written contracts and instructions involving the personnel working for it. While it often is legal to have verbal employment contracts, these are undesirable because they are difficult to pin down. The sensible rule in any kind of agreement is to put it in writing so that everyone involved will have a clear, unchanging statement of the conditions of the arrangement.

The real estate brokerage business makes extensive use of the *independent contractor* form of employment. This arrangement treats the "employee" as an independent, self-employed entity, at least for federal income tax purposes. Because of the importance of this type of contract we will devote considerable discussion to it in this chapter.

INDEPENDENT CONTRACTOR

In most businesses, those who do the work are considered employees: they are assigned jobs to do, directed in those jobs, and paid for their work. The firm withholds federal and, when applicable, state and local income taxes from their paychecks, and pays the employer's share of FICA (social security) taxes. The employer also makes payments, as required by the laws governing the place of employment, into unemployment insurance funds, workmen's compensation funds, and the like. Many businesses offer other fringe benefits such as partially or fully paid pension contributions, health and life insurance, profit sharing, and so on.

Nature of Independent Contractor

However, there is another kind of "employee," the *independent contractor*, whose treatment with respect to the matters discussed in the previous paragraph is quite different. The independent contractor is looked upon as a separate business entity who contracts his services to others. His employer pays him for his services, but no more. The independent contractor himself, at least for income tax purposes, is considered to be self-employed. He pays all his FICA taxes himself. He makes estimated tax payments of his income taxes, because they are not withheld from payments made to him. He may not be eligible for unemployment or disability benefits unless he pays into the funds himself. Any pension plans or insurance programs that he has he pays for himself. He is not eligible for profit sharing plans or other fringe benefits.

Advantages of Independent Contractor Relationship

From the point of view of the employer, the use of independent contractors instead of people with employee status appears to be very economical. There is no encumbrance with the paperwork and associated costs of withholding income taxes, and the employer is not required to pay FICA taxes or to contribute to unemployment or compensation funds. Since the employer is prohibited from giving independent contractors fringe benefits, he is spared this possible additional cost of employing people. Since FICA taxes and other mandatory contributions can come to as much as 10% of total payroll, the savings can be quite substantial, to say nothing of the additional 10% to 30% that is saved compared to most firms that have fringe benefit packages. A result of this has been a trend in the real estate business for salespeople to be employed as independent contractors rather than as employees.

Independent Contractor and U.S. Internal Revenue Service

Given the obvious benefits to the employer of having a work force on independent contractor status, one might wonder why there are any working people at all on employee status. The answer rests with the legal definitions of the employee and independent contractor and, most particularly with the distinction as interpreted by the United States Internal Revenue Service (IRS). As we all are reminded every spring at tax time, the IRS is the tax collecting arm of the federal government. As we all are at least minimally aware, the IRS tends to operate with a fairly loose rein, and is responsible for interpreting as well as enforcing the tax laws. Since more taxes can be collected from situations where employees exist instead of independent contractors, a fairly severe body of law and regulation has emerged defining the exact circumstances under which independent contractor status will be recognized.

Definition of Independent Contractor Status

One significant point here is that the status of independent contractor can only be sustained if, in fact, the actual employment situation fits the IRS definition. It is not enough simply for an employer and employee to agree that independent contractor status exists and to go on from there. To be sure, a *necessary* condition for such status is that it is recognized to exist by the employer and individual involved, but this is not enough; the duties and responsibilities of the independent contractor also must be consistent with the IRS definition.

The key element of the definition of independent contractor hinges on the word *independent*. In order for one to have independent contractor status, one must be seen to be acting in a largely independent manner, free from much of the direction and control that would normally be associated with an employer-employee relationship. This factor comes directly to bear upon the control the employer exerts over the employee. On the one hand, even in an independent contractor arrangement, some control is recognized, since it is necessary to have some definition of the task to be performed and the service for which payment is made. However, the independent contractor is supposed to be largely independent in the means he uses to achieve the goal, given that it falls within broad limitations that can be imposed even by an independent contractor agreement.

Controlling the Independent Contractor

Briefly, control can be exerted over an independent contractor so far as the result to be accomplished by the relationship is concerned, but control cannot extend to the means, details, and specific techniques used by the contractor to achieve the desired result. In real estate brokerage contexts, this means that an independent contractor agreement can specify that the contractor is being hired to list and sell real estate on behalf of the company. He can be required to follow certain procedures, so long as they are generally accepted courses of action within the industry. He can be required to abide by all laws and regulations that apply, such as license and agency law, contract law, and so on. He can be specifically prohibited from certain activities; for example, an independent contractor can be hired to list and sell houses, but prohibited from listing and selling commercial property.

All these considerations represent genuine control, but note that this also assumes that the contractor himself is a professional who can be trusted to handle the details of getting the required job done. Thus, control in the area of these details cannot be exerted in an independent contractor relationship. The contractor cannot be required to hold open house every so often, to hold a particular listing of his open, to be any particular place at a particular time. This would prohibit the requirement that the salesperson do floor duty or attend any meetings called by management. He may do so voluntarily, of course, but he cannot be forced to as a condition of his employment. He cannot be required to drive a certain size, make, or quality of automobile. He cannot be required to wear a certain uniform, or dress in certain color combinations that are intended to promote identity with the employing firm. His hours of work cannot be controlled. He cannot be required to attend training sessions, professional meetings, or other meetings. The broker cannot have any substantial control over the priorities the contractor assigns to the listings, prospects, clients, and customers that he is working on.

The IRS Definition of Independent Contractor

Current law specifies five conditions that will allow a real estate salesperson to qualify as an independent contractor to the U.S. Internal Revenue Service. The salesperson and his employment situation must meet all five conditions or the individual will be considered to be an employee for federal income tax purpose. The five conditions are:

1. The independent contractor must have *absolute* control over the number of hours worked and the manner in which they are scheduled.
2. The independent contractor must have a written contract with the broker, and the broker must provide the contractor written information describing the contractor's self-employment and income tax obligations.

3. The independent contractor must maintain a separate place of business.

OR

at least one-third of the value of the contractor's service must be due to property provided by the contractor

OR

the independent contractor must be a licensed real estate agent, a licensed insurance agent, or a direct seller.

4. At least 90 percent of the contractor's income must be related to sales rather than to the number of hours worked.

5. The broker employing the services provided by the independent contractor must file the legally required information tax returns.

Provision 3 defines a *real estate licensee* as an independent contractor, provided that the other four conditions are also met. Provision 5 requires the broker to file periodic returns with the Internal Revenue Service showing how much was paid to each independent contractor; however, no withholding or employer-related taxes will have to be paid by the broker. Provision 2 assures that the contractor is aware of his status, and that there is a written agreement available that defines his independent contractor status. Provision 4 in effect requires that the contractor earn his income from commissions and not from salary paid for hours worked.

Provision 1 is the most significant. By requiring that the contractor have absolute control over time and scheduling of work, his independence is assured. This means that brokers are not able to schedule independent contractors to work assigned floor duty, open houses, or other duty unless they specifically agree to it.

Provisions 2 through 5 pose no serious problems, since they relate directly to the manner in which the brokerage business currently is conducted. Employment contracts can be written to include the necessary information required by provision 2 and virtually all real estate licensees qualify under provision 4 anyway since practically all of their income is from commissions. However, this provision is likely to generate scrutiny of any kind of draw arrangements with independent contractors. If a draw of some kind is desired, the contracts defining it should be airtight: the draw must be a legally collectible loan, and it would be preferable if there were no mention at all of future commissions being used to pay it off. Otherwise, the IRS may contend that by requiring that future commissions be used to pay off the loan, a disguised draw has been created. A better arrangement would be to provide a specific repayment date for the loan, regardless of commissions earned by the contractor.

Compensation of the Independent Contractor

It is essential that an independent contractor not be paid in any manner that might be construed as salary. Normally, all he can be paid are commissions he has earned. It usually is all right for some form of incentive to be used, such as a bonus or larger commission split once a certain level of commission income has been reached, but these must be based entirely upon the performance of the independent contractor himself. This rules out any form of profit sharing. In some sales arrangements it is customary to pay a small salary to be supplemented by commissions; this cannot be done in an independent contractor arrangement and is not a prevalent practice in the real estate brokerage industry anyway.

Sometimes it is advantageous for a salesperson to be paid a *draw*, which actually is an advance against future commissions. In the case of an independent contractor, there must be very careful arrangement of any draws, and the contractor's liability to repay such draws at some future date, regardless of future commission income, should be unquestionable. This means that one way of handling draws is to make them in the forms of loans, in which a legal, contractual method of repayment is spelled out and legal liability for repayment is obvious.

Expenses

The independent contractor must be left liable for all his expenses. He cannot be provided a car or other essentials of the business, and office space should be made available only with the full intention that it is there to be used or not, as the contractor wishes. In any case, office space provided must not be construed as requiring the contractor to spend any particular amount of time in it or to appear as if all or most of his function is performed in the broker's office. With real estate salespeople that is little problem, since they have to spend so much time out on their own soliciting listings and showing property. The independent contractor is required to pay his own license fees, professional dues, and other fees, although an employer may pay these for those on employee status.

Benefits

The independent contractor may be provided with office services such as secretarial service and telephone availability so long as he is not required to use it. Any expenses of this nature that he accumulates outside the broker's office, however, cannot be reimbursed. The independent contractor cannot be given the usual run of fringe benefits that an employee might expect, such as pension plans, group insurance plans, sick pay, or paid vacations. All of these are defined by IRS as benefits available only to employees. The contractor's vacation time cannot be controlled by the broker either; he must be left free to schedule his working hours, days, and weeks as he sees fit.

The broker is not required to pay FICA taxes for independent contractors, nor need he withhold income taxes; however, he should ascertain that the contractor himself pays these taxes properly and when due, so as to reinforce the independent contractor status. The broker may not pay other government-run insurance premiums on behalf of the contractor, such as unemployment insurance, disability compensation insurance, and the like unless it is specifically required by state law, even for independent contractors. (Tax and other laws in some states do not recognize the independent contractor relationship in the same manner as does the IRS.)

Information

Finally, the broker is entitled to information from the independent contractor only so far as it pertains directly to the conduct of business. He may require that listings and sale contracts be submitted in a timely manner and in certain form. He may require any information he needs to assure that the salesperson is abiding by the law. He may not require that the contractor work full time for him (although no state permits a sales licensee to be in the employ of more than one broker at a time), nor may he prohibit the contractor from doing other, non-real estate brokerage work in addition to his sales position.

The key determinant of the independent contractor "is not what you *say*, but what you *do*." If any of the provisions of the independent contractor relationship are violated, the contractor will be considered an employee by the IRS, and IRS may then levy back taxes, unpaid FICA taxes, and penalties and fines for failure to abide by tax laws. Loss of independent contractor status in this manner, then, can be a very expensive proposition, especially to the brokerage firm. Therefore, particular effort must be made to assure that the independent contractor is one in more than name only, and that the control exerted over him is consistent with the definition.

PROBLEMS WITH THE INDEPENDENT CONTRACTOR RELATIONSHIP

The advantage to the independent contractor relationship is that it saves the brokerage firm a lot of money that otherwise would be paid in taxes and book-keeping costs. The contractor benefits by being able to act independently, and by the recognition that real estate sales is a very independent line of work, in which individual effort and responsibility and self-supervision must loom large. The major disadvantage to the contractor is a greater personal responsibility for his own well-being, lack of fringe benefits, and additional recordkeeping requirements, since he must handle his entire tax and self-insurance program himself. However, some contractors actually will find these to be advantages, theorizing that their independent situation allows them considerably more control over their own lives and destinies.

Limited Control

The major problem to the brokerage firm is the obvious one of having limited control over the sales force. Some firms set up independent contractor relationships and then proceed to control the contractors as though they were employees. This works only so long as the IRS doesn't get wind of it, and it is poor business practice to use as a significant foundation of the firm's organization the hope that the tax man doesn't find out something illegal is going on.

When highly skilled and talented salespeople are involved, there is little worry, since they can be relied upon to act properly. Many firms, which hire inexperienced sales personnel as employees may reduce commission splits to account at least partially for the additional expense they incur. The employee status allows full control by the broker. He can require attendance at meetings and training sessions, floor duty, open house, and all other forms of adherence to his wishes with no worries, since the people involved are classified as employees. Once they have proved themselves and earned independent contractor status, it is given to them; by this time the broker has some assurance that they have the experience and ability to conduct themselves properly with little supervision.

Encouraging Desired Activity

In some areas, however, it would be nice to have control. Sales meetings are important for communication purposes, and most sales managers like all salespeople to attend. It is essential that at least one licensee be in the office at all times to handle calls and walk-in business, so it is necessary to have some reliable means of scheduling floor time among the sales force to see to it that somebody is in the office.

The usual answer is to make it obvious to employees and independent contractors alike that there are real benefits to be had from attendance and floor duty, even though independent contractors cannot be specifically required to do either. Of course, a contractor who does not seem to be doing his part can simply be let go when his contract expires, and if this happens a few times the others will get the message that their continued employment may depend on their willingness to engage in "voluntary" activity that meets with the approval and desires of management. However, such a situation cannot be the overt policy of the brokerage firm, because it will be interpreted as excessive control.

This kind of problem has no easy solution. Some brokerage firms try to make the floor duty and other "required" activity as attractive as possible, so that voluntary compliance is no problem. Floor agents usually have first priority on all walk-in and call-in business that occurs during their duty period. Many firms receive listing and sales leads through the officers and managers who are not active salespeople; referral of these calls and requests to active agents can be based upon floor duty time or other factors, so long as it is provided simply as incentive, with no specific promises. Firms that do have some salespeople in employee status may schedule them for such duties, while allowing independent contractors to request such activity if they want it. This leaves the matter entirely up to the contractor, which conforms with the proper requirements but is only successful where it is possible to fill all such duties with employees if no contractors wish to volunteer.

THE SALESPERSON'S CONTRACT

The contract of employment between the brokerage and the salesperson should be written. Depending upon the laws prevailing in the state where the firm is located, a verbal agreement may or may not be legal. Even if it is, the written instrument is far preferable because it provides a specific piece of evidence that each party can refer to whenever necessary. Furthermore, contracts employing independent contractors should be written if only because they may be the only foolproof evidence with which the independent status can be proved to the satisfaction of the IRS.

The contract (an example is presented in Figure 5–1) should be drawn up by the firm's attorney to reflect exactly what the firm and the contracting salesperson agree upon and to assure that all legal requirements are properly met. A standard form can be drafted by the attorney which the firm can use for a number of its salespeople. However, it must be remembered that not all salespeople will be doing the same types of things, so there often will be a need for different types of agreements with different members of the sales force.

It is possible for the attorney to draw up a multiple-purpose agreement with blank spaces where particular provisions referring to a specific sales position can be written in. In such a case, the attorney also should draft versions of the wording to be inserted in these spaces. If an agreement calls for wording that has not been prepared by the attorney, he should be consulted.

Salesperson's Status and Responsibility

The contract should mention a number of specific things. The status (independent contractor or employee) must be detailed, as the contractual requirements of each will differ considerably. If the salesperson is an employee, there should be a reasonable summary of the specific duties required and the manner in which the employee is to be controlled by the firm. The independent contractor's agreement has to be more general on this point. The contract should specify the manner in which the salesperson is to be paid by the firm, as well as how and when. Since his income will be shares of commissions that he brings into the firm, the manner in which those commissions are split with him should be detailed. If there are any bonus or incentive payments agreed upon, they should be included. Reference to the policy manual (described in Chapter 7) can be made in the contract. The employee can be required to abide by the rules and provisions set down in the manual, but for the independent contractor the manual must remain a guide, and not a direct order.

Renegotiation

Contracts employing salespeople can be designed to be renegotiated from time to time. This can be accomplished by making the contract for a

DOVER REALTY COMPANY

1776 Twelfth Street, Waltham, Xxxxx 12345   (908) 555-4321

BROKER - SALES ASSOCIATE CONTRACT

INDEPENDENT CONTRACTOR

THIS AGREEMENT made this _____ day of _____, 19____,
by and between DOVER REALTY COMPANY, hereinafter referred to as Broker, and
_____, hereinafter referred to as Sales Associate,
for and in consideration of their mutual premises and agreements and for their
mutual benefits.

W I T N E S S E T H:

WHEREAS, said broker is engaged in business as a general real estate
broker in the City of Waltham and County of Roman, State of XXXXXXXXXXXX, and is
duly qualified to and does operate a general real estate brokerage business
and is duly qualified to and does procure the listings of real estate for sale,
and prospective purchasers, and has and does enjoy the good will of, and a
reputation for fair dealing with the public, and

WHEREAS, said broker maintains an office in said City, properly equipped
with furnishings and other equipment necessary and incidental to the proper
operation of said business, and staffed with employess, suitable to serving the
public as a real estate broker, and

WHEREAS, said Sales Associate is a duly licensed real estate salesman and
enjoys a good reputation for fair and honest dealing with the public as such, and

WHEREAS, it is deemed to be to the mutual advantage of said Broker and
Sales Associate to form the association hereinafter agreed to under the terms
and conditions hereinafter set out,

Figure 5-1. Independent Contractor Broker-salesperson Agreement.

THEREFORE, for and in consideration of the premises and of the mutual convenants hereinafter contained, it is mutually agreed as follows:

1. Broker agrees to make available to the Sales Associate all current listings of the office, and agrees, upon request, to assist the Sales Associate in his work by giving advice and providing full cooperation in every way possible.

2. Broker agrees that the Sales Associate may share with other Sales Associates all the facilities of the office now operated by said Broker in connection with the subject matter of this contract, which office is now located at 1776 12th Street, Waltham, XXXXX.

3. Sales Associate agrees to work diligently and with his best efforts to sell all real estate listed with the Broker, to always solicit additional list-ings and customers, and otherwise promote the business of serving the public in real estate transactions to the end that each of the parties hereto may derive the greatest profits possible; it being understood that Sales Associate's only renumeration shall be by way of sharing in commissions collected as a result, in whole or in part, of his activities as hereinafter provided.

4. Sales Associate agrees to conduct his business and regulate his habits, so as to maintain and to increase the good will and reputation of the Broker and the Sales Associate, and the parties hereto agree to conform to and abide by all laws, rules and regulations, and codes of ethics that are binding upon or applicable to real estate brokers and real estate sales-men.

Figure 5-1. *(Continued)*

DOVER REALTY COMPANY INDEPENDENT CONTRACTOR AGREEMENT page 3

5. The commissions to be charged for any services performed hereunder shall be those determined by the Broker, and the Broker shall advise the Sales Associate of any special contract relating to any particular transaction which he undertakes to handle. When the Sales Associate shall perform any service hereunder, whereby a commission is earned, said commission shall, when collected, be divided between the Broker and Sales Associate, in which division the Sales Associate shall receive a proportionate share as set out in the Policy Manual of Dover Realty Company and the Broker shall receive the balance. In the event of special arrangements with any client of the Broker or the Sales Associate on property listed with the Broker or controlled by the Sales Associate, a special division of commission may apply, such rate of division to be agreed upon in advance by the Broker and the Sales Associate. In the event that two or more Sales Associates participate in such a service, or claim to have done so, they shall agree as to how the amount of the commission over that accruing to the Broker shall be divided. In no case shall either party be personally liable to the other for uncollected commissions, but when the commission shall have been collected from the party or parties for whom the service was performed, said Broker shall hold the same in trust for said Sales Associate and himself to be divided according to the terms of this agreement.

6. The division and distribution of the earned commission as set out in Paragraph 5 hereto, which may be paid to or collected by either party hereto, shall take place as soon as practicable after the collection of such commission from the party or parties for whom the services may have been performed.

7. The Broker shall not be liable to the Sales Associate for any expenses incurred by him, or for any of his acts, nor shall the Sales

Figure 5-1. (*Continued*)

Associate be liable to the Broker for office help or expense, and the Sales Associate shall have no authority to bind the Broker by any promise or representation, unless specifically authorized in writing in advance in a particular transaction. Sales Associate shall pay all of the cost of his own real estate license and bond, and of his dues for membership in the National Association of Real Estate Boards, and State Real Estate Association, the local Board of Realtors and any other dues, any applicable occupation tax, and notary bond, if any. It is specifically agreed that Sales Associate shall furnish his own automobile and pay all expenses thereof and that Broker shall have no responsibility therefor. Sales Associate agrees to carry public liability insurance upon his automobile with minimum limits of $100,000.00 for each person and $300,000.00 for each accident and with property damage limit of $25,000.00. Sales Associate agrees to furnish Broker a certificate prepared by the insurance company certifying that such insurance is in force and obligating the insurer to give Broker notice before cancellation.

8. This agreement does not constitute a hiring by either party. The parties hereto are and shall remain independent contractors bound by the provisions hereof. Sales Associate is under the control of Broker as to the result of Sales Associate's work only and not as to the methods or means by which such result is accomplished. This agreement shall not be construed as a partnership, and neither party hereto shall be liable for any obligation incurred by the other except as provided elsewhere herein. Broker shall not withold from Sales Associate's commissions any amounts for taxes or any other items. Broker shall not make any premium payments or contributions for any workman's compensation or unemployment compensation for Sales Associate.

Figure 5-1. (*Continued*)

9.   (a) This contract and the association created hereby, may be terminated by either party hereto, at any time upon notice given to the other; but
the rights of the parties to any commissions which were earned and collected
prior to said notice, shall not be divested by the termination of this contract.
Upon termination of this agreement, Sales Associate shall not be compensated in
respect to any commission resulting from the exercise of a sale after the
termination of said agreement.

(b) Upon termination of this agreement, Sales Associate further
agrees not to furnish to any person, firm, company or corporation engaged in
the real estate business any information as to Broker's clients, customers,
properties, prices, terms of negotiations nor Broker's policies or relationships with clients and customers nor any other information concerning Broker
and/or his business. Sales Associate shall not, after termination of this
agreement, remove from the files or from the office of the Broker any maps,
books and publications, files or data, and it is expressly agreed that the
aforementioned records and information are the property of the Broker.
Sales Associate shall be entitled to photostats of certain instruments
pertaining to transactions in which Sales Associate has a bona fide interest
and Broker shall not unreasonably withhold the same from Sales Associate.

10. (a) Heirs, Successors and Assigns. This agreement shall be binding
upon and the benefits shall insure to the heirs, successors and assigns of the
parties hereto.

(b) Notices. All notices provided for under this agreement shall
be in writing and shall be sufficient if sent by certified mail to the
following listed addresses of the parties hereto or to such other address as
shall be designated in writing to the other party:

Figure 5-1. (Continued)

DOVER REALTY COMPANY INDEPENDENT CONTRACTOR AGREEMENT page 6

BROKER: DOVER REALTY COMPANY
                  1776 Twelfth Street
                  WALTHAM, XXXXXXXX   12345

SALES ASSOCIATE: _____

(c) <u>Governing Law</u>. This agreement shall be governed by the laws of the State of XXXXXXXX.

(d) <u>Assignment</u>. This agreement is personal to the parties hereto and may not be assigned, sold or otherwise by either of them.

(e) <u>Waiver</u>. That the failure of any party hereto to enforce at any time any of the provisions or terms of this agreement shall not be construed to be a waiver of such provisions or terms, nor the right of any party thereafter to enforce such terms or provisions.

(f) <u>Entire Agreement</u>. That this agreement constitutes the entire agreement between the Broker and Sales Associate, and that there are no agreements or understandings concerning such agreement which are not fully set forth herein.

(g) <u>Severability</u>. That if any provision of this agreement is invalid or unenforceable in any jurisdiction, the other provisions herein shall remain in full force and effect in such jurisdiction and shall be liberally construed in order to effectuate the purpose and intent of this agreement, and the invalidity or unenforceability of any provision of this agreement in any jurisdication shall not affect the durability or enforce-ability of any such provision in any other jurisdication.

WITNESS the signatures of the parties hereto the day and year first above written to duplicate.

BROKER: SALES ASSOCIATE:

DOVER REALTY COMPANY   by_____   _____

Figure 5-1. (*Continued*)

relatively short period of time, such as a year. The periodic renegotiation of the contract will give both salesperson and manager the opportunity for frank discussion of the salesperson's performance and also will provide management with an incentive tool. The salesperson can be told during a contract period that if his work achieves a certain level he may expect a new contract which reflects, perhaps, a better commission split or a more generous incentive program for him. Also, if a salesperson is performing poorly, he will know that his contract may not be renewed if he does not improve.

Termination

It is particularly important that the contract spell out the manner in which it may be terminated. For example, if the salesperson does not achieve a certain minimum level of activity, the firm may terminate the agreement before it expires. If he resigns, the contract should spell out what responsibilities he has to the firm by so doing. Severance pay (for employees) should be mentioned. There may also be language guaranteeing the salesperson renewal of the contract if certain performance goals are met. It is poor policy to keep people guessing until the last minute about their continued employment, and they feel much more secure if they know that their contract guarantees their job if they do it well enough.

Support and Benefits

The contract should point out what supportive services the brokerage firm will provide for the salesperson, especially if they are better or worse than those normally provided by firms in its area. The employee salesperson's contract should list the fringe benefits, if any, that the employee will receive. If it is a contract for a new employee, it may specify required training sessions, the specifics of draws against commissions, and other special provisions, including the eventual change of status to independent contractor when experience and competence permit. It is wise to agree in the independent contractor's contract that he will be responsible for paying self-employment taxes and making the quarterly payments of estimated taxes required by the IRS of self-employed people. Finally, signed copies of the agreement should be in the possession of both the firm and the salesperson.

SUPPORT PERSONNEL

Nearly all full-time and part-time support personnel will be classified as employees, but most when-needed service providers can be treated as independent contractors. This means that in addition to salaries for support personnel, the firm must withhold income taxes and social security payments from employees' salaries, and must pay the employer's share of social security, workers' compensation, unemployment insurance and the like. Employees may be offered participation in pension, health insurance, life insurance, and other fringe benefit plans the firm may have, and the firm may choose to pay part of the cost for these on behalf of employees. Employees also may be eligible for profit sharing plans if the firm has them and wishes to include these personnel in them.

DISCUSSION QUESTIONS AND PROJECTS

1. Get samples of the employment agreements used by one or two of the major brokerage firms in your area. If they use the independent contractor system, examine the agreements to see if they include any provisions that might violate the independent contractor status.
2. Why do brokerage systems prefer the independent contractor status for their salespeople?
3. What would be the advantages and disadvantages of treating the sales force as employees instead of independent contractors?
4. What are the major problems associated with independent contractor status from the brokerage firm's point of view?
5. From the salesperson's point of view, what are the advantages and disadvantages of being an independent contractor?
6. Can you find any brokerage firms in your area that do not use a written contract between the firm and the salesperson? Do they encounter any problems? If so, what problems are the most significant?
7. What means of compensation would be inconsistent with the independent contractor's status? Why?

A Case Study

INDEPENDENT CONTRACTOR

This story is probably not precisely true, but there is more truth in it than fiction. And it's an instructive tale.

A large midwestern real estate brokerage firm was investigated by the IRS to determine whether or not its sales force fit the legal definition of the independent contractor. The investigators poked around for several days, and finally informed management that they wanted to meet with the entire sales force to report the results of their investigation. "How about the day after tomorrow at 10 AM?" asked the manager. "Fine," replied the investigators.

At the appointed time, the investigators entered the crowded bullpen room. "Is everyone here?" they asked, "Yes," replied the manager. "I called each one and told them to be here, and they're all present."

"Well," said the chief investigator, "If all of them came here because you told them to, then by definition they are employees. If they really were independent contractors, you could not have required them to attend this meeting. So, according to our calculations, your firm owes several hundred thousand dollars in back taxes and penalties."

The manager's response to this has not been revealed.

REFERENCES

FISHER, FREDERICK J., *Broker Beware: Selling Real Estate Within the Law*, ch. 2–5. Reston, VA: Reston Publishing Company, Inc., 1981.

PHILLIPS, BARBARA, "Office Management for Brokers," in *The McGraw-Hill Real Estate Handbook*, ed. Robert Irwin, ch. 33. New York, NY: McGraw-Hill Book Company, 1984.

Real Estate Office Management: People Functions Systems, ch. 9. Chicago, IL: REALTORS® National Marketing Institute, 1975.

GROSS, JEROME S., *Encyclopedia of Real Estate Forms*, ch. 6. Englewood Cliffs, NJ: Prentice Hall.

SHENKEL, WILLIAM M., *Marketing Real Estate* (2nd ed.), ch. 12, 13. Englewood Cliffs, NJ: Prentice Hall, 1985.

SIX

PERSONNEL SELECTION

Recruitment Sources

The Selection Process

Support Personnel Selections

Termination

Choosing the people who will work in the brokerage firm is of prime importance to its continued success. In this chapter we will consider the selection process and the means available to the firm of assuring the selection of the best qualified people. Because of their importance and the specialty of their skills, we will devote most of our discussion to the selection of salespeople. We will also give some consideration to the unpleasant business of terminating unsatisfactory personnel.

RECRUITMENT SOURCES

It is likely that most members of the public at large will not be qualified to assume a particular position that a firm has available; most people will lack the necessary skills, the interest in the work, or both. Therefore, the firm should try to concentrate its recruitment efforts in those places where the desired person is most likely to be found.

The Firm Itself

The current staff of the firm should never be ignored as a source of people to fill new positions, particularly if they are replacement or growth positions. The advantage here is that promotion from within involves people who already are familiar with the firm and its methods and who are known to the management. They are most easily evaluated because management has had a long history of working with them directly and closely, and they will require relatively less training. The cost, both in money and time, of finding someone within the firm is very low, since no advertising has to be done and relatively little formal interviewing or getting acquainted is needed.

If, however, promotion within the firm occurs the person involved will be leaving his old job vacant, and it is not likely that someone the firm is willing to promote would have been in a job that subsequently will become expendable. Therefore, in-house promotion usually means that while a certain job has been filled, another will open up, and eventually the firm will have to look outside itself to fill its staff completely. However, it may be that the vacated job will be easier to fill, and so the firm will benefit overall. As an example, if a member of the sales staff is promoted to sales manager, another salesperson will have to be found. However, salespeople are easier to find than good sales managers.

A big advantage of in-house promotion is that if it is known well in advance that a certain individual will be promoted, a lot of time is available to "groom" him for that position while he continues in the one he already has. It also can be a morale booster, especially for the individual affected. Handled properly, the promotion may make other staff members also feel better because the firm has demonstrated that its first loyalty is to its own people.

On the other hand, in-house promotion can impair morale if several people think they are capable of handling the job and only one can be chosen.

Those who are passed over will have to be handled with care for some time, since they may well feel that they have lost esteem or the appreciation of management. Furthermore, promotion from within can be carried too far. If the best person for the job is not someone who is in the firm already, then choosing someone from inside is detrimental because the firm will be overlooking better people simply because they are not already in the firm. Finally, jobs created by *expansion* are less likely to be adequately filled from within because they will call for skills, knowledge, and abilities that are new to the company and so might not be found in abundance in the staff members already present.

Other Firms in the Business

Newcomers to the real estate brokerage business will be surprised at the amount of job-hopping that goes on, especially among salespeople. As a consequence, it is not necessarily considered in bad taste for a company to try to entice into its fold superior producers at other companies. The firm is not going to improve its relations with other firms by doing this, but at the same time it should be evident that most other companies are doing the same thing.

The reason is that while countless people may have real estate sales licenses, only a very few mature in the business to become good producers. Those few effective people are in high demand, and they are well known in the local business. Therefore, this kind of recruiting is not very expensive or time-consuming. The natural association that real estate brokerage people have with one another in their daily work usually is enough to get the word around as to who is satisfied where he is and who might be available if the right offer were to come along.

Frequently, when a firm develops a vacant position—new or existing—and a candidate from within the firm is not available, management can easily come up with a list of potentially desirable people who are presently with other firms. This is particularly the case when the position is due to expansion, and the firm is necessarily looking for a person with experience in the new area. Such a person can best be found in another firm that already has developed the same area.

Other Related Businesses

A person who is very successful at selling something other than real estate may be a good prospect for a real estate sales position; he has the ability to sell and to survive on a commission pay scheme. Successful sales experience in any field is a good predictor of successful real estate selling, for to a very real extent, a good salesman can sell anything.

Other businesses may also be good sources of certain management personnel, since management is to some extent a universal skill. Particularly good sources in different businesses are large companies with relatively limited promotion opportunities. A highly motivated person eventually gets frustrated in such surroundings; the company is so large that he is never able to move to a position high enough for him to feel he is controlling or operating something significant. Also, in large companies many executives who are capable and eager eventually find themselves bogged down at some relatively high level of management above which they know they have little chance of advancing. People like this may find the smaller size of the typical real estate firm attractive. They can be in control of a significant part of the smaller firm and can see the results of their efforts much more clearly.

Schools, Colleges, and Other Training Centers

This source is not always available to a firm. To make most effective use of schools and other educational institutions that produce graduates with the skills desired, the company is best located near them. Then it takes little effort to call once or twice a year to find out whether or not there are promising graduates available, and to make known the firm's needs.

But even if such an institution is not nearby, it may be advantageous to contact the closer ones and to make the firm's needs known to them. This applies especially to colleges and universities, as more and more are introducing real estate subjects into their programs of study. Graduates will have acquired a lot of formal knowledge but relatively little actual experience in the business, so they will need additional training once they are on staff. However, they will have had a considerable introduction to the field and are likely to be interested in and eager for the jobs they take.

People recruited from such sources do not need to have intimate knowledge of the local business. Whether they graduate from a local institution or one some distance away, any decent training provided them by the firm will include a rigorous introduction to the market they will be dealing in. Their lack of local knowledge is a disadvantage in that they will require more training than someone already experienced, but they make up for it with the general knowledge of the business and its nature that they acquired in the classroom. Also, they are likely to be aware of the latest developments in the field and so may well bring knowledge and skills that will prove valuable. However, they may be too eager to put *all* they know to work, and it may be necessary to include in their training by the firm some suggestions concerning the knowledge they have that ought to be put aside, at least temporarily.

The General Public

It is usually expensive and not very rewarding to solicit applications from the general public. Most people recruited from this source will have no experience in real estate and no demonstrated talent. They must be trained from the very beginning, and most will have to get licensed before even the training can begin.

However, many firms are quite successful in recruiting in such a general manner. Usually, they protect themselves by having an associated real estate school (in states that allow them to do so) and requiring interested people to pay their own way through the preliminary and prelicensing training. Then the firm will select the most promising students as potential associates, thus using the school as both a recruiting and a screening device. Other firms use advertising and other recruitment of the general public to attract people who may have an interest in real estate. Once they contact them, the nature of the business is explained and discussed and promising applicants are urged to take licensing preparation courses as a requisite for further consideration, either at the firm's own school or, if it doesn't have one, at some other.

This source of applicants is feasible only for the firm that is structured so that it can handle a fairly large training program and is willing to invest the necessary time and money in promising but unskilled applicants. A smaller firm rarely can handle this type of recruitment. However, since good salespeople are so scarce, a firm may find that this method of recruiting is worthwhile if only a small percentage of the people processed through the program turn out to be good real estate salespeople.

THE SELECTION PROCESS

Whatever sources the firm uses, applicants for an available position will begin to appear once information about the position circulates. If none do, it will be because the information being sent out does not describe the position attractively, because the position itself is not attractive (usually because the pay and other benefits are not competitive), or occasionally because nobody wants the job enough to apply for it. The latter problem is likely to crop up only when the job is very unusual—not a frequent occurrence in the real estate brokerage business—or in areas with populations so small that a limited labor force exists.

If an unusually large number of applicants appears, then the position is being described too attractively, the pay and benefits are too high, or the local area is experiencing relatively high unemployment and a lot of people are just looking for *any* job.

In the first case, care should be taken to describe the position honestly at the outset; otherwise time will be wasted interviewing people who will lose interest when they discover the position is not as good as it sounds. There is also a risk of hiring someone who may not find this out until after he has taken the job, and who may then resign quickly, leaving the firm to go through the whole process all over again. If the firm is offering too attractive a pay and benefits package, it may end up spending more money than it should to fill the position.

Of course, sometimes a firm will deliberately offer better than average pay because it is seeking better than average peformance in the job. If this is the case, it should be made known at the outset, when information about the position is first made available. Generally, if superior performance is being sought, it should be rewarded with performance bonuses, productivity bonuses, or some other kind of payment that does not have to be made unless the person hired actually does perform to the unusually high standards desired.

In this case the person has an incentive to perform well, and the firm is not obligated to pay for exceptional performance unless it gets it. A careful effort should be made to define, at the very beginning, just what constitutes the superior performance desired and exactly how it will be rewarded. High sales can easily be measured and rewarded, but it is much more difficult to define superior performance of a typist, a switchboard operator, or other support personnel.

When unemployment increases in an area, people become less selective in seeking jobs. When this happens, the real estate business may experience an influx of people desiring to become salespeople, as well as more activity from licensees whose activity had been minimal. This will mean more work for the brokerage management as it tries to sift the potential producers from a larger supply of applicants, but there is no easy way to avoid this except by insisting on a record of sales or even real estate experience. Sometimes, of course, the slack in the local economy involves the real estate business itself. If it is bad enough, applicants may be discouraged simply because they do not see any genuine opportunity in the work. Just that sort of thing happened in the early 1980s, when soaring interest rates resulted in a dramatic fall both in new home construction and sales and in resales of older homes. Rather then hiring more people, most brokerage firms laid people off and also found that the rate of voluntary resignations from their sales forces increased rapidly.

The Application

When first contact is made with a prospective employee, it usually is wise to have him fill out an application form, an example of which is shown in Figure 6–1. The application should ask for the applicant's name and address, as well as his social security number and home telephone. It should list the names and relationships of his immediate family. His current employment should be given, as well as his previous employers going back at least five years. These are necessary for background checking and for indications of stability in job performance. It should reveal whether he currently is licensed, when he became licensed, and whether or not he had previously held licenses.

Educational background should be included, especially any courses or other studies that are related to the real estate business. Finally, some information about the applicant's financial status should be included. Salaries and other pay at previous jobs will give some indication of financial objectives; other information, such as assets on hand and debts, will demonstrate financial responsibility.

A brokerage firm should keep a supply of applications on hand at all times, since worthwhile applicants may occasionally walk in the door to inquire about a job. Whenever an application is taken, some information about the firm and the job should be given to the applicant. Real estate sales positions require

D DOVER REALTY COMPANY

1776 Twelfth Street, Waltham, Xxxxx 12345   (908) 555-4321

APPLICATION FORM

ACTION_____ _____

POSITION_____

DATE RECEIVED_____

      Thank you for considering Dover Realty Company. Please provide the infor-
mation requested below. All information that you give will be held in the
strictest confidence. However, in order to enable us to evaluate your application
fully, we also will ask you to give us permission to contact references and
previous employers and to secure a credit report on you.

FULL NAME_____SOCIAL SECURITY #_____

ADDRESS_____

TELEPHONE: Home_____Work_____DATE OF BIRTH_____

If you have a real estate license,   PLACE OF BIRTH_____

list type, state, number, expiration date:_____

DEPENDENTS (Give name, age and relationship):

_____

_____

_____

_____

List former residences for the last 10 years (address, city, how long there)

_____

_____

_____

_____

List all employment for the last 10 years, including your present job(s).
Give name, address and telephone of employer; your job there; approximate
monthly earnings; dates of employment and your reasons for leaving:

_____

_____

_____

_____

_____

Please note any that you would prefer that we do <u>not</u> contact. Explain why.

_____

Figure 6-1. Sample Application Form.

EDUCATION: List schools, when attended, degrees (if any), grades or years attended, major (for college): _____

_____

_____

List all course work that you have completed in the REAL ESTATE area:

_____

MILITARY RECORD (dates, branch, type of discharge, present status):

_____

Do you have any health problems? If so, list them here, along with treatment taken: _____

_____

List make, model and year of your automobile: _____

_____

List any business, social, or community service organizations that you belong to, including how long, and any offices or other positions you have held and now hold: _____

_____

_____

List at least three people we can contact as references, giving name, address, telephone and relationship to you: _____

_____

_____

In a short paragraph, tell us why you want to join Dover Realty, why you want to be in the real estate business, how much you know about the business, and what you expect to get out of it: _____

_____

_____

I certify that to the best of my knowledge, the information that I have given in this application is true and accurate.

SIGNATURE: _____

Figure 6-1. (*Continued*)

certain kinds of people with certain abilities and tolerances. It is only fair to an applicant to make sure that he is as knowledgeable as possible about the type of work involved. A good practice is to have a one- or two-page letter that briefly describes the real estate sales field and the company's particular situation. This can be given out along with the application, or mailed to applicants who write or telephone about jobs. Since it is relatively inexpensive to print up and send out this material, it should be handed out freely to anyone expressing an interest. An example of such a form letter is shown in Figure 6–2.

It should be pointed out that our discussion here, for purposes of completeness, concentrates on the processing of applicants who have relatively little experience. Obviously, dealing with experienced applicants may not have to be so involved. First, they are much more aware of the nature of the job they are applying for, so much of the explaining and description can be passed over. Second, their abilities already may be known to the firm's management to some extent by reputation, since successful salespeople are noticeable in the local business environment.

The Introductory Interview

Once the application has been filled out by the applicant and examined by the firm's interviewer, an initial personal interview can take place. If possible, it is advisable that the applicant have time to read over any available material describing the position, the company, and the nature of the business. The application and initial interview can be handled during the same visit. In such a case, the applicant can be instructed to fill out the application, and while the firm's interviewer is looking it over the applicant can be reading the other descriptive material given him. When this is done, both interviewer and applicant will have some questions to ask one another.

The introductory interview occurs between strangers who may not have known of one another's existence a few minutes before. Therefore, it cannot be expected to be a circumstance in which detailed personal matters are discussed. Its main purpose is to give both parties the opportunity to get some important impressions. This should be the interviewer's objective, although he also should make certain that the application is complete and ask any questions that are immediately brought to mind by the information provided on the application.

Necessary Qualifications

Throughout the application procedure, the applicant is free to say "No"; that is, he can say that he no longer is interested and terminate the process. The firm also decides at each step whether to proceed or terminate the process. After the initial interview, the firm should proceed only if the following conditions are met:

1. *The applicant should have the personality and desire necessary for a chance at success in the business.* Clues to this lie in what he says and the manner in which he acts.

D DOVER REALTY COMPANY

1776 Twelfth Street, Waltham, Xxxxx 12345   (908) 555-4321

We are pleased that you have expressed an interest in becoming an associate with Dover Realty Company. The purpose of this letter is to describe our firm to you more fully and to give an idea of what to expect in a career as a real estate associate, and what we at Dover Realty expect of our own associates.

Before you can become associated with our or any other company in a sales position, you must hold the proper license. If you are not licensed, you should make arrangements to take the licensing examination as soon as possible. There are many schools specializing in providing the necessary instruction to applicants for licenses, and we have one here at Dover; our tuition fee is $150.00 for the full six-week course that meets twice weekly for three-hour sessions. An advantage of taking your course from us is that you will meet some of our people and can get to know us better; however you may take your course, if you need it, wherever you like.

All Dover Realty associates are required to own and use a late-model, air-conditioned automobile which is clean and undamaged. While most associates use four-door sedans, some use luxury vans or station wagons. You should expect at least a three to six month period of no income as you undergo training and begin to do your first sales work. For new associates we can arrange a small draw on future commissions, not to exceed $750 per month; as your commissions begin to come in, 50% of your commission earnings will be retained by the company until your accrued draw has been paid off. If you leave the Company while still owing on the draw, our draw arrangement will make you legally liable to pay off the balance within one year, and an interest rate of 18% of the unpaid balance will be charged, beginning with the date of your resignation. In no case will draws continue for more than six months after initial association with the firm. At present it is our policy not to renew contracts of associates who do not earn at least $10,000.00 per year in commission to themselves.

Our commission arrangement is that the associate receives 50% of all commission income that he brings into the firm. We pay an additional override of 5% of commissions brought in in excess of a total of $40,000 per year, and a 10% override (a total of 60%) on any commissions in excess of $75,000.00 that an associate brings into the firm in one year. These overrides are payable on June 30 of the following year, providing that the associate is still under contract to our firm.

You should expect to spend at least four to six weeks in training after associating with us. We expect our associates to be knowledgeable professionals, and to undergo serious training and learning that will make them so. A new associate spends an initial probationary period as an employee of the firm,

Figure 6-2. Sample Informative Letter to Applicants.

during which he undergoes our training program and begins his early sales experience. Upon satisfactory completion of this phase (usually four to six months)
be becomes a full associate. All our associates are <u>independent contractors</u>:
that is an arrangement which allows great professional flexability. For tax
purposes, an independent contractor is self-employed and, so, must pay estimated
taxes to both Federal and State Government during the year, must pay self-
employed tax (instead of Social Security withholding), must arrange his own
personal health, life and automobile insurance, and, generally, must handle his
finances himself. None of these will be withheld from commission checks paid by
the Company. However, during the probationary period the new associate is
classified as an employee, and income and Social Security taxes will be withheld.

Because you will be responsible for your own finances, and because of the
nature of commission income, you should be prepared to provide from your own
savings or other sources available to you the income you will need to maintain
the living standard you desire during the time you are on draw, and until your
commission income reaches suitable levels. You should always keep a fairly
large reserve of savings on hand to tide you over slack periods; proper management of your personal finances is absolutely essential to a successful career
in real estate.

Real estate sales requires hard work. We do not normally hire associates
who will be unable to devote their full time to their work with us because we
do not believe it is the kind of job that you can take up only when it is
convenient. Associates may find themselves working at all hours of the day or
night and there is an abundance of work on weekends. All of our associates are
expected to list properties as well as to sell them, and they are expected to
spend a considerable amount of their time soliciting business from both buyers
and sellers. Many aspects of this job are not glamorous, but they must be done,
and done well, if success is to follow. Many people new to the business experience initial success by involving friends, relatives and acquaintances in deals,
but this source soon dries up. The successful associate is the one who is able
to deal with the public at large.

At Dover Realty we insist on the highest standards of ethical conduct and
honest dealing. Our reputation is our most treasured possession, and we want our
associates to value their own reputations just as highly. We do not engage in
high-pressure tactics, nor do we try to sell people property that they may not
really want or need. Our business is not just selling--it is <u>service</u>. We
insist on friendly service, conscientious assistance and advice, and careful
attention to all details by our Associates.

Again, we thank you for your interest in the real estate business and in
Dover Realty. Now that you know more about both, you are better able to judge
if this is for you. If it is, we will be happy to discuss it further with you.

Figure 6-2. (*Continued*)

Overly forceful or negative personalities are to be avoided. People do not like to be bullied by salespersons, and there is no point to sending them out with a salesperson whose best ability seems to be to talk them out of buying. A salesperson should demonstrate considerable confidence in his ability and knowledge; he will be acting alone much of the time, and has to be trusted to do so. Also, this type of personality creates confidence in him within the people he deals with, and this is a very important quality for success in real estate brokerage. The applicant's demeanor and appearance should be pleasing.

Actual physical appearance is not so important, since even people who might be thought quite ugly can dress to cover whatever flaws they may seem to have, and a good personality can hide it completely. However, mode of dress is important. Peculiar clothing styles are to be avoided, as are general uncleanliness and slovenliness.

2. *The applicant should show a strong interest in the real estate business.* This is not an easy line of work in which to become established, and a person who does not have a strong interest is likely to lose heart and quit early on. Merely the desire to make a lot of money is not enough: Everybody wants to make a lot of money, but not everyone has the desire to make the sacrifices and do the work necessary. An applicant who chooses the real estate field because it interests him is preferable to one who just needs a job.

3. *The applicant should know what he will be getting into in the real estate business.* A lot of people think real estate looks attractive because they imagine themselves showing attractive homes to attractive people, and generally earning their money by taking pleasant afternoon outings. They are horrified to learn that they will be expected to solicit listings from total strangers; to conduct open houses; to spend a certain amount of floor time at the office; to conduct business at all hours of the day and night, especially evenings and weekends, to show ten or twenty homes to a prospective buyer, possibly without making a sale; and to find prospective buyers by themselves. Those with strong nerves may remain long enough to learn that they must obtain licenses before they can partcipate in the business at all; that even after the weeks of study necessary for passing the licensing examinations they will know only the rudiments of the skills they will need; and that the period of training and learning they will need for success will barely have begun when they obtain their licenses.

If this has not frightened them away, they will discover that while the commission form of payment in real estate sales offers the opportunity of unlimited income, it also carries with it unlimited personal responsibility for one's financial well-being: If they do not list and sell, they do not earn any income. People starting out in the real estate sales field ought to have savings enough to sustain them for at least six months. Even if they are successsful right away, the time delay between the signing of deals and their eventual closing—which is when the commissions are paid—can be several weeks or months. Also, they must be prepared to deal with the feast-and-famine character of real estate sales, and to withstand the poor periods that afflict even the most successful salespeople.

4. *The applicant should be a stable individual with the motivation and desire to succeed in the real estate business.* Success requires that in all but emergency cases the salesperson's job has first call on his time at all hours of the day, seven days a week, all year long. He must be prepared to drop whatever he may be doing to meet with a prospect, show property, iron out a problem. Many licensees work very peculiar hours. During the week, prospects often require that they meet with the salesperson early in the morning or sometime in the evening, for they are at work during the day. A considerable amount of business is done on weekends, when prospects are free to look at property.

A salesperson's family life and home life are subject to constant interruptions. This would suggest that people who are relatively footloose, and not bound by family ties would make better salespeople, but in practice the reverse usually is true. Salespeople with family responsibilities know that their loved ones are dependent upon them, and so they are motivated to work hard to provide for them. This reasoning holds both for men and women. While a woman with a family may *appear* to be a housewife first and a worker second, the money she earns is just as important to the family as that brought in by others, no matter how "traditional" the family may consider itself.

Some younger people may have difficulty in the real estate business. Most successful sales personnel are family people, in their late twenties or older, who have held one or two other jobs previously and are looking for something more independent and interesting. Unattached younger people, who have only themselves to look out for, may be satisfied with relatively low productivity. When they have families to support they begin to think of increasing their earnings every year.

5. *Finally, the applicant must meet the basic requirements.* He must be licensed, or able to become licensed within a reasonable period of time. He must have the savings necessary to sustain him before commission income begins to come in. He must have the necessary tools of the trade, including a comfortable automobile to use when showing property.

Testing

Some firms prefer to measure the applicant's potential by using various kinds of tests. A formidable battery of test is available, although there are very few designed to measure potential success in the real estate business itself, and their reliability is not especially good. Real estate selling is somewhat of an art, and it is difficult to measure a given person's potential for success. Pehaps as reliable is the "seat of the pants" evaluation; an experienced manager somehow feels that he can tell who will succeed and who will not, although he may find it very difficult to explain why.

The firm should use whatever measures it feels most comfortable with. Whether or not extensive and sophisticated testing techniques are used, mistakes will be made: Some people will go unnoticed who later will prove to be successful, while others will be identified as prime prospects who later fail. Experience tells in the long run, and whatever forms of evaluation management feels are best are the ones that should be used. It should be pointed out, however, that some intuitive measures may be illegal. For example, overlooking women or blacks specifically because they are female or black is discrimination and violates a host of federal laws, as well as many state and local laws. It also violates good business practice. There is no valid reason why persons of certain racial, sex, or ethnic characteristics should perform any better or worse than anyone else; discrimination leads to exclusion of many capable people who could contribute profit and professionalism to the business.

Investigation

If the applicant has remained in the running so far, some investigation of his background should be made. The thrust of this phase is to get a better picture of his reliability, honesty, and general ability. Previous employers are good sources of this information. Application forms also ask for references, but it is not likely that the applicant will list people he thinks will give him a poor rating, so information from such a source should be given less weight.

It is good practice, if the application process gets this far, for the firm to secure the applicant's permission to run a credit check. Credit bureaus can lay bare someone's most intimate financial secrets, and the manner in which a person handles his personal finances often gives good clues to his other abilities. If he is organized and relatively conservative in this area, one might expect him to be equally careful in other aspects of his life. Similarly, a poor credit record reflects disorganization and poor judgment and management ability. In the real estate business, it also reflects something else: a potential lack of ability to understand personal finance and the management of borrowing. Since borrowing usually is an essential part of most real estate transactions, it might be expected that one who cannot control or manage his own borrowing satisfactorily would not be particularly suitable to advise others.

A particular concern of the investigation should be the applicant's stability; satisfactory explanations of all job changes should be found, and the ratings given by previous employers should be sought out. An applicant who has had a lot of jobs, especially in a variety of lines of work demonstrates a potentially unsatisfactory record. Care should be taken, however, to avoid the mistake of assuming that the applicant's objective at those times was a career. Certainly jobs held while he was in school or college should be discounted, since his objective at that time was to get an education, and he is likely to have taken whatever work was available that would not interfere with that goal.

Some applicants will show numerous job changes which, upon investigation, prove to have been better and better jobs every time. This demonstrates ambition and self-confidence, since the person was willing to take some risks to improve his situation. It can also show that the applicant might be likely to move on to better things later on as well, so if such an applicant appears the firm ought to think of the possibility of providing him with better situations within the company as his skills and abilities increase. A striver is a good person to have, but he also is difficult to satisfy.

If negative reports are received from previous employers, they should be weighed carefully. Everyone makes mistakes, and even the best performers may at one time have found themselves in untenable situations. If most reports are favorable and one is not, this probably is the case, and it can be further investigated in the final interview. If most reports are negative, the interviewer should try to find out why; there may be extenuating circumstances that ought to be considered.

In order to save time and effort, a checklist should be used when a background investigation is done. A fairly general list of questions to be asked can be provided. If this list is longer than that which will be used for a particular contact, the inapplicable questions can be crossed out before the contact is made. Usually the contact is by telephone, since telephoning is fast and convenient. Some contacts may refuse to divulge information to a strange voice on the telephone, in which case a letter on company letterhead usually will be sufficient. The letter can outline the information needed, or a form can be made up and enclosed. The applicant can be asked to sign a number of form letters requesting that information on him be given. These could be sent to the contacts ahead of time, with a cover letter noting that the interviewer will call within a few days to ask for the information. A disadvantage of this advance notice is the possibility that the contact and the applicant may get together and rehearse the proper answers, but this is a slight risk.

Less convenient is personal contact; it takes a lot of time by the interviewer and can be quite impractical if travel to other cities is required. However, a face-to-face interview with a contact can yield a rich lode of information, since people are more willing to talk in person if they have the time.

The investigation also should assemble proof of claims by the applicant as to educational background, licenses held, and other earned designations and professional recognitions. It should include some information as to the applicant's general health, although often satisfactory information of this nature can be included on the application form and observed in the initial interview.

Final Interview

By this point, relatively few of the original group of applicants will still be in the running. These should be interviewed once more, this time in considerable depth. This interview can be much less formal than the first; applicant and interviewer have met and they both know that the interview is serious.

While this interview can be conducted in the office, it is best if it is done at the applicant's home, especially if he or she has a family. Real estate sales is not a nine-to-five job with a weekly paycheck, so it will have a considerable effect on the applicant's family. An interview at home allows the interviewer to experience the applicant's home situation and to gauge whether or not there may be unusual stresses there because of the nature of the job. A supportive family, especially a spouse, is a valuable asset to anyone in such work, and their existence is a strong plus factor. They will help him to get through slack periods and will not make unusual demands upon him because of the nature of his work.

The interviewer should make sure that the applicant's family knows the nature of the job and the particular ways in which it will affect them. If they are unaware of it, there may be reason for concern, since it is to be expected that a conscientious person would want those closest to him to know the full impact that such a job would have on their lives.

The final interview should be designed to get a better idea of the applicant's motivations and personality. The first interview was too short and too formal for this, and the other investigation and testing generated only second-hand information in this area. Specific questions and problem areas that appeared to the interviewer during the investigation process should be discussed, but only in general terms so as not to divulge information contacts thought that they were giving in confidence. The attitude of the interviewer should be that of a listener and not a talker. The applicant will have taken pains to present himself in the best light possible; once the interview has become relaxed his guard will begin to slip. The more he talks, the more he will say about himself and the more the interviewer will learn.

The Choice

When all applicants have been through the interviewing process, the choice will be made as to which will be hired. This should be done as quickly as possible, and all applicants still under consideration should be notified of the decision, although it is not necessary to tell unsuccessful applicants the identity of the person hired. The information is best given by telephone, with a follow-up letter. It must be stressed that the entire interviewing and selection process should be conducted as rapidly as possible. Not only is this fair to applicants, who ought not to be kept waiting for overly long periods of time, but it also assures that prime prospects will not take other positions in the intervening time.

In the earlier interviewing stages other applicants will have been dropped from consideration, and once they have been they should be informed immediately. While giving such a message is not a pleasant task, it has to be done, and with practice it can be done with a minimum of stress. It is best to be relatively honest, although sometimes the reasons may be sensitive and best kept understated. A follow-up letter should be sent to each applicant turned down. It is particularly important that if it is necessary to turn down an appplicant who is a member of minority or a female, the letter point out the reasons very specifically so there is no question of discrimination.

SUPPORT PERSONNEL SELECTION

Selection of support personnel should be given the same care as that of salespeople. Generally the first contact will come as a result of advertisement or other information intended to solicit potential employees. The applicant should be required to fill out an application form that assembles important information that can be used to make the hiring decision. Minimum information should include name, address, social security number, and names and relationships of immediate family members. Previous employment going back several years should be given, along with education and special training that is relevant to the job being applied for. The applicant should be asked to give two or three references, particularly previous employers who can be contacted.

A particular firm may choose to augment these questions with several others that may be considered important. Application forms in a standardized format are available at stationery or office supply stores, or the firm can prepare its own. In a pinch, the salesperson's application can be used; the inapplicable portions can be crossed out or ignored.

Some information about the job should be given to the applicant as well.

A copy of the job description is usually enough. It should describe the duties, the salary range (if this is not flexible or negotiable), and the necessary qualifications for the job. If the job is one that will offer opportunities for promotion to more responsible positions, this should be mentioned.

Checking the applicant's qualifications should follow the same pattern as that shown earlier for salespeople, although a less intensive background search may be adequate, depending upon the job being filled. A final interview of the best candidates should be conducted. If possible, all personnel who will be working with the applicant should be introduced, but this is not always practical.

Testing

For some jobs, such as typing and stenography, it is possible to give simple and straightforward tests that measure aptitude and skills. Some employers also like to give more subtle tests, such as psychological ones, but these are much harder to grade and sometimes require the use of specially skilled personnel for evaluation and even for administration. Use of these kinds of tests should be kept in context; it should be remembered that the only sensible objective is to measure suitability for a particular job, and many psychological factors will have no bearing.

Review

Once the application materials have been reviewed, the decision is made whether or not to continue the application procedure. Application review should be done quickly, in fairness to the applicants and also because an applicant is not likely to retain a favorable impression of a firm that dallies in its initial relationship with him. If it is decided at this point to terminate discussion with an applicant, he should be notified immediately, preferably by telephone with a formal letter to follow. The tone should be polite; the applicant should be thanked for responding and for considering employment with the firm and the turn-down itself should be worded gently and politely.

Compensation of Support Personnel

Many firms regard their support personnel as necessary evils and are determined to spend as little as possible of their resources on them. This attitude is highly inefficient. Support personnel are useful; they should be employed when it is profitable to do so, and their worth to the firm should be recognized. This is not to suggest that fabulous wages should be paid, but it is not good business to try to get away with the lowest pay scale and the cheapest labor. A quick glance at the "Help Wanted" section of the local newspaper and a few calls to employment agencies and other sources of information will quickly establish the general range of salary that must be paid in the locality for the kind of personnel being sought. An offer to employ at the lower range of salary will bring forth relatively inefficient or inexperienced applicants who may well provide less useful work per dollar than someone more capable who must be paid more. On the other hand, a high salary will attract capable people, but they may be able to do more than is really needed. In either case, money may be wasted.

Good performance should always be rewarded. Support personnel who do their jobs well are valuable, and keeping them happy will keep the level of their work high and, just as important, will keep them on the job. Any new employee, no matter how skilled or competent, must undergo some period of initial training to establish familiarity with the job, the firm, and the particular demands that the position will make; no two jobs are exactly alike in every respect. Once the employee is acclimated to the job, he can be trusted to do what is necessary with a minimum of assistance or supervision. If the employee leaves the job, a replacement must be found and trained, and this process cannot help but cost the company money and valuable time. This makes it worth money to keep capable and satisfactory employees, even though they may end up being paid more than a replacement would cost. A careful analysis of what they do and their value to the firm generally will show that they actually are doing quite a bit more for the company than a new person would be able to.

TERMINATION

Not all salespeople will be good enough for a firm to keep. Some will violate the law or will engage in practices the firm discourages. Others may work hard and proceed correctly but just won't be able to produce enough income to make it profitable for the firm to keep them. In these cases it becomes necessary to terminate their employment with the firm.

Firing people is a distasteful responsibility of management. From time to time it has to be done if the firm is to be operated properly. No matter how carefully the process is carried out, there always exists an element of cold-bloodedness about it that makes most managers uncomfortable. Firing people ranks at or near the top of the manager's list of things he least likes to do.

Firing someone should always be done in person, and by the manager who works most closely with that person. The terminated employee or contractor is entitled to the opportunity to talk over the situation and to learn firsthand what the reasons are. Some firings are automatic, especially when violations of law or ethical conduct or the firm's policies occurs. In fact, many firms write into their employment contracts language listing specific violations that will be cause for immediate termination by management. It is absolutely essential that all personnel be aware of actions that are forbidden and will result in their being fired. It does nobody any good for the individual to discover after he had innocently done something that "our firm does not like that sort of thing."

The most difficult firing occurs when a sincere, hardworking person has to be let go because of poor productivity. This happens most often with salespeople who are fairly new to the business and who are discovering that the work simply is not what they are suited for. Often, arrangements can be made ahead of time to set some standards of performance so that the individual can monitor his progress as he goes along. In many cases, those who are not measuring up will eventually resign voluntarily, as they will know that their performance is not suitable.

Firings should be conducted in private and person to person. It is difficult to imagine any situation that would justify the public embarrassment, anger, and ill feeling that would occur if someone were to be fired in the company of others who are not his direct superiors. Usually the salesperson involved will know that he has not been performing well or has violated a provision of his contract, and the actual firing will be no surprise. By far the best technique is to explain the situation to the individual and to ask for a letter of resignation. In that manner, the records will not contain letters from management that spell out particular violations, and there is no risk that they will fall into unauthorized hands. If necessary, management can keep a separate set of private files, available only to select members of management, that provide more detail about the performance of the person who is fired. Records such as these should be kept under lock and key, or in a bank vault safety deposit box to which only authorized people have access.

Some people who are fired will seek employment elsewhere, and future employers may ask the brokerage firm for its information about the person. In such cases it is imperative that the firm take great care, especially if the information they have to give is derogatory. If a salesperson is fired for breaking the law, and there are public records of hearings or court activities in which he was found guilty, the firm can mention these with no fear of slander or libel. However, any other information given out that reflects poorly upon a person's ability or character *must* be fully documented. The firm should be prepared to prove, in a court of law, everything it says about someone.

DISCUSSION QUESTIONS AND PROJECTS

1. Interview one or two managers of large brokerage firms in your area. What do they think is their best source of new salespeople?
2. From the same source, find out what they think is the kind of person they look for when they hire salespeople. What characteristics do they think are most important? What characteristics should be avoided?
3. If you are using this book in a classroom situation, divide the class into groups of two people each. One person "interviews" the other, taking down all pertinent information and making a decision as to whether or not the person being interviewed should be hired.
4. From the same source as in (1), find out the application procedure they use. Collect and evaluate all the materials used in the application process.
5. Why is a background investigation of a prospective salesperson important? What kind of information should be sought?

6. Assume you are the sales manager of a real estate brokerage firm. Draw up a list of the qualifications and characteristics you would look for in an applicant for a salesperson's position if that applicant has no previous real estate selling experience.
7. If a firm can afford to hire only one support person on its staff, what duties should that person be given?

REFERENCES

HALL INSTITUTE OF REAL ESTATE, *Managing a Real Estate Team*, appendix F. Hinsdale, IL: The Dryden Press, 1980.

NATIONAL ASSOCIATION OF REAL ESTATE LICENSE LAW OFFICIALS, *Guide to Examinations and Careers in Real Estate*, ch. 2. Reston, VA: Reston Publishing Company, Inc., 1979.

PHILLIPS, BARBARA, "Office Management for Brokers," in *The McGraw-Hill Real Estate Handbook*, ed. Robert Irwin, ch. 33. New York, NY: McGraw-Hill Book Company, 1984.

Real Estate Office Management: People Functions Systems, ch. 7, 8. Chicago, IL: REALTORS® National Marketing Institute, 1975.

Real Estate Sales Handbook (9th ed.), ch. 3. Chicago, IL: REALTORS® National Marketing Institute, 1983.

SHENKEL, WILLIAM M., *Marketing Real Estate* (2nd ed.), ch. 12. Englewood Cliffs, NJ: Prentice Hall, 1985.

SEVEN

THE POLICY MANUAL

Purpose of the Policy Manual

Arrangement of the Manual

The Policy Manual and Independent Contractors

Revision

Example

In any organization it is essential that staff be aware of management objectives and policy, at least as far as each staff member's contribution to the attainment of management goals and objectives is concerned. In most large firms, the individual employee's contribution is carefully described in the job description, and he is not concerned with anything beyond the particular limits of his own position. Brokerage firms, however, tend to be fairly small, and employees of these firms must assume a large variety of duties. The entire sales force of a brokerage firm—usually representing the majority of its total staff—operates quite independently and, indeed, performs a great many activities outside the firm's own offices. Consequently, they are operating in an unsupervised situation, and it is absolutely essential that a clear and precise statement of the firm's policy be made available to them, both in the matters of doing business with the public and in matters of intracompany operation. A well-run brokerage firm will accomplish its objective by producing a written *policy manual*. The policy manual need not be very long; it is usually provided in a looseleaf format so that amendments and changes can be made easily and the manual can be kept up to date.

PURPOSE OF THE POLICY MANUAL

The function of the policy manual is to assure that each salesperson is given the best possible guidance in respect to the firm's operating procedures and the manner in which he should perform in order to reflect the desired image of the firm. Many firms operate without a policy manual; this usually is a mistake. The advantage of the written manual is that it provides a clear statement of the firm's objectives and policies, as well as providing clear written rules by which the sales force conducts itself.

The manual should cover all significant aspects of doing business in the company's manner. It should cover any particular variations from the normal practice that the firm chooses to impose upon its own operation. It should provide a precise but thorough outline of the compensation policy within the firm and of the manner in which the relationships among the sales staff and between the sales staff and other branches of the firm should be conducted. The ideal policy manual provides sales staff members with a tool they can use so that they will be able to perform their duties according to the firm's criteria with very little or no supervision. The policy manual can also be used as a recruiting tool. It can be displayed to prospective staff members as a convenient and concise means of explaining the firm's policies and the working surroundings and conditions that they might expect. A good policy manual can also be a training device.

Since the sales force represents the company, the policy manual should properly present its business philosophy. It should describe all that the salesperson should do, as well as pointing out those activities the salesperson should not engage in. The manual should try to anticipate the normal problems the salesperson may encounter in his duties, so that he will be properly equipped to handle them in the manner in which the company wants them handled.

ARRANGEMENT OF THE MANUAL

The policy manual should be divided into several parts. One would describe the company itself, including perhaps a brief history, a description of the company's current status, and a short description of the current goals and objectives. Another section would deal with the manner in which the salesperson should approach the public, both in the solicitation of listings and the handling of sales. A third section would cover all that the salesperson should be expected to know with respect to his dealings within the company. This section would describe compensation practices and the manner in which various problems that might arise within the firm would be expected to be handled. In all cases, the salesperson should be given a clear understanding of the manner in which he is expected to behave under various circumstances so as to properly represent the company he works for.

Following are a number of topics and questions that should be covered in a policy manual:

1. Company history, objectives
2. Listing procedure
   a. Use of company contract
   b. Protection of listing prospects
   c. Listing presentation kit
   d. Solicitation procedure
3. Selling procedure
   a. Use of company contract
   b. Protection of prospects
   c. Solicitation of prospects, screening
   d. Advertising
   e. Offer procedure
4. Office procedures
   a. Open houses
   b. Floor time
   c. Intra-office handling of client- and prospect-sharing
   d. Sales meetings
   e. Signs
5. Compensation procedure
   a. Commission sharing arrangements
   b. Bonuses
   c. Incentives
6. Brokerage industry practice
   a. Multiple listing procedures
   b. Joint listing policy
   c. Cooperation with other firms
   d. New homes, subdivisions
7. Other
   a. State license law
   b. REALTOR® Code of Ethics (for REALTOR® member firms)
   c. Other necessary material.

THE POLICY MANUAL AND INDEPENDENT CONTRACTORS

Since independent contractors cannot be held to the kinds of rules and regulations a firm may use for its employees, the policy manual should be worded accordingly. Only matters of law and recognized ethical considerations should be worded imperatively (e.g., "Sales associates *must not* . . ."). Wording on other matters of policy should be given in less restricted form: "Associates should try to . . .," "Associates probably will find it useful to . . .," and similar approaches are better in that they are not in the form of commands but rather appear to be suggestions. This kind of wording is much less severe and allows the affected associate to feel that the manual is designed as a guide and aid to successful business practice rather than a set of rules of conduct. It also is wise to include explanations of policy where they will be useful to give the associate a better understanding of policy and procedures.

REVISION

Revision of the manual should be undertaken whenever necessary, but not until there has been proper discussion and consideration of the changes to be made. Some may be needed just to make things clearer than the original statement, but some changes may also be designed to implement significant changes of policy. Proper management technique dictates that these changes be well advertised in the firm and, whenever possible, thoroughly discussed by all who will be affected by them.

Changes should not be made for their own sake, but in response to genuine need. A poor policy or one that simply is not getting done what it should ought to be changed. Good policy ought to be left alone. The growth and development of a business often will create situations where changes in policy are necessary, and changes in business conditions, laws, and other external factors may also have this effect. But any change, no matter how big or small, should be looked at carefully and thoroughly. It is better to stick with a policy that is not perfect than to try something that has not been thoroughly analyzed. Consistency is an important feature of comfort in any environment, and change usually starts out as disruptive to some extent even if everyone agrees that it is needed and favors it. These stresses, therefore, should be avoided except when they are absolutely necessary.

EXAMPLE

An example of a policy manual is provided in Figure 7–1, which begins on page 120. It should be noted that this example, for the sake of brevity, does not cover all the things that should be mentioned in most manuals; the intention here is

DOVER REALTY COMPANY

1776 Twelfth Street, Waltham, Xxxxx 12345   (908) 555-4321

POLICY MANUAL

INTRODUCTION

This manual is to be used by authorized personnel of Dover Realty, Inc. It contains confidential information which should be treated as such. All sales personnel should be completely familiar with the contents of this manual and should regulate their daily practice by it whenever possible. This manual is a general guide and does not cover all possible situations. It is designed to keep friction and misunderstanding to a minimum. Whenever questions arise that cannot be resolved by policy presented in this manual, they should be referred to the appropriate officers of Dover Realty, Inc. for action.

HISTORY

Dover Realty, Inc. was organized on March 2, 1980 to provide the finest and highest caliber of professional service to the homeowning community of our city. Dover Realty prides itself on its ethical approach to the real estate business and its concern for the satisfaction of all its customers, whether buyers or sellers. Our policy and the hard work we have done have had excellent results; from a beginning when we employed five full-time salespersons, we have grown to have a staff of over 25 sales associates. Our listings and sales total over $15 million per year and we are growing rapidly. We expect all who are associated with our firm to reflect our ideals and ambitions, to our mutual benefits.

GENERAL

Our firm subscribes to the code of ethics of the National Association of REALTORS® and the rules and bylaws of the local Real Estate Board. All associates are expected to be familiar with these and to apply them rigorously in all aspects of their professional lives.

Figure 7-1. Sample Policy Manual.

All associates should have an attractive, comfortable and clean automobile large enough to use for showing property comfortably. The costs of buying and maintaining the automobile are the responsibility of the associate. The associate also will be responsible for the cost of meals, entertainment, travel, business cards, sign stickers and MLS books.

Dover Realty will provide desk space, secretarial services, contract forms, telephone service at the office, advertising and literature, within reasonable limits. Dover Realty will handle paperwork concerning license renewals and REALTOR® memberships, though each individual salesperson will be responsible for the costs associated with the fees involved.

The office will be open from 8:30 am to 6:00 pm Monday through Saturday. Keys are issued to sales associates to enable them to use the office facilities at all other times when needed. When sales associates are away from the office they should check in every hour or two for messages; whenever possible instructions should be left with the receptionist for contacting sales associates who are out of the office.

SALES MEETINGS

Sales meetings are held every Monday morning at 9:30 am; they usually will last an hour or longer if need be. Attendance at these meetings is strongly advised since they are the forum in which much useful information will be made available. Associates who have information or questions that may be of interest to other associates are encouraged to make them known at the sales meetings. Special training sessions or other special-purpose meetings may be called at other times, and associates are urged to attend them.

LISTING POLICY

Listings are the bread-and-butter of the real estate brokerage business and sales associates are encouraged to make considerable effort to secure them. Listings must be taken on the company's listing contract form, and the listing description sheet must be completely filled out; these, along with at least two photographs of the listed property, should be submitted to the sales manager for copying and distribution to the other sales associates.

Figure 7-1. (Continued)

Normally, NO OFFER MAY BE SUBMITTED TO A SELLER UNTIL THE LISTING HAS BEEN SUBMITTED TO THE SALES MANAGER AND NOTIFICATION DISTRIBUTED TO THE SALES FORCE. Listing commissions will not be paid unless this procedure is followed. In unusual circumstances a sales associate may obtain a signed listing at the time the offer is presented, but only if it is patently necessary to do so in order to safeguard the company's right to a commission.

All original contracts must be kept by the sales manager, although copies can be run off and distributed when necessary, according to his judgment.

The associate securing the listing is entitled to advertise it in his name, and has the responsibility of servicing it properly. Improper servicing of listings will result in the listing being assigned to another sales associate.

Lock boxes are in the custody of the sales manager's secretary and should be signed out whenever they are taken and signed in when they are returned. DO NOT LOSE THEM. They are company property.

All listings are the property of Dover Realty, Inc. An associate who does not service his listings properly may find them reassigned to others. Associates who resign must leave all unsold listings with Dover Realty, Inc.

LISTING PROCUREMENT PROCEDURE

When a prospect for listing appears, company policy is to provide for an informal appraisal of the property and a presentation of the company's services to be made by the listing agent. An associate may "protect" a potential listing once the procurement process has gone so far as to have an appraisal presented to the owner; the associate has 15 days from that time to secure the listing. After that time, any of the company's associates may try to secure that listing.

Listing associates should endeavor to get complete information on all property they list, keep sellers informed of what the company is doing for them, and advise the seller on things he can do to facilitate the sale. The associate should be sure that the seller understands all terms of the listing and the manner in which the property will be sold. The listing associate must present ALL offers received on property he has listed, and must do so personally.

Figure 7-1. (*Continued*)

Associates should strive to secure listings on an exclusive-right-to-sell basis for a 90-day period. Any listing of less than 60 days, or nonexclusive, must be cleared with the sales manager.

All sellers should be notified of the progress of their listings every ten days or so. The listing associate is responsible for proper care of vacant property.

Dover Realty, Inc. does NOT accept "net" listings. Negotiations for other than our standard commission must be with the sales manager.

COMMISSION SCHEDULE

Single family, duplex, other small rental units - resales 7%

"   "   "   "   "   "   " - new   5%

Building lots in developed subdivisions -   8%

Undeveloped land regardless of acreage   - 10%

Commercial or office property - negotiated with sales manager

OFFER POLICY

All offers submitted on Dover Realty listings must be presented to the seller as soon as possible and in no case more than overnight. If the listing associate is unavailable to present the offer, the associate who has solicited the offer may do so if approved by the sales manager. Offers received from other firms may be assigned to sales associates by the sales manager, if the listing associate is unavailable.

Offers submitted by prospects recruited by Dover Realty sales associates should be written up on the Dover Realty sales agreement form.

No offer will be taken unless it is properly executed and is accompanied by an earnest money check or some other statement of earnest money to follow. The check should be made out to Dover Realty and must be deposited in the Dover Realty trust account at Second City Bank within 24 hours of receipt.

Acceptance of offers by owners is indicated by their signature on the sales agreement. Out-of-town owners must acknowledge acceptance by telegram. An offer must be accepted in full for it to become a contract; if any changes are made before the offer is accepted, it constitutes only a counter-offer and must be submitted to the original offeror as soon as possible for perusal.

Figure 7-1. (*Continued*)

ALL OFFERS SHOULD BE SUBMITTED AS SOON AS POSSIBLE, even if it means waking people up in the middle of the night. It is unlikely that something so important to a client will be an unwelcome interruption.

ALL OFFERS MUST BE PRESENTED AS SOON AS THEY ARE RECEIVED. Until a seller has accepted an offer he is entitled to see all offers. Prospective buyers must never be given the details of other offers, although the fact of their existence may be used as an enticement to quick action and good terms. It is illegal to hold back an offer for any reason except explicit instructions from the seller himself. Under no circumstances should a sales associate try to act in place of the seller or make his decisions for him.

As brokers, we represent the seller. No attempt should be made to influence prospective buyers that we are on their side or will negotiate on their behalf against the seller. Once a contract is signed it is our duty to see to it that both sides live up to it.

The sales agreement should be complete and proper. EVERYTHING agreed upon MUST BE IN WRITING. Sales associates should make every effort to seek out potential problem areas and solve them in the negotiation process. A sale which does not close is no better than no sale at all and may be worse: instead of perhaps being able to make a better agreement with someone else, we are unable to do much of anything until an agreement that was bad in the first place has fallen through.

PROSPECTS

Within the company a sales associate may "protect" a prospect <u>once that prospect has been shown property</u> by him or her. Telephone contact or other contact without showing property will not provide protection except under circumstances approved by the sales manager. Prospects who visit an open house are not considered to have been shown property except when negotiations get underway concerning the open house property itself. A prospect who has not been shown property by an associate for over eight consecutive days is no longer protected. The sales manager may reassign prospects if they are being handled improperly by the associate responsible for them.

Figure 7-1. (*Continued*)

The sales manager, officers of the company, receptionists and secretaries do not actively sell property. Any calls received by them from prospects will result in the prospect being assigned to an active sales force member. Calls coming in to a specific associate will be referred to him or her; if the associate cannot be found and the prospect is unprotected, the prospect will be assigned.

First priority in assignment always goes to the associate on floor duty at the time the call comes in. In some circumstances the sales manager will decide to assign the prospect to another associate, but this will only be done for good reason.

PROSPECT SHARING

Associates may agree to share prospects, but should avoid doing so unless it is necessary. A necessary situation might arise when an associate will have to be out of town, is ill, or is otherwise occupied. The sharing associates must agree on potential commission splits, and this information should be relayed by BOTH to the sales manager before such sharing begins.

FLOOR TIME

Each sales associate will be asked to spend one four-hour period per week of floor time in rotation with all other sales associates. Associates agreeing to floor time who do not take advantage of assigned floor time may switch assignments with another associate, if one day's notice is given to the sales manager and he approves. The associate on duty receives all cold calls for which an associate's assistance is necessary. Calls to another associate who is not present will be referred to the associate on duty and he is free to work with all unprotected prospects he finds in this manner. Protected prospects should be given the assistance necessary if an attempt to contact the protecting associate is unsuccessful. If a prospect must be shown property during an associate's floor time, the associate must find a replacement floor agent to fill in for him while he is gone.

If an associate on duty is required to show property to another associate's protected prospect, he should do so only after attempting to contact the protecting agent and after trying to get the prospect to wait until the protecting associate is available. If a sale results

Figure 7-1. (Continued)

from such a showing, the associate on duty will be entitled to one-third of the sales commission and the protecting associate the other two-thirds.

A complete log of all incoming calls should be kept by the duty associate. Additionally, a full log of all calls made trying to locate other associates asked for by callers should be kept, including a record of everyone spoken to in the search and the instructions that may have been received from such calls for finding the associate called for.

OPEN HOUSES

Each sales associate is encouraged to hold an open house at least once every other weekend. Choice of listings to be held open is left to the associate, except that new listings should be given preference. Normally a new listing should be held open on one of the first three weekends after the listing is obtained, if it has not yet been sold. If an associate is unable to hold a new listing open within this time, open house on that listing may be assigned to another associate by the sales manager.

Prospects recruited at open houses should be screened to assure that they are not protected by another associate. This screening process must not make the prospect aware of our prospect protection system, and it is up to the sales associate doing the screening to find out the necessary information given this restriction.

TELEPHONE

Telephones are provided for the use of all sales associates. Unlimited local calling is permitted. Long distance calling is permitted without restriction to relay offers. Other long distance calling is generally permitted without restriction so long as the sales associate is prepared to defend his long distance calling whenever asked. All long distance calls must be entered on the telephone log, including the agent making the call, the city and number called, the name of the person(s) called and the purpose of the call. Efforts should be made to use cheaper station-to-station and off-time rates when practical. Calls to submit offers should be made person-to-person at the soonest possible time after the offer is received, regardless of the time of day or rate structure in effect.

Figure 7-1. (*Continued*)

COMMISSION SPLITS TO ASSOCIATES - BASE COMMISSIONS

    (1) Sales of Dover Realty listings by Dover Realty sales associates. In these we retain the full commission.

           Listing associate's commission is 25% of total commission if an offer is accepted within 30 days of listings. $22\frac{1}{2}$% of total commission after 30 days. On listings referred to a sales associate by a non-selling member of the firm, a 10% share of the total commission is paid. Selling associate's share of the commission is 25%.

    (2) Sales of Dover Realty listings by other firms. In these the firm receives 55% of the total commission. Dover Realty listing associate's share of the total commission is the same as in (1) above.

    (3) Sales of other firm's listings by Dover Realty sales associates. In these the firm receives 45% of the total commission. The selling associate for Dover Realty will receive 20% of the total commission.

COMMISSION INCENTIVE PLAN

    Productive associates are rewarded with a commission bonus plan as described below. The bonus is calculated as a percentage of the base commissions earned each quarter in accordance with the commission schedule above. Bonuses are calculated according to the schedule below. Bonuses earned are payable 90 days after the end of the month when they are earned, provided that the associate is still associated with Dover Realty Company.

If the Base Commissions earned are

at least	but less than	the bonus will be
$4000.00	$4500.00	3% of the base commission earned
4500.00	5000.00	4% " " " " "
5000.00	5500.00	5% " " " " "
5500.00	6000.00	6% " " " " "
6000.00	7000.00	8% " " " " "
7000.00	8000.00	12% " " " " "
8000.00	10,000.00	18% " " " " "
over 10,000.00		25% " " " " "

Figure 7-1. (Continued)

merely to provide a sample. In a manual for actual use, a number of topics not found in the example, such as those listed earlier in this chapter, should be discussed. Each topic ought to be covered on a separate page or set of pages to facilitate revision. This also is aided by a looseleaf format, especially if one intention is to include in an appendix reprints of articles or information of current interest. The manual need not be a work of art; copies of a neatly typed manuscript are perfectly adequate.

DISCUSSION QUESTIONS AND PROJECTS

1. From brokerage firms in your area, assemble as much information as you can about their policy manuals. Which areas of the business seem to receive the most attention? Why is this so?

2. Obtain a copy of one of the brokerage firms' policy manuals. Go over it carefully, prepare an analysis of its strengths and weaknesses, and make suggestions for improvement.

3. Are there major firms in your area that do not use policy manuals? If so, how do they handle the communication of the things that a policy manual usually contains?

REFERENCES

DOOLEY, THOMAS W., "The Real Estate Office of Tomorrow," in *The McGraw-Hill Real Estate Handbook*, ed. Robert Irwin, ch. 36. New York, NY: McGraw-Hill Book Company, 1984.

FISHER, FREDERICK J., *Broker Beware: Selling Real Estate Within the Law*, ch. 2, 4–9. Reston, VA: Reston Publishing Company, Inc., 1981.

GOLDSTEIN, PAUL, *Real Estate Transactions*. St. Paul, MN: Foundation Press, 1985.

HALL INSTITUTE OF REAL ESTATE, *Managing a Real Estate Team*, ch. 10, appendices G, H. Hinsdale, IL: The Dryden Press, 1980.

PHILLIPS, BARBARA, "Office Management for Brokers," in *The McGraw-Hill Real Estate Handbook*, ch. 33. New York, NY: McGraw-Hill Book Company, 1984.

Real Estate Office Management: People Functions System, ch. 9. Chicago, IL: REALTORS® National Marketing Institute, 1975.

Real Estate Sales Handbook (9th ed.). Chicago, IL: REALTORS® National Marketing Institute, 1983.

SHENKEL, WILLIAM M., *Marketing Real Estate* (2nd ed.), ch. 4. Englewood Cliffs, NJ: Prentice Hall, 1985.

EIGHT

LISTING MANAGEMENT

Contract Form Design

Listing Contracts

Establishing the Right to the Commission

Listing Policy

Listing Information

Setting Commission Rates

Dissolving Listing Contracts

Listings are the mainstay of the brokerage business. They determine the success of the business and are the source of its income. All firms should have specific policy concerning the obtaining of listings, the kinds of listings solicited, commission rates and policy, and listing information exchange with other firms.

CONTRACT FORM DESIGN

The real estate brokerage makes intensive use of two types of contracts: *listing contracts* and *sales contracts*. The first is the contract between the potential seller of property and the broker hired to solicit buyers. The second is the contract between the buyer of property and the seller; this contract usually is negotiated with the help and assistance of the broker or brokers involved. Normal practice requires salespeople to fill out these contracts, explain them to the people involved, and, occasionally, engage in active negotiations involving the contracts, although the latter generally is confined to listing contracts only. Therefore it is essential that the sales force be perfectly familiar with the contract forms used for these purposes by the brokerage firm and with the situations in which they are authorized to deal with them on their own.

Contract forms should be printed, with the appropriate blanks to be filled in to suit them to each situation. It is essential that these forms be designed to be clear and concise. Fine print is no longer an essential to a well-written contract and, indeed, is often looked upon with some disfavor by today's courts, especially if it appears that the use of a lot of legalistic language and wordiness is designed to confuse one or more of the parties to the contract.

The contract forms used by the brokerage firm should be designed with the assistance of a competent attorney who is well versed in the purposes they are to serve. Under no circumstances should they be designed without such professional help! In some states, professional organizations within the brokerage industry (notably the state REALTORS® organizations) may have produced such forms, with the assistance of attorneys, for the use of their members. If so, these forms should be given serious consideration. However, if an already prepared form is not absolutely suitable for a given firm's purposes or policies, it should be amended (with an attorney's assistance) as necessary and then put to use. This is far preferable to using an even slightly inappropriate contract form.

It must be emphasized that a real estate license does not confer upon its holder the right to practice law, and that the drawing up of contracts usually is considered legal practice. State laws usually allow licensees to draw up and assist in the preparation of contractual arrangements using preprinted contract forms whose language has been approved by an attorney, but it rarely is advisable to go any further. If complications arise, an attorney should be consulted and his advice followed. The professional brokerage firm always will have some sort of arrangement with a competent attorney allowing for consultation in just such instances.

The broker is held legally responsible for the contracts he provides, enters into, and assists in arranging; therefore errors are to be avoided at all costs. While attorneys' fees and retainers may seem expensive, they are a pittance compared to the potential losses that can be suffered by not consulting the attorney when one should have done so.

LISTING CONTRACTS

The listing contract is the contract between the broker and the client whose property he is being hired to rent or sell. As such, it is his bread-and-butter contract, because it gives him his stock in trade: real estate for which buyers or other users are to be found. An example of a listing contract form is shown in Figure 8–1. While details will vary from one state or firm to another, it is a good representation of a simple, clear form that can be used in the residential brokerage business. All listing contracts should include the following:

1. *A legal description of the property involved.*
2. *The legal name(s) of the owner(s).* If there is more than one owner, all should be listed and all should be a party to the contract either by direct assent (signature) or by power of attorney granted to someone else who then will sign for them. In such a case, copies of all relevant powers of attorney should be attached to the contract.
3. *The objective of the contract.* In a listing for sale, this would be a statement that the broker is being hired to solicit buyers for the listed property.
4. *The terms under which the broker may offer the property.* This is an all-inclusive category, comprising the selling price and all special terms of the sale. These might include whether or not the seller will permit a loan assumption, will take back any (or all) financing on the property, or will be required to be paid in cash. Will the seller pay points on VA loans? Are there any other special circumstances, such as a date before which the seller does not want to leave, or certain fixtures that the seller does not intend to sell along with the property? All these should be spelled out in the listing contract.
5. *An expiration date.* Licensing law in many states requires an expiration date in all listings, and it is always advisable to put one in.
6. *The manner in which the commission is to be calculated and when and how it is to be paid.*

The sample contract form shown in Figure 8–1 has another useful feature, the "information card" that is printed on it. This section, in the top half of the sample form, provides space for the listing salesperson to insert all the relevant information concerning the property needed for effective marketing. It is a simple matter for the brokerage to copy that part of the form and distribute it to all other salespeople for insertion in their listing books. A copy of this information can be relayed to cooperating brokerages as well.

An important point should be made at this time. While the contract is very specific as to the items mentioned in it, the broker's responsibility (and almost always the law as well) requires him to transmit *all* offers to the seller,

D DOVER REALTY COMPANY

1776 Twelfth Street, Waltham, Xxxxx 12345   (908) 555-4321

SPECIAL SERVICE—SALES MANAGEMENT AGREEMENT

In **Consideration** of the services of DOVER REALTY CO., hereinafter called the Agent, and efforts on his part and at his expense to obtain a purchaser for me for the property described herein, undersigned seller does hereby grant to said agent a term of _____months from date, the **exclusive right to sell** the following described property situated in the City of _____ ,
County of _____ , Xxxx to-wit:

Encumbrance		Term		Size of Lot		F	R	S	S
Original Date		How Payable		Addition			Lot		Blk.
To Whom		% Int.		Faces		Contour			
Style		School		Carpets			Color		
Material		Transportation		Drapes			Fireplace		
Age	Condition	Stores		Oven			Range		
Approx. Sq. Ft.		Taxes		Washer Conn.			220		
Bedrooms	Baths	Ins.		Disposal			Dishwasher		
Dining Room	Break. Room	Remarks:							
Living Room	Den								
Heat	Air								
Attic Fan	Hot Water								
Garage or C.P.									
Storage									
Foundation									
Termite									
Fence									
Vegetation		Occupant					Phone		
Street		Owner					Phone		
Curb		Address							
Sewer		Salesman		Phone			Keys		
Alley		Date Listed		Expires			Possession		
File No.	Address			E	O	Location		Price	

Interest, rents, taxes and insurance, if policies are acceptable to purchaser, are to be pro-rated from date of transfer. In the event a sale is obtained by said Agent, seller hereby agrees to convey said property by a good and sufficient grant deed to the purchaser thereof at the time required by the contract of sale.

When the agent has produced a purchaser on the terms set forth in this agreement, or on other items acceptable to Seller, or if Seller directly or through any other agent should during the term hereof sell or exchange said property, or if the Seller, after the expiration of this agreement should deal with, sell or exchange said property to any person to whose attention said property was brought through the efforts or services of Agent or on information secured directly or indirectly from or through Agent during the term of this agreement, then Agent shall be conclusively presumed to be the procuring cause of such sale or exchange, in any of which cases Seller agrees to pay Agent a commission of_____% of the selling price of said property. In all of said cases payment shall be made to Agent at his office in Waltham, Xxxxx

Seller hereby acknowledges the receipt of a copy of this agreement.

Waltham, Xxxxx

Seller _____
Seller _____
Address _____

_____ 19____   Telephone _____

As the duly appointed Agent for seller and in consideration of the appointment thereof by the Seller I do hereby agree during the term hereof, to make efforts to sell said property, including the following:

1. To advertise in a newspaper this or other property for prospective purchasers. Agent does not promise to advertise any specific individual property but to advertise such properties as will aid in securing prospects for seller's property.
2. To immediately prepare and process a complete sales management file.
3. To advise within the first 30 days_____brokers and salesmen of other real estate firms dealing in similar priced properties of the existence of this listing.
4. To discuss at my regular property sales management meetings the selling price and progress being made toward the sale.
5. To advise seller of the opinions of the salesmen who inspected the property as to the advisable selling price.
6. To cooperate on an agreed upon commission basis with any Realtor that generally cooperates with other Realtors on the same basis.

DOVER REALTY COMPANY

By _____

Figure 8-1. Listing Agreement Example.

even if they do not meet the conditions set down in the listing contract. This is because the broker is hired to solicit offers, and the manner in which the contract tells the broker to offer the property does not restrict the seller to accepting only such an offer. He is free to negotiate with any potential buyer the broker brings, and frequently the seller ends up settling for terms that do not exactly match those outlined in the contract.

Expiration

A listing will expire on the date mentioned in the contract. However, the broker may, in the contract, reserve an interest in all parties to whom he has given information about the property for a certain length of time after the listing has expired. However, he cannot expect to retain his rights with respect to buyers he contacts or shows the property to after the expiration of the listing. Also, the broker is hired to find a certain buyer—specifically, one who will meet the conditions of the listing contract. When he finds such a buyer, he has performed his duty and earned his compensation. However, even if the broker finds a buyer who agrees without reservation to all the conditions of the listing contract, the seller is not obliged to deal with the buyer, although he *is* obliged to pay the broker the agreed upon fee because the broker has done what he was hired to do.

Types of Listings

Listing contracts are of various types, categorized in the manner in which the commission is paid, to whom it is paid, and the extent to which the broker's employer is responsible for paying a commission.

An *open* listing is one in which the principal agrees to compensate the agent only if the agent actually finds the buyer with whom the principal finally deals. A single owner may have open listings with many brokers, since he is obliging himself to pay only upon performance, and the broker makes his effort at his own risk.

An *exclusive agency* listing is one in which the princpal agrees to employ no other broker, and if the property is sold by any licensed agent a commission will be paid to the listing broker. State license law usually requires that any other agent must work *through* a broker having an exclusive listing; the participating brokers must then agree on a means by which they will share in the commission. However, the commission always will be paid to the listing broker, who then may pay a share to the other brokers(s) who cooperated in the deal.

An *exclusive-right-to-sell* listing guarantees that the princpal will pay the broker a commission regardless of who actually sells the property. This applies even if the principal finds the buyer himself, with no aid at all from the broker. Note that under the exclusive agency listing, the principal would not have to pay a commission if he found the buyer himself.

Usage of the term *exclusive listing* varies from one place to another. In some localities the term refers to an exclusive agency; in others it refers to the exclusive-right-to-sell; and in still others it refers to both types interchangeably.

Net Listings

A *net* listing is one in which the principal agrees to receive a given net sum, with the full excess by which the sale price exceeds the net amount going to the broker as his commission. In many states net listings are illegal; in many others they are not illegal, but are "frowned upon" or otherwise disapproved of in some quasi-official manner. The big problem with net listings is that the agent is strongly tempted to act in his own interest rather than that of his employer. To illustrate, suppose a net listing contract with a proposed net to the seller of $30,000 is agreed upon. By law, any time the broker solicits an offer he must report it to the principal. However, let us assume that an offer of exactly $30,000 is made; if the broker transmits it, the seller probably will accept, and the broker will receive no compensation. Clearly there is the temptation to hide that offer and any subsequent offers until one yielding a satisfactory excess over the listed price is received.

Obviously, such action flies in the face of the agent's legal responsibilities to his employer. A further source of trouble with net listings would arise when an unscrupulous agent deals with a seller who is not knowledgeable. There may exist an opportunity for the agent to convince the seller to sign a net listing at a low price, thereby guaranteeing the agent a large commission when he finds a buyer who will pay true market value.

Termination of Listing Contracts

Listing contracts are agency contracts, and as such can be terminated by a variety of events. These are divided into two categories, termination by *action of the parties* and termination by *law*. Termination by action of the parties includes the following:

1. The contract is terminated by *performance* when both parties perform their duties as prescribed, and the event for which the agency is created ends. In the real estate business, a listing agency contract would be terminated by performance when there is a "meeting of the minds" between the principal and the third party found by the agent. Sometimes, however, the contract will specify some other event (usually title closing, in the event of a listing for sale) as the actual termination of the contractual relationship.

2. The parties may *mutually agree* to terminate the relationship before it would have been terminated by performance.

3. The agent may *resign*. In this case, the agent may be liable to the principal for damages due to his breach of the contract, but he cannot be held to perform under the contract.

4. The principal may *discharge* the agent. Once again, the principal too can be liable for damages due to his breach of the contract, but he cannot be forced to continue the employment of the agent.

The agent may resign or the principal may discharge the agent without penalty if it can be proved that the other party was not properly discharging his duties under the contract. An agent would be justified in resigning if his principal, for example, did not provide him with enough information to do his job well or required that he perform some illegal act in the execution of his duties. An agent could be discharged justifiably if it could be shown that he was not faithful to his duties or was acting contrary to the interests of the principal.

Termination of the contractual relationship also occurs automatically, *by law*, with the occurrence of certain events, such as the following:

1. *Death of either party* terminates an agency relationship.
2. If either party becomes *legally incompetent*, the agency relationship ceases.
3. *Bankruptcy* of either party, making continuation of the relationship impossible, terminates the relationship.
4. *Destruction of the subject matter* terminates any agency relationship. In real estate this would include such events as a house burning down or the discovery that there is another claim on the title that would make it impossible for the owner of the property to pass good and marketable title.

ESTABLISHING THE RIGHT TO THE COMMISSION

The broker earns his commission when he produces a buyer (or tenant) with whom the owner reaches agreement concerning a sale or lease. From then on, the risk that the buyer may not end up going through with the deal rests with the owner. However, many listing contracts in use today spread that risk by specifying that the commission on a sale is payable at the closing of the deal: if there is no closing because the buyer defaults, there is no commission earned. On rentals, the commission often is based fully or in part upon the monthly rental payments made by the tenant; if the tenant breaches the lease, no rent payments are made, and no commission is due on them. However, if the sale does not close, or the tenant is forced out, and the blame rests with the property owner—the broker's employer—the broker usually has a good case that he is entitled to the full commission anyway. Furthermore, as we have discussed, if the broker finds a bona fide buyer or tenant who is willing to agree to the owner's conditions as expressed in the listing, the broker has earned his commission even if the owner refuses to deal with the party making the offer.

Conditions for Right to Commission

If the broker's principal refuses to pay him a commission the broker feels he has earned, he may sue in court to receive it. In order to be successful, he must prove three things:

1. That he was *licensed* throughout the time beginning with the solicitation of the listing until the closing of the deal and the passing of title (or the notification by the principal that he would not accept an offer which met the terms of the listing agreement).

2. That he had a contract of employment with the principal. The best evidence here is a written contract, and some state licensing laws require that listings be written to be enforceable.

3. That he was the "efficient and procuring cause" of the sale. In effect, this means that he actually brought about the sale within the terms of the listing contract. In an open listing it would mean that he actually found the eventual buyer. In an exclusive listing, he must have found the buyer or the buyer must have been found by a licensed agent. An exclusive-right-to-sell listing effectively defines the broker as having earned a commission when and if the property is sold.

4. If no sale occurs, the broker still may be due a commission. In this case, he cannot qualify under (3) above, since no sale occurred. Therefore he must be able to prove one of two things:

    (a) The broker was the "effective and procuring cause" by bringing the seller a bona fide (genuine, good faith) buyer who made the seller an offer which met all the seller's terms as specified in the listing contract. However, the seller refused the buyer's offer.

    (b) The seller accepted an offer for which the broker was the "effective and procuring cause." However, the sale never went through because of something that was the seller's fault. Such a thing could range from blatant seller default to discovery of a flaw in the title that made the sale impossible.

Disputed Trust Money

If a seller refuses to pay a commission, the broker cannot withhold his commission at closing, nor can he withhold his share of earnest money proceeds upon a default by a buyer, if the seller demands the full earnest money payment. Remember, these trust monies are not the property of the broker but belong to others, and all he can do is disburse them as instructed. Of course, once he has disbursed them he may sue to recover the amount he thinks he is entitled to. If he should withhold these monies for himself against instructions, he may be in violation of his duties as trustee or escrow agent.

License Status

The requirement that an agent be licensed in order to collect a commission is usually broadly interpreted. He must have been licensed from the very beginning of the transaction (when he first began to solicit the listing) until his duties were effectively terminated (in some cases this can occur before actual closing).

In one case, a sales licensee had passed the examination for licensure, and had been notified, but it was several days before the license actually was issued to his broker. During that time he solicited a listing from a friend, although he delayed the actual arrangement of the listing contract until after his license had been issued to and received by his broker. The property was sold, and the seller refused to pay the commission. The licensee lost because it was shown that he had begun solicitation of the listing before his license had been issued, even though it was clear that he had met all the qualifications for licensure and that his license was in the process of being issued by the Real Estate Commission.

Existence of Listing

Determination of the existence of a listing is less clear-cut. Many states require that listings be written; however, most states allow the existence of implied contracts even though no written agreement exists. This usually requires specific action by the property owner in the case of implied listings.

In one case, an owner posted a sign on his lot stating: "For Sale by Owner, Call 555-5555, Brokers Protected." The words *brokers protected* were construed by the court to extend an open listing to all interested brokers, upon which the seller would pay the normal commission paid for such sales in that area. In another case the sign instead said "For Sale by Owner. Call 555-5555, or See Your Broker." Some states have construed this as offering an open listing as well, but others say that it implies that a buyer can consult *his* broker, who will work on the *buyer's* behalf, and who will be paid by the buyer.

In another case, Smith was chatting over the back fence with his neighbor Jones, who knew that Smith made his living as a licensed real estate broker. In the course of the conversation Jones said: "If I could get $50,000 for this place I'd sell it!" No other mention of that subject was made. A few days later Smith brought Jones a buyer who offered $50,000 for his home, and Jones sold. The court ruled that Jones was not liable for a commission because no contract existed; Smith and Jones had never expressly agreed that Smith was being employed to sell Jones's property. If Jones had said, "I'd pay a 6 percent commission to anyone who brought me a buyer who'd pay $50,000 for this place," then he probably would have created a listing contract.

Of course, in states where all listings are required to be written, he would not have. However, in most of these states, the posting of a sign by an owner which states that brokers are protected, or some such language, is usually enough of a "written" instrument to satisfy the law.

In the final analysis, it is always best to have a written listing contract that spells out all conditions. These will carry the greatest possible weight in court and are very difficult to argue against; so much so, in fact, that their existence will convince most parties to go ahead and live up to the written contract rather than waste their time and money in a useless court proceeding.

Cause of Sale

Showing that the broker brought about the sale may be easy or difficult. In an exclusive-right-to-sell listing, the fact that the property was sold usually is enough to satisfy this requirement. Disputes arise with other kinds of listings and usually concern whether or not the broker, or someone else, caused the sale. If the listing agreement allows the owner to find his own buyer without having to pay a commission (exclusive agency or open listing), dispute can often arise. The mere fact that a buyer saw the broker's sign in someone's yard and then proceeded to negotiate directly with the owner usually is not enough to establish that the broker had enough personal involvement in the transaction to be entitled to a commission. However, if the eventual buyer contacted the broker and was directed by him to the property, the broker usually has established his claim on that buyer.

It is extremely wise for brokers to keep careful lists of all prospects they have come in contact with for any property they have listed. When a prospective buyer has been shown a property, many brokers send the owner a letter naming the prospect and telling when the showing occurred; the broker keeps a copy of each of these letters in the appropriate files. This has the double effect of providing evidence, if need be, that the prospect had dealt with the broker and also letting the owner know that the broker is conscientious about keeping him up to date on the progress of the selling effort.

LISTING POLICY

Naturally, it is in the best interest of the real estate brokerage firm to use the exclusive-right-to-sell listing contract whenever possible, and many firms insist on it and will not enter into any other kind of agreement. While it may appear that the best feature of this arrangement is that the broker gets paid even when the seller finds his own buyer, this rarely happens. Homeowners, especially, are not very adept at arranging or concluding advantageous sales of their property and so pose relatively little threat to the broker in that respect. However, the exclusive-right-to-sell listing makes it easy for the broker to get the seller to refer all inquiries to him, since the seller will not feel there is much point to negotiating a deal for which he will pay a commission anyway.

This might lead to an argument that since owners are not as good at selling as brokers, the exclusive agency listing (which allows the owner to sell by himself commission-free) is not a great threat and can indeed be used as a marketing device by assuring the seller that he will pay only for effective selling by the broker, while the broker remains assured by experience that only rarely will the seller succeed. However, there is a serious flaw in this reasoning, which makes brokers relatively reluctant to use the exclusive agency. It encourages the seller to try to sell himself, and therefore encourages him to keep to himself all leads he obtains. While it is true that he may not make much of these leads, they will be lost to the broker, who is much more capable of turning one of them into a genuine and satisfactory buyer. The owner himself usually is a valuable source of leads; he or someone in the family usually is at home, and the "For Sale" sign will attract potential buyers who may direct initial inquiries to the owner.

With an exclusive-right-to-sell listing, the broker can tell the owner, "Refer all leads to me. Make me do my job; there's no sense in your doing it for me." In this manner he will get the leads the owner accumulates, and so will have the best opportunity to do the most effective job. Additional instructions to the seller might also be in order, all of them designed to get him to let the broker have his leads as soon as possible. For example, the seller should impart as little information as possible. At best, he should tell the prospect to contact the broker and perhaps get the prospect's name and telephone number and relay those to the broker. In that manner, if the prospect does not voluntarily contact the broker, the broker has the information necessary to enable him to initiate contact. The seller should not offer to show prospects around on his own and should politely refuse requests for showings by saying that it is an inconvenient time or making some other suitable excuse.

Use of the Open Listing

The basic nature of the open listing appears very unattractive to the broker, since he receives no payment at all unless it is his firm that finds the buyer as well as secures the listing. However, there are circumstances under which the open listing can be useful. Primarily, it is handy when an owner really does not want to list, but the broker has found or is relatively certain that he can find a prime buying prospect. In such a case, the broker might be willing to risk an open listing and might find that securing one is not terribly difficult, since the seller is not committing for a commission unless the particular broker involved finds a satisfactory buyer.

A typical ploy is to open-list the property at a price higher than that which the owner is asking on a for-sale-by-owner basis to account for the commission at no perceived loss to the seller. While the offers the broker brings in might not be that high, once he confronts the owner with a genuine offer, the owner will face a serious decision. He has an offer that may not be as much as he was asking, once he has paid the commission. On the other hand, he may not have any reliable prospects of his own. Of course he can always refuse, but few brokers would be uncomfortable in the position of one who has a reasonable offer on property that an owner wants to sell.

The open listing is particularly effective when dealing with owners who are trying to sell their real estate by themselves to avoid a commission payment. However, it has its severe limitations and generally is not a good arrangement for a broker who does not have definite prospects in mind and who is merely willing to take the risk that his selling efforts will pay off under the limited protection an open listing gives. For example, an open listing does not deny other brokers access to the owner; at any time another broker could obtain an exclusive listing or another open listing on the same property. Of course, another broker's later exclusive listing would have to respect the access of a broker with an open listing so long as it is valid and has not expired, but in such a case the broker with the open listing would be at a severe competitive disadvantage.

One particular use of the open listing is in the listing of new homes from builders. Many builders are willing to pay a commission to a selling broker, but they are reluctant to give a single brokerage firm exclusive agency. In many cases an open listing is the only way to get a written agreement from a builder that he will pay a commission. The brokerage firm usually does not work an open listing as vigorously as it would an exclusive one, and the firm's sign rarely will be allowed to be put on the property. Still, by securing builders' open listings, the firm increases the inventory of homes available for its salespeople to show.

Restrictions on Sales Force Listing Practice

The sales force is encouraged to list property and usually is provided with listing contract forms for that purpose. However, no one should be given such a role without the experience necessary to handle it properly, and it is good practice to limit the degree to which salespeople can negotiate listings to their experience and capabilities. Many firms require that all listings be approved by the sales manager before they become binding; this gives the manager the opportunity to look them over and to arrange for alterations where necessary.

By law, real estate sales commissions are negotiable. However, this does not prevent the firm from, in effect, quoting a fixed listing commission when asked. Most particularly, if any negotiation of a commission rate other than the one usually quoted and secured is to be done, it should be done by management or by trusted and competent salespeople only—those who can be counted on to make the same decisions management would. There are times when departure from a fixed commission schedule may be advisable, but this discretion does not belong with the sales force.

For Sale Signs

The For Sale sign is one of the best means of advertising the brokerage firm and should be used in most circumstances. The exact use and design of this valuable tool is discussed in the next chapter, but some mention of its use is necessary here. First, some localities prohibit them and in others their use may be legal but not traditional. This occurs particularly in prestigious neighborhoods where residents may feel that the signs, no matter how handsome or unobtrusive, detract from the appearance of the community. A For Sale sign cannot be erected on an owner's property without his permission, and if the use of one is intended, permission to use it should be a part of the listing contract. Recent practice has evolved the use, by some firms, of very large and impressive signs that actually have to be *erected* in the true sense of the word: a posthole digger has to dig a real hole, and a large signpost is inserted. In such cases, the brokerage firm assumes responsibility for the damage done to the lawn or grounds by the sign. Smaller signs on wire stakes or narrow wooden posts do much less damage, but if any is done the broker will be responsible for necessary repairs. On the rare occasions when a listing expires and the property is not sold, the broker should remove his sign immediately.

When the property is sold, it is general practice to put a SOLD label on the sign; once again, this is very effective advertising on the part of the broker. It is advisable to stipulate in the listing contract that the SOLD sign can remain on the property until the deal is closed, or even until the new owner takes possession. Brokers differ in their practice as to when to put the SOLD label on. Some do so as soon as the seller has accepted a deal; others wait until financing has been approved.

LISTING INFORMATION

When a salesperson obtains a listing it is necessary for him to obtain as much information as possible concerning the property and the features and terms under which the seller is willing to transact. The listing contract form shown in Figure 8–1 has a large part devoted to such description, and forms of that kind are in frequent use around the country. The information section also can be copied onto large cards or sheets, which salespeople can keep in their files to give them the most up-to-date information on all listings in the firm.

An example of a filled-out information form is provided in Figure 8–2. Note that it enables the determination of a considerable amount of information concerning the listing at a glance. Salespeople familiar with an information sheet such as this one will be able to refer to it with ease.

SETTING COMMISSION RATES

Until the late 1960s, it was fairly common practice for local organizations of brokerages to establish uniform schedules of commission rates that were to be observed by all firms in the organization. Since these groups tended to include all of the major firms in the area, the rate schedules they set also tended to dictate the norm. However, by the end of the 1960s action by the Anti-Trust Division of the United States Justice Department had established that such policies were in restraint of trade and therefore illegal, and that from that time on, commission rates had to be genuinely negotiable between broker and employer. This, of course, does not mean that the individual firm cannot set up its own schedule of commissions for various kinds of deals; doing so simply constitutes the same sort of things as publishing a firm's "price list." Customers are free to try to negotiate differing rates from the firm's schedule and to attempt the same with other firms.

Nevertheless, commission rates tend to be relatively standardized in a given area, although it is much more likely that these rates are set competitively than by collusion or agreement. Generally speaking, firms that charge higher than "going" rates will lose business to those firms whose rates are lower. Firms charging less than the going rate often find that their commission fees are not enough to sustain the business in the long run. Either they go out of business or they eventually raise their rates closer to the prevailing level.

The "Right" Commission Rate

What, then, is the reasonable rate that should be charged? This is a question that cannot be answered definitely because local and other considerations will have a significant effect. However, surveying the various real estate markets in the nation can lead to some generalized conclusions. The prevailing

Encumbrance $66,787.09	Term 28 years ($663.45 PITI) Size of Lot 48 F 48 R 113 S 113 S
Original Date 8/30/88	Addition Marlowe Field	Lot 17	Blk. R
To Whom Waltham Federal	How Payable $663.45 P+1	% Int. 9.5

	Faces east	Contour flat
Style Patio Ranch	School Tennyson, Main High	Carpets yes	Color rust/white
Material Stucco and cedar	Transportation walk	Drapes yes	Fireplace yes
Age 2 years Condition excellent	Stores all, Waltham Mall 1 mi.	Oven double wall	Range built-in
Approx. Sq. Ft. 1383	Taxes $1182.44	Washer Conn. yes	220 yes
Bedrooms 2 Baths 2	Ins. $348	Disposal yes	Dishwasher yes

Dining Room no	Break. Room yes
Living Room yes	Den yes
Heat nat.gas	Air elect.
Attic Fan no	Hot Water elect.
Garage or C.P. 2-car carport	
Storage yes, in carport	
Foundation slab	
Termite Curry Pest Control	
Fence Cedar privacy 9'	
Vegetation see remarks	
Street cul-de-sac	
Curb yes	
Sewer yes	
Alley no	

Remarks: Lovely Marlowe Field patio townhome. lush landscaping, premium carpeting, living and master bedroom papered, deluxe appliances and appointments. Custom drapes stay with house as does all custom lighting. Covered flagstone patio off den and kitchen. Assumable loan; seller will consider 2nd mortgage for part of equity. Owner moving overseas, will consider selling some of furniture.

Occupant Jackson and Vera Marshall	Phone 555-0001
Owner same	Phone same
Address 12108 Cedar Road	
Salesman Chatham Phone 555-9991	Keys lockbox
Date Listed 9/30/88 Expires 9/30/88	Possession negotiable

E	O	Location
		Southwood

File No.	Address	Price
DR – 8199	12108 Cedar Road	$96,500

Figure 8-2. Listing Information Sheet.

commission rate in most markets appears to be 6 to 7 percent on resale homes (that is, homes being sold by people other than builders). However, in markets where home prices are notoriously high, such as Washington, D.C., Los Angeles, San Francisco, San Diego, and others, the commission rate tends to be lower: 5 to 6 percent. Still, these lower commission rates may result in higher *dollar* commissions paid since they are based on much higher than average prices. As an example, a home selling for $60,000 in Little Rock, Tampa, or Abilene will yield a commission of $4,200 at a 7 percent rate, while a similar home in a major California city may fetch $150,000 and yield a commission of $9,000 at a lower 6 percent rate.

Market forces in every locality will tend to force commission rates to a reasonable level. If commission rates are too low to allow reasonable profit, there will be pressure on brokerages to charge more. Eventually, one or more will begin to charge a higher rate and the others will follow because they think they will be better off with the higher rate than with the extra business they may obtain by continuing at a lower rate. Similarly, if rates are too high, some firms will switch to lower rates as a means of getting more business. They will find that even at the lower rate they are making enough to stay in business profitably and so will stay at the lower rate, and their competition eventually will force other firms to reduce their rates as well.

Of course, other considerations will apply in addition to long-run market forces. In the short run, the local real estate market may be active or very slow. When there is a lot of business available, there is less pressure to reduce commissions since firms are operating about as intensively as they can and do not see any point in reducing rates to capture business that they do not have a reserve capacity to handle. In slow markets, commission cutting may occur as firms try all available means to capture what little business there is. Even if it means temporary losses, this may be preferable to closing down if it is expected that a recovery in the market will occur in a reasonable period of time.

Typically, about half of the total commission volume brought into a firm is paid out to the sales force as their share. If a firm considers cutting its commission rates below those charged by others, it will have to be prepared to absorb nearly all the drop in revenue per sale by itself, since a reduction in the share per sale that is paid to salespeople will encourage them to leave for another firm that is continuing to pay better commissions. As we will see in Chapter 12, a firm operating in a normally competitive market will find it has a relatively small amount of its total revenue that it can consider to be profit—typically no more than 10 or 15 percent. Consequently, there is relatively little extra money to work with if commission cutting is to be considered.

Varying Commissions

To some extent, commissions can be adjusted to reflect the difficulty of obtaining the listing and, subsequently, the sale. Commission *rates* on very high-

Table 8–1   Commission Amounts, Commission Rates, and Property Sale Prices

Sale Price of Property	COMMISSION RATE NECESSARY TO YIELD COMMISSION OF:	
	$5,000	$100,000
$ 20,000	25%	—%
50,000	10	—
75,000	6⅔	—
100,000	5	100
250,000	2	40
500,000	1	20
1,000,000	0.5	10
5,000,000	0.1	2
10,000,000	0.05	1

priced homes may be negotiated to considerably lower than the normal rate, since the dollar value of the commission still will be quite high (see Table 8–1). For example, a home sold for $420,000 at a 4 percent commission will yield a total commission of $16,800; to earn the same amount of commission selling $60,000 houses, the firm would have to make four sales at a 7 percent commission rate. If the expensive house is no more than four times as difficult to sell than a $60,000 house, then the 4 percent commission is reasonable. In a similar vein, commission rates on very expensive commercial property may be as low as 1 or 2 percent; nonetheless, a 1 percent commission on a sale of a $10 million shopping center is $100,000, which is a handsome reward and a considerable incentive.

Commission *rates* on land, farms, and very inexpensive properties may also be higher than normal because these properties are more difficult to sell, and in the case of land and farms may require considerably more sophisticated and complicated negotiations and deals than sales of single family homes.

Some firms may adopt a sliding commission scale even with listings of homes. An example is the 7-5-3 scale used by some firms in areas where the typical commission is 7 percent. The firm secures an exclusive-right-to-sell listing; however, depending on who sells the house, the commission varies. If it is sold by another firm through a cooperative deal, the commission is the regular 7 percent rate. If it is sold by the firm that listed it, the commission is 5 percent. If the owner sells it himself, the commission is 3 percent.

Such a plan is a two-edged sword. On the one hand the listing firm puts itself at a slight advantage over competing firms, since it can bring in slightly lower offers that may be accepted because the lower commission rate will mean a satisfactory realization for the seller. On the other hand, the seller is allowed to retain some incentive to do his own selling, since he saves on the commission thereby, and so the listing firm may lose the prospects that the seller himself obtains.

Flat Fee Commissions

A fairly recent innovation has been the establishment of *flat fee* brokerages. Generally, these offer limited services such as placing a sign in the yard, advertising the property, and giving limited advice to the seller when he is in the process of negotiation and closing. All calls received by the firm are referred to the property owners, who are responsible for the actual selling effort. In effect, the flat fee firm provides a centralized listing source for buyers and relatively little more. The buyers are attracted by the firm's advertising, which features the low commission and the suggestion that a lower commission means the seller will be willing to accept a lower price than if he had to pay a normal commission out of his proceeds. Local brokerage firms have registered considerable upset with flat fee firms, contending that their limited service hardly qualifies them to be considered genuine real estate brokerage firms, even though such firms are required to be licensed.

It is true that such a firm is little more than a referral service, and it is likely that the market eventually will recognize them as such. They will serve a purpose for those who do not want full brokerage service, and for bargain hunters who would not have dealt with a full service brokerage anyway. Typical flat-fee charges vary quite a lot from place to place, but generally range between about $400 and $1,000 or so, depending upon the area and the amount of actual service offered.

Special Commission Payment Arrangements

Normally commissions are paid in cash at the time of closing; however, there is no reason other than sensible business practice to prevent different arrangements. In cases where sellers may be in a cash pinch, brokers can arrange to have the commission paid to them over time and, in effect, end up lending the commission to someone else for a period of time. Commission payments can be made in forms other than cash as well—virtually anything of value has been taken at one time or another by a broker somewhere. An occasional arrangement is for the broker to receive as his commission partial ownership of property for which he has negotiated the sale.

In some cases there are advantageous income tax reasons for the buyer to pay the commission, and a deal can be negotiated wherein it is recognized that the buyer pays the brokerage fee and the seller, in return, accepts a lower price that reflects the lack of a commission. When a broker or salesperson buys real estate for himself, he may find it advantageous from an income tax standpoint to forego his share of the commission in return for a lower price.

Whenever there is to be a deviation from the manner and amount of commission stated in a listing contract, the new arrangement should be written and signed by all parties involved. Frequently this can be done on the sale contract; if not, then a separate amendment to the listing contract should be formally drawn up. Brokerage firms should study carefully any proposal that involves a delayed payment of the commission or a noncash payment. A business needs cash to keep going, and proliferate use of special commission arrangements may result in a poor cash flow. A firm may find itself with a lot of commissions owed to it and holding a lot of noncash assets that it took instead of cash commissions, with no ready money with which to pay current bills, obligations, taxes, and payrolls.

Expenses and Unsold Listings

In normal practice, the brokerage firm pays all the fees and expenses it incurs in making a sale out of the commission it is paid. However, if the listing expires unsold there is no commission, and the broker absorbs the expenses incurred in advertising and other services. He has not been able to provide a service to the seller, and so receives no compensation.

Sometimes, however, the property is unsold because the employer dismisses the broker before the listing contract expires. Listing contracts should contain language to clarify what is to be done in these cases. Clearly, it is of little advantage to a brokerage firm to insist on keeping a listing when the owner of the listed property is dissatisfied with the firm and its services, even though a strict reading of most listing contracts would show that the owner has the legal responsibility to retain the firm's service until the property is sold or the listing expires. Most firms will allow a dissatisfied property owner to cancel a listing contract provided that the broker is reimbursed for the out-of-pocket expenses incurred. Some require the payment of part (or, rarely, all) of the commission—based on the listing price—as a condition for termination of the contract.

The exact manner in which such problems are handled is a delicate matter. Too forceful an insistence on its rights by the brokerage might create further dissatisfaction and possible adverse publicity. If some way to dissolve the contract can be found without causing more trouble, it should be undertaken. If the seller is left with the feeling that he has been fairly treated, he may use the broker's services again at a later time, and he may say favorable things about the firm to others.

DISSOLVING LISTING CONTRACTS

Sellers may want to dissolve listing contracts for a variety of reasons, and each should be handled differently. If the seller simply gets cold feet and decides for one reason or another that he no longer wishes to sell, relatively little effort should be made to get him to change his mind. Doing so is a direct attack on his judgment. Instead, a gracious withdrawal is in order. The broker should mention that there will be no charge for the expenses incurred, and that he hopes that the seller will list with the firm if and when he later decides to sell. Because of the brokerage's efforts on his behalf, the seller probably will feel obligated to the firm and may even steer other business toward it.

If the seller wants to dissolve the listing so that he can list with another firm, a little more resistance may be employed. He should be shown how much the firm has already done and how well the sales activity on his property compares to that of similar properties in the market. If there is evidence that another firm has been actively soliciting the seller during the listing period, it could be pointed out that such activity is illegal, implying that the seller might want to think twice about dealing with a firm that breaks the law.

If the seller simply is dissatisfied with the brokerage's efforts, considerable examination is necessary. If the seller's objections are valid, then some disciplining or reprimanding of the firm's sales force is in order for being lax in their duties. Or it may be that the seller is a complainer. In either case, there is little point in continuing the relationship, and it should be terminated as painlessly as possible. However, a third possibility is that the seller simply is unaware of what is involved in selling real estate. Action that the firm knows is proper and will lead to a buyer in a reasonable time may not seem adequate to him. In this case, what the firm is doing should be explained in clear and simple terms. There is no need to go into a long lecture about the brokerage business. Frequently, some evidence showing how long it took and what had to be done in other successful sales will be satisfactory.

On rare occasions, the firm will decide that a contract should be dissolved. The reasons are varied, but usually will have to do with a seller who is difficult to deal with or a property that turns out to be very difficult to sell. In either case, the firm determines that the listing simply is not worth the effort. A common solution in such cases is to stop making any effort and to let the listing expire unsold. However, this is very unprofessional, and it certainly is not fair to the owner. Although it may be more awkward to do, ethical business practice demands that the firm discuss such problems with the property owner and, as diplomatically as possible, resign from the listing contract.

DISCUSSION QUESTIONS AND PROJECTS

1. Obtain copies of the listing contracts and information cards used by several firms in your area. Are there any improvements you think should be made in any of them? Compare them to find what you think are the best and worst ones. Why do you think so?

2. What sort of policy should a brokerage firm have with respect to suing sellers of property who refuse to pay commissions the firm is legally entitled to?

3. What are the prevailing commission rates in your area? Are there any firms that regularly charge higher or lower commissions? Are they more or less successful than the others in getting listing business? If there is a difference in their success, is it primarily due to the difference in commission rates? Why or why not?

4. Interview one or two sales managers to find out the reasons they would give for refusing to cooperate on a transaction with another brokerage firm.

5. Are there any brokerage firms in your area that use the flat fee commission? Are

they successful? Compare the services they offer to those of full commission firms.

6. Examine real estate practice in your area to determine whether or not there is much use of the open listing. Is it confined to one or a few kinds of property? Why or why not?

7. What is the common practice in your area for allocating expenses of the brokerage if a listing expires unsold or is dissolved before sale? Are any of these expenses charged to the owner of the listed property?

8. Are net listings in common use in your area? If so, is there any evidence that brokers use them to gain larger profits?

9. Under what conditions do you think it would be advisable for a brokerage firm to reduce its overall commission rate?

10. Under what conditions do you think it would be advisable for a brokerage firm to negotiate a smaller than usual commission rate on a particular listing?

A Case Study

COMMISSION RATES

Morris J., the sales manager of a medium-sized residential brokerage firm in Atlanta, Georgia, is speaking:

"Our basic commission rate is 7% of the sale price. We've considered being flexible, or going to a 7-5-3 schedule, but we don't think it will have much of an effect on our business. Most sellers in this market are used to the 7% rate. They may not like it, but it's the rate that most of the major firms in this area charge. We certainly aren't making what I consider to be outrageous profits, and I'm convinced that we couldn't make it as a business for much less. We don't waste much money around here, and we pay our people well, which means that they bring in good business for us. If we reduced our rate, most of the reduction would have to come out of the salesperson's share, and we'd probably lose our best people to other firms because of it.

"There are a few outfits here that have a 7-5-3 schedule, or which negotiate lower commissions frequently. I don't think they have very skilled sales forces. We picked up a very productive person from a firm that had gone to a generally lower commission rate, because we could offer her more money for each sale she made. We don't cooperate on sales with commissions lower than 7%, unless the other brokerage will pay us the same amount that our share would have been with the standard rate. A few have done so, but I don't see how they can stay in business long. The 7-5-3, in my opinion, is just a gimmick. I would guess that 4 out 5 sales in this area are cooperated, so most listings would carry 7% anyway. However, the seller will be harder to convince when a cooperated contract comes in, because he'll be thinking of that extra 2 or 4 percent he could save if his broker sells or he sells himself. I'd rather have a 7% exclusive right-to-sell, and keep the seller out of the process. When we're left alone to do our best, we do very well!"

A Case Study

TERMINATING A LISTING

Sales manager Morris J. is speaking again:

"In our experience we've found that the best way to deal with a seller who has listed with us and wants out is to let him go with a friendly handshake. They have all kinds of reasons. Sometimes they just don't like what we're doing. Often they get cold feet; selling a house is a pretty big event in lots of peoples' lives, and you have to treat them well and care about them and their feelings.

"I always tell our people to try to put themselves in the other guy's shoes when they're handling a listing. If they do, they can understand how one seller may think that his deal is the only one in the world, and he ought to get the best care and consideration possible. Of course, we handle a lot of them at once and sometimes the seller just doesn't think he's getting enough attention. We try to explain what we're doing and how much we are prepared to do, and often it works. But if the guy decides he wants out, we usually let him go without a fight.

"Our philosophy is that if we keep things friendly and understanding, at least we've got someone out there who has had a good experience with us. We've found that a pretty good number of people who 'fire' us come back later. Sometimes they've tried to list with someone else, and found that we were doing a better job for them. If they just got too nervous, they usually come back when they've thought it over. Occasionally one will get rid of us because he's got a private deal cooking, and he doesn't want to pay us a commission. But that really doesn't happen very often, and we just chalk it up to business experience.

"We've found that a good strategy with people who are nervous or are getting cold feet is to agree to put the listing on 'hold' for a couple of weeks. We don't actually terminate, but we just let things lie long enough for the seller to do whatever thinking he has to do. We promise him that if at the end of two weeks he still wants out, we'll let him out of the listing. Quite a lot of them decide to go ahead with it, but they never forget that we were willing to go along with them."

REFERENCES

FISHER, FREDERICK J., *Broker Beware: Selling Real Estate Within the Law,* ch. 4. Reston, VA: Reston Publishing Company, Inc., 1981.

GOLDSTEIN, PAUL, *Real Estate Transactions.* St. Paul, MN: Foundation Press, 1985.

HANSOTTE, LOUIS B., "Real Estate Contracts," in *The McGraw-Hill Real Estate Handbook,* ed. Robert Irwin, ch. 22. New York, NY: McGraw-Hill Book Company, 1984.

Real Estate Office Management: People Functions Systems, ch. 14. Chicago, IL: REALTORS® National Marketing Institute, 1975.

Real Estate Sales Handbook (9th ed.), ch 6, 8, 9. Chicago, IL: REALTORS® National Marketing Institute, 1983.

SHENKEL, WILLIAM M., *Marketing Real Estate* (2nd ed.), ch. 6, 7. Englewood Cliffs, NJ: Prentice-Hall, Inc., 1985.

WIGGINTON, F. PETER, *The Complete Guide to Profitable Real Estate Listings: Programs of the Pros,* ch. 2–5. Homewood, IL: Dow Jones-Irwin, 1977.

———. *Residential Real Estate Practice,* ch. 4-6. Indianapolis, IN: The Bobbs-Merrill Company, Inc., 1978.

NINE

MARKET OPERATIONS

Sale Contracts

Offers

Cooperating with Other Brokerage Firms

Franchising

Information Services

Settlement

Defaults

When property has been listed for sale, the marketing procedure begins. In this chapter we will consider some of the policy matters brokerages must deal with in their marketing operations. A sale contract form must be developed, and policy on handling negotiations must be made. Since these are governed to a considerable extent by contract law and the law governing the making and acceptance of offers, these legal requirements will be discussed.

A specific procedure often handled by brokerage firms is preparing documents for and conducting settlement of real estate transactions. Discussion of the basics of this procedure will be included. Finally, brokerage policy must be considered for one of the more unpleasant risks of the business: default on contracts by the brokerage's clients and customers.

SALE CONTRACTS

When real estate is sold, seller and buyer will enter into a contractual arrangement governing the terms of the sale. It is very rare that the deed will be passed to the buyer and the transaction closed as soon as it is negotiated, because both parties usually have a lot of legal and other work to do before title can be properly passed. Therefore, there is a need for what is usually called the *contract of sale* to determine the manner and the time in which title eventually will be passed. This contract determines all the conditions that may surround the passing of title. It may also include various kinds of contingent arrangements allowing one or both of the parties to back out of the arrangement if unexpected events occur or if certain arrangements cannot be made that are necessary for the completion of the sale.

The actual sale contract is referred to by a variety of names, depending upon the locality in which it is being used. *Contract of sale, sale agreement, offer and acceptance,* and *binder* are some of the names used. No matter what it is called, however, it will contain essential information:

1. The identities and interests (buyer or seller) of the parties.
2. The description of the property.
3. The sale price and manner of payment.
4. The terms of the sale (all conditions, contingencies, etc.).
5. A date by which closing is expected to be effected.

Although the broker is not a direct party to this contract, he may be instrumental in drawing it up, because his experience with such matters is often much greater than that of the parties involved, especially in residential sales. He should take special care to be sure that the contract says what the parties want it to, and that they understand what it says.

Most brokers will use a preprinted form for such contracts as a precautionary measure, since spaces are provided for all the information and conditions usually required. However, in most states such a form is not required, and it is quite legal for a sales contract to be written to suit the particular deal. Some states regard the drawing up of contracts to be exclusively the province of members of the legal profession. In such states brokers who are not attorneys usually are allowed to assist in the filling out of preprinted contract forms, but may not write contracts from scratch. If such an arrangement were necessary, the parties or the broker would have to hire an attorney to draw up the document for them.

In some cases, particularly involving nonresidential sales, the terms of a sale can be very complicated. In such cases, where preprinted contracts are little used, the contract should be drawn up by an attorney or at least approved by an attorney before being put into effect. This is especially important in investment-oriented transactions because even the terms of the sale can have an effect on the income tax situation of both buyer and seller. An improperly drawn contract can cost thousands or even millions of dollars to the unfortunate parties, and it is not likely to earn much respect for the brokerage firms involved.

Contract Form

In most brokerages a preprinted a contract is used, since it is unlikely that salespeople will be able to prepare sale contracts from scratch. The form should be simple and direct, and it should contain space for including all necessary information. This type of contract is usually quite suitable for the brokerage that specializes in residential sales, which tend to be straightforward and follow a fairly standardized procedure.

Salespeople can be trained to anticipate the kinds of contingencies and terms that frequently will be encountered, and the forms can be designed to make their inclusion simple and problem-free. Figure 9–1 displays such a form. Section 1 of the illustrated form, as an example, provides a simple way of entering the most common financing contingencies that appear in these contractual arrangements.

Land Contracts

A *land contract* (also called *agreement for purchase and sale, land sales contract, installment land contract, contract for a deed,* and others) is a form of purchase contract for real estate that is often confused with deeds. This arrangement allows the purchaser to pay for the property in installment payments made to the seller; however, *no deed is given at the time of sale.* This means that the seller continues to hold title to the property. Generally, the contract will allow the seller to remove the buyer from the property if the buyer defaults upon the payments; since no title has been transferred, no foreclosure proceedings are necessary.

A land contract specifies that the seller will pass title in a deed to the buyer at some agreed upon point. Sometimes it is not until all payments have been made in full, but it also can commit the seller to provide a deed at any agreed upon time during the payment period. Land contracts (which can apply to all real estate, and not just to land) are not as widely used as they once were, but they can often be useful in the consummation of some transactions, so brokers should be aware of them. They are particularly useful in cases where buyers cannot secure mortgage financing and sellers are willing to be paid in installments but are reluctant to pass title without having already received at least a substantial amount of the price in payment. They also are used frequently in land sales arrangements where land is subdivided and sold, but actual development and building are not expected to occur for a period of time.

Since a land contract allows the buyer to take possession of the property while title remains with the seller, a *sale* technically does not take place until some later date when a deed actually is transferred by seller to buyer; therefore, land contract sales have become quite popular in some areas where rate escalation is being practiced. In such cases it is absolutely necessary that the land contract be properly worded, especially since it will be the *only* evidence of any transfer of interest for a long time. It is essential in transactions such as this that the wording of the contract be drawn up by an attorney knowledgeable in such matters.

OFFERS

A particular feature of the contract of sale is that as it is being prepared it often is used as an instrument by which *offers* are made during negotiations. For example, if a buyer wishes to make an offer on a listed property, he and the broker will draw up a sale contract that the buyer will sign. The contract will include all the provisions and conditions the buyer is willing to agree to, and it is presented to the seller for his reaction. If the seller is willing to accept the offer as it stands, he signs it. Once the prospective buyer is notified that the seller has agreed to the offer, it becomes a binding contract between them.

But suppose the seller does not agree to the buyer's complete offer; for example, he may agree to everything except that he wants a higher price, or a later closing date, and so on. In that case, the seller may prepare a *counteroffer* by redrawing the contract to reflect his desires. He then signs the redrawn contract, and it is presented to the prospective buyer. This process of offer and counteroffer may go on for quite some time until the parties reach agreement, in which case a binding sale contract will exist between them. If they do not reach agreement, then neither has any responsibility to the other.

Alterations

It is common practice that if the party receiving the offer requires only minor changes to be made, these changes are made on the submitted offer itself by scratching out the items to be changed or deleted, and then writing in the new or changed items. The document is then signed by the *offeree* (the party to whom the offer was made), and he initials each of the changes he has made. It then is submitted to the original *offeror* and if he is willing to go along with the changes

D DOVER REALTY COMPANY

1776 Twelfth Street, Waltham, Xxxxx 12345   (908) 555-4321

CONTRACT OF SALE

You are authorized to submit the following offer to purchase the property known as:

_____ more completely described as:

_____ upon the following terms:

1. PURCHASE PRICE: The Buyer agrees to pay for the property the sum of . . . . $_____
as follows:

A. ☐ NEW LOAN: Conventional ☐   FHA ☐   VA ☐   Other ☐   Payable for_____ years.

The down payment shall be . . . . $_____

Subject to the Buyer's ability to obtain a loan on the property in an amount not less than . . . . $_____
Unless otherwise specified, all loan cost and prepaid items shall be paid by Buyer. If said loan is not
available or is not closed, Buyer agrees to pay for loan costs incurred including appraisal and credit
report unless failure to close is caused by Seller.

B. ☐ LOAN ASSUMPTION:

Equity in cash in the amount of . . . . $_____

Subject to the Buyer's ability to assume existing loan in the approximate amount of . . . . $_____

currently payable at approximately $_____ per month, including_____ principal,

_____ interest, _____ existing taxes and _____ existing insurance. Payments on
existing loan to be current at closing.

C. SPECIAL CONDITIONS REGARDING FINANCING:

2. LOAN APPLICATION: Buyer agrees to make application for new loan or for loan assumption, if applicable, within_____ business days from
date of acceptance. Buyer hereby authorizes Dover Realty, Inc. to obtain any necessary information to assist Buyer in securing financing.

3. EARNEST MONEY: Buyer herewith tenders $_____ as earnest money, which shall apply on purchase price/or closing costs if
this offer is accepted. This sum shall be deposited by Agent and if offer is not accepted or if title requirements are not fulfilled, it shall be promptly re-
funded to Buyer. If, after acceptance, Buyer fails to fulfill his obligations, the earnest money shall become liquidated damages, WHICH FACT SHALL
NOT PRECLUDE SELLER OR AGENT FROM ASSERTING OTHER LEGAL RIGHTS WHICH THEY MAY HAVE BECAUSE OF SUCH BREACH.

4. CONVEYANCE: Conveyance shall be made to Buyer, or as directed by Buyer by general warranty deed except it shall be subject to recorded restrictions
and easements, if any, which do not materially affect the value of the property.

5. ABSTRACT OF TITLE INSURANCE: The owner(s) of the above property, hereinafter called Seller, shall furnish, at Seller's cost, a complete abstract re-
flecting merchantable title satisfactory to Buyer's attorney; however, Seller shall have an option to furnish Buyer, in place of abstract, a policy of title
insurance in the amount of the purchase price, and submission of an abstract shall not constitute a waiver of this option. If objections are made to title,
Seller shall have a reasonable time to meet the objections or to furnish title insurance.

Buyer_____

Seller_____

Dated_____

Figure 9-1. Sale Contract - Offer and Acceptance Form.

6. PRORATIONS: Taxes and special assessments, due on or before the closing date, shall be paid by the Seller. Current general taxes and special assessments shall be prorated as of closing date, based upon most current information available from County Assessor's office or upon the last tax statement, whichever may be applicable. Insurance, interest and rental payments shall be prorated as of closing date.

7. CLOSING: Closing date to be approximately _____

8. POSSESSION: Seller shall vacate the property and deliver possession to Buyer on or before _____ days after the closing date. Seller agrees to pay rent to Buyer at the rate of $ _____ per day until possession is given after closing date. The enforcement or collection of any rental payments contained herein must be handled directly between Buyer and Seller.

9. WARRANTIES: Buyer certifies that he has inspected the property and is not relying upon any warranties, representations or statements of Agent or Seller as to age or condition of improvements, other than those specified herein. Seller certifies that to his best knowledge and belief all plumbing, heating, air conditioning, built-in appliances, and hot water tank are in working condition except as specified herein. Buyer shall have the right prior to closing to have any of the above mentioned items inspected at his own expense if he deems it necessary. If Buyer fails to have such inspections made within 5 days prior to closing, then he shall be deemed to have waived such right of inspections and agrees to accept the property in its present condition. The risk of loss or damage to the property by fire or other casualty occurring up to the time of transfer of title on the closing date is assumed by the Seller.

10. TERMITE CLEARANCE: Seller, at his expense, will furnish Buyer with termite clearance by a licensed termite control company.

11. OTHER SPECIAL CONDITIONS:

DOVER REALTY COMPANY will not be responsible for any agreements by the Buyer, Seller, or Agent except those written herein. Neither will the company be responsible for any guarantee (written or verbal) covering roofs, plumbing, heating, air conditioning, appliances or any other equipment or portion of the property.

12. This Offer is binding upon Buyer if accepted within _____ days from date.

13. Permission is hereby given to send a letter of introduction on my behalf to our new neighbors.

Selling Broker _____   Buyer _____

Selling Associate _____   Buyer _____

The above offer is accepted on _____, 19____. I/We agree to pay the below named agent a fee of _____ for professional services rendered in securing said offer. If for any reason the earnest money provided for herein is forfeited by Buyer under the provisions hereof, same shall be divided equally between Seller and Agent after payment of incurred expenses.

Listing Broker/Agent _____   Seller _____

Listing Associate _____   Seller _____

THIS IS A LEGALLY BINDING CONTRACT WHEN SIGNED BY BOTH BUYER AND SELLER

155

he initials all of them, and the contract in its revised form becomes binding on the parties.

A serious problem with this practice is that the erasures, new items, and initials can become messy and even indecipherable, causing confusion. It is much better practice to fill out a new form if an offeree wishes to counteroffer with any substantial changes. Whether or not that is done, once a final agreement has been reached it always is wise to rewrite it, as it was agreed upon, on a fresh form or sheet so that the final agreement is as neat and legible as possible. This is particularly important because other parties such as mortgage lenders and perhaps even a court of law may have to view the document, and they may not be so familiar with the negotiations or the handwritten appendages to a messy contract form.

Nonbinding Nature of Offers

An offer is not binding upon anyone. Until it is accepted *without any changes* by the offeree, the offer does not bind the offeror to anything. He may withdraw the offer at any time so long as it has not been accepted in full. If the offeree makes a counteroffer, he legally has *turned down* the original offer, and that offer ceases to exist. This is so even if the offeree has agreed to some of the provisions of the original offer: He has no choice, legally, but to accept the offer in full as it stands or to turn it down. He cannot accept part of it. Therefore, if an offeree makes a counteroffer, legally the roles become reversed. The offeree is now an offeror, since he now is making an offer to the party who originally had made an offer to him. All offers and counteroffers are governed by the same rules of law; they are not binding upon the parties who make them until they are accepted *in full* by the parties to whom they are made.

The reason offers are not binding until accepted is that they are *not* contracts. Even if an offer states that it will remain open for a certain length of time after it is made, it can legally be withdrawn before then. Consider the following example: Jones lists his house with Broker Smith at an asking price of $80,000. Brown makes an offer of $72,000 for the house. Jones is satisfied with all the provisions of the offer except that he thinks the price is too low, so he counteroffers with the same offer Brown made to him, except that the price is $76,000. In the counteroffer, Jones states that it will remain open for three days. The next day a different prospect, Green, offers $80,000 for the house; Jones and Broker Smith have heard nothing from Brown with regard to Jones's counteroffer of $76,000.

Since Brown has not yet notified Jones or Smith that he accepts the counteroffer of $76,000 they may notify Brown that the offer of $76,000 is withdrawn and then go ahead and accept Green's offer of $80,000. For that matter, they can tell Brown that they have received an offer of $80,000 and encourage him to offer more if he wishes. But note that even though they stated that the offer to Brown would remain open for three days, they are not obliged to keep their word, since the promise was not contained in any binding contract. In fact, the courts have consistently ruled that such language in an offer says no more than that the offer will definitely expire at a certain time if it is not accepted by then; it does not promise that the offer will remain open that long, but only that it cannot remain open any longer than that specified time.

Let us use this example to explain a few more characteristics of offers. First, once Jones decided to counteroffer at $76,000, he turned down Brown's original offer of $72,000. At that point, this original offer ceased to exist. If Brown had immediately turned down Jones's counteroffer, Jones could not then decide to accept Brown's first offer and bind him to it; to do that Brown would have to make the offer again, because Jones had turned it down and thereby had "killed" it. Jones may, of course, make a second offer to Brown that is simply repeats Brown's first offer to him. That is legally a new offer, and there is no obligation upon Brown to accept it, since his own similar offer had been turned down originally.

Notification of Acceptance of Offer

A great many real estate licensees find the laws concerning offers confusing, but that need not be. Simply stated, offers are not contracts and carry no obligation upon the offeror until they are accepted in full. At that point they no longer are offers; they have become contracts. Offers that have not been accepted can be withdrawn at any time. Once an offer is turned down, it ceases to exist; the making of a counteroffer by an offeree automatically is a rejection of the original offer.

A final point concerns the exact moment in time when an offer becomes a contract. This occurs at the time the offeror is *notified* that the offer has been accepted in full by the offeree. It is not enough for an offeree to sign an offer and then put it in his desk drawer without telling anyone; the offeror is entitled to notification that he has created a binding contract upon himself. Any form of notification is suitable, so long as it can be shown that the offeror received it and understood it to mean that his offer was accepted.

It is good practice, once an offer is accepted, for the broker to telephone the offeror and notify him, thereby establishing that the contract exists. Later, a signed copy of the contract can be given to him at a convenient time. It should also be noted that the signed contract can be mailed to the offeree. In this case, notification is considered to have been legally received at the moment the document enters the mails. Offers can also be accepted by telegram or any other means of communication. Finally, an offeror can specify certain forms of notice that he must receive if the offer is to be made into a contract by the offeree. For example, the offer may require the written acceptance be put in the hands of the offeror before it is construed to have become a contract.

COOPERATING WITH OTHER BROKERAGE FIRMS

It is common practice in the brokerage business for brokers to sell one another's listings cooperatively; that is, a broker may find a buyer for another broker's listing, and the two will split the commission upon closing of the sale. Exclusive agency and exclusive-right-to-sell listings give the listing broker all agency access to the property and require that other brokers desiring to find buyers work through the listing broker. In many states, the licensing law requires that brokers respect one another's listings; in states that do not have this legal requirement, it is technically possible for another broker to sign a listing contract even though an exclusive listing already exists. In that case, if the second broker sells the property, the owner will be obliged to pay full commissions to *both* brokers.

Requirements of Cooperation

When brokers cooperate on the sale of a property listed by one of them, it is essential that certain arrangements be worked out in advance—particularly the manner in which the commission will be split. The seller will pay the con-tracted commission to the listing broker, who then will pay the selling broker the agreed upon share. If he does not, the selling broker must sue the listing broker. The seller of the property is no longer obliged once he has paid the proper commission to the listing broker. License law prohibits the listing broker from paying a commission share directly to the *salesperson* from another firm. He pays the other firm its share of the commission, and then that share is split by that firm with its salespeople.

A brokerage firm is not legally obliged to cooperate on its listings unless it chooses to do so; at least there is no law *specifically* requiring cooperation, although provisions of some license laws can be interpreted to suggest that cooperation should be required. However, there is some concern that in areas where cooperation is routinely practiced (and in most areas of the United States it is) it could be a violation of agency law *not* to cooperate. For example, if a competing broker appears with an offer that the seller probably would take, is it appropriate to the listing broker's agency responsibility to refuse to allow that offer to be presented simply because it comes from another broker? Questions such as these have not been satisfactorily answered by the courts.

These problems do not affect firms whose policy is not to refuse cooper-ation. Even so, some of these firms may not care to cooperate with *certain* other brokerages of whose practices they do not approve or with whom they have had unhappy experiences. This might be done entirely in good faith; the firm is convinced that its clients will be better off to avoid dealing with firms that it does not care to cooperate with. It is best that the listing contract contain language allowing the listing broker to cooperate with other brokerages of its choice, since this will eliminate the conflict with agency law. Sometimes the seller himself will desire that only the listing broker be allowed to handle the sale, in which case refusal to cooperate becomes part of the listing contract itself.

Multiple Listing

A great many communities have *multiple listing* arrangements among brokers. These are private contractual arrangements among groups of brokers who agree among themselves to establish a system of listing cooperation. Usually, the member brokers are not required to put all their listings into the multiple listing program; those that they do put in are automatically made available for cooperative sale by all other member brokerage firms and their salespeople. The arrangement specifies the manner in which the commission will be split and sets certain requirements for all listings to be submitted.

Common requirements are that listings be exclusive-right-to-sell, and that certain information about the listed property be submitted. The multiple listing service then assembles all active listings into books that are distributed among the member firms. A great many multiple listing groups also keep their listing files on computer. Individual brokerage firms have access to the computer files by using terminals provided by the multilist or their own computer equipment tied in to the multilist files by special phone lines. In this manner, each firm has up-to-date information about all multiple listed property; usually a book is obtained for each member of the sales force, who then has a large inventory of property for sale.

Multiple listing books are updated frequently, often weekly in larger and more active markets. The multilist's computer file of listing may be updated as often as daily. In addition, the computer files can "flag" listings as impending closings, sold, or with other restrictions. Some cities' markets may be so large that several multiple listing arrangements may exist simultaneously, each covering a specific geographic area and having members who specialize or sell in that area. The information required for the listing usually is exhaustive, so that the salesperson using it can be as well informed as possible about the property. This information should include the name of the listing salesperson, so that others may contact him to arrange for showings.

Because of their widespread use, multiple listing arrangements are powerful tools and often can be used as impressive persuasion to property owners to list the properties they wish to sell. The image of an entire population of salespeople being provided with the information needed to effect the sale of a property is a powerful inducement.

A particular advantage of computerized multilist files is that they can be used for much more than merely containing a file of existing listings. The power of the computer is often used to make available easy sorting of listings in many ways. A salesperson can enter a prospect's desires, price range, location preferences, etc., and the computer quickly searches the listing files and prints out all those which match the prospect's needs. By "flagging" listings as to status, the files also can carry closing and sale information, thereby building up a useful file of recent sales. This kind of information is handy for appraisers as well as brokerage firms.

Multiple listing arrangements are not free. Frequently they are sustained by reserving a small percentage of each commission on a multilisted transaction to be paid by the listing broker to the multiple listing service. Others are paid for by direct membership fees charged to brokers. The books are sometimes provided as part of the total package and sometimes are sold, as requested, to firms or to individual salespeople. Recent developments have included the storage of multiple listing information on computers, with an access terminal in each member brokerage's office. With such a setup, the brokerage's salespeople can receive printed output that is up to date as of the same day and arranged however they like: by area, price range, features, and so on.

Most multiple listing services also include information about recent sales and closings, giving sale date, closing date, sale price, and financing arrangements. This kind of information is extremely valuable not only in keeping the listing book up to date between editions, but also as a barometer of market activity.

Cooperation Process

Although a brokerage may allow access to its listings to other firms, it still remains the contractor with the seller and is responsible for all selling activity that takes place. When another firm desires to show a listed property, it will contact the firm or the listing salesperson in that firm to arrange for an appointment. It is generally thought to be unethical (and in some staes illegal) for one firm to contact the owner of property listed by another without first clearing the contact with the listing firm. Frequently the practice is for the listing salesperson or someone else in his firm to contact the owner, arrange for the appointment, and say who will be arriving to show the property. Then the salesperson from the other firm is contacted and told of the arrangements.

Some brokerages will give others permission to make direct contact, but it is better not to. For one thing, by insisting that all dealings with a seller be made through the listing broker, the brokerage is able to keep track of all activity. Once the other brokerage's prospect has been shown the property, it is considered good and ethical practice to let the listing brokerage know how the visit went and what the prospect's reaction was.

When an offer is made by a prospect from a cooperating brokerage, it is mandatory that the offer be transmitted through the listing firm unless unequivocal permission to do otherwise has been granted. The listing salesperson almost certainly will want to be present when the offer is presented and very often will actually present it himself without any representative of the offering brokerage present. Furthermore, if the offer is rejected and a counteroffer made, this will usually be taken by the listing brokerage's salesperson to the counterpart at the cooperating brokerage, who then will submit it to the prospect. In this manner, all dealings between prospect and seller will pass through all involved salespeople.

FRANCHISING

One of the most significant developments in the real estate brokerage industry in the 1970s was the rapid growth of regional and even nationwide franchised networks of brokerage firms. Franchise firms are established in many parts of the country and are actively expanding their markets to include new areas. It is a continuous matter of concern to many brokerage firms to consider the advantages and disadvantages of affiliation with franchises.

The franchise is not free. The brokerage firm pays an initiation fee that may range from a few hundred to several thousand dollars, depending upon the particular franchise firm chosen, the services contracted for, and the size and nature of the brokerage firm. After that, a regular fee of some kind is paid to the franchising company. Usually it is a percentage of the firm's gross commission income, although the formula can be varied to consider only the firm's gross profits, the "company dollar" (see Chapter 12), or some other measure. The fee also can be a regular, flat, unchanging periodic fee or a combination of a flat fee and a percentage of income.

In return, the brokerage firm receives a number of benefits. Most significant is a nationally or regionally oriented identification, since the brokerage will use the franchise's signs and identify itself with the franchise network. The franchise system makes possible general advertising that is well beyond the means of a single brokerage firm. One example is television. Many franchise networks advertise themselves nationally in prime time, with the cost of the spot spread over the fees recieved from hundreds of affiliated firms. Similar national advertising campaigns are conducted in other media as well, and they are designed to promote a professional and successful image that will rub off on each franchise brokerage.

Franchise networks also operate sales training programs and management training programs that benefit members, and they supply a variety of other useful services. Most national franchise organizations have nationwide referral services (described in the next section). They may also provide their members with ancillary selling tools such as homeowner's warranty programs.

There are disadvantages to the franchising program as well. Many brokerage firms find the cost too high. Either they do not have the profit margin to allow for the additional costs or they feel that the benefits received do not justify the price they will have to pay. In many areas, franchise networks have found greater success in signing up medium or small firms. The larger firms already have established name identification in their market areas and they do not feel a need to trade it, at a price, for the different identification the franchise offers.

Identification itself is a problem in some franchise situations. While the member brokerages remain independent in virtually all areas, the franchise advertising creates the impression in the public mind that they all are somehow branches of the same firm. The individuality of the brokerage may therefore be submerged, since the advertising features the franchise name, with the name of the individual brokerage firm either missing (in regional or national advertising) or added in smaller, less noticeable type (in the brokerage firm's own advertising).

If a prospect sees the firm's sign on a property for sale, he will notice the franchise name on the sign more often than the smaller presentation of the firm's name. If he later decides to call and hasn't written down the firm's telephone number from the sign, he will look under the franchise name in the yellow pages. There he will see a block ad featuring the names of several firms; if that doesn't remind him of the actual listing firm's name, he may call one at random. As a result, a prospect who should have been generated for the brokerage firm through the visibility of its For Sale sign may end up with another firm. Since in these situations people tend to call the top number on the list, there is a slight advantage for brokerages with names such as AAA Realty. This may be quite an advantage if the franchise's own advertising creates a lot of interest, since people will look in the telephone directory to find out how to make contact.

Therefore, it remains for each firm to decide whether or not affiliation with a franchise is to its advantage. The costs and the benefits should be weighed very carefully, and if possible interviews with current and former and members of the franchise should be made before a decision is finalized.

INFORMATION SERVICES

Several kinds of referral and advertising services are available to brokerage firms—if they are willing to pay the price for them—to aid in their search for potential sellers and buyers. A number of nationwide referral agencies have been set up to provide a network of referral arrangements. Some simply monitor moves made by homeowners, collecting information on their destinations and sending it to the agencies' subscribers in destination cities. The subscribing brokerage then contacts the prospective arrival and offers to help him in the search for a new home.

More sophisticated arrangements connect various brokerage firms in a loose nationwide network. When a member firm lists a home being sold by an owner who is moving to another city, the arrangement provides for notification of the member firm or firms in the destination city. Often the listing brokerage will refer the seller directly to the other firm, with a strong suggestion that he select that firm to find his new home. In this manner, information is exchanged along the network, and member brokerages, especially in areas where a lot of people are moving in, receive a good source of buying prospects.

Some of these network agencies also publish "homes magazines" for the market areas in which they operate. These describe properties currently listed by member firms and give a lot of standard information about the area that the reader moving there may find useful. These are sent to the prospect and often also are given away free at locations around the towns they describe. Typical distribution locations are airports, bus stations, hotels, motels, and restaurants— all of which are likely to be frequented by people contemplating a move to the particular city or town. Free distribution of these materials is also a potentially valuable outlet for locally oriented advertising, since the brochures are likely to be picked up and read by a large number of local residents as well.

Referral services are useful to firms that operate in markets to which a lot of families are moving. However, the local firm can generate its own referrals, by contacting local firms and employers that are expanding and are recruiting new employees from outside the brokerage's market area. Some of these companies will be more reluctant than others to divulge the names of newly arriving employees, but others may be quite cooperative. A particularly good source is a company that is moving its entire operation to the brokerage's town or opening a new facility that will require the transfer of people from other areas. Instead of getting references one by one, the brokerage can try for an arrangement whereby the incoming company will give it the names of transferees as they are reassigned.

SETTLEMENT

In order to conclude a real estate deal, a lot of paperwork and other arrangements have to be concluded at the same time. Then the seller will issue a deed to the buyer, transferring title to him. Usually the buyer and the seller meet with an agent and sign all necessary papers to effect the settlement.

It used to be traditional for settlement arrangements to be made by the brokerage company that handled the transaction; if more than one was involved, it generally was handled by the listing firm. However, in current practice in many areas, settlements are handled either by the financial institution making the mortgage loan to the buyer, or by specialized firms set up for the express purpose of settling real estate transactions. These firms are known by a variety of names, such as *title company, escrow agent,* or *abstract company.* Whether the brokerage firm settles its own brokered transactions or uses the facilities of another firm, the settlement process should be familiar to the brokerage management. Frequently the firm's customers will not understand all of the settlement process, and they will turn to the brokerage for explanations. Also, the brokerage is involved in negotiating the transaction and "nursemaiding" it through to settlement. If it understands the process, it can help to expedite matters and make useful suggestions when changes in the original transaction have to be made before it is settled.

Reporting a Transaction to the IRS

The Federal Tax Reform Act of 1986 requires that the terms of many real estate transactions be reported to the U. S. Internal Revenue Service. The objective is to assure that both buyer and seller correctly report the tax implications of the transaction on their returns.

The responsibility for reporting this information lies with the closing agent for the transaction. If a brokerage firm handles the closing, it must make this report. As noted above, however, in many instances settlements are handled by other closings agents. When they are, it is those agents and not the broker who must make the report.

Even though the broker does not handle the closing, the law provides for some situations in which the broker *still* may be required to report details of the transaction to the Internal Revenue Service. The law actually provides a "ranking" of the parties responsible for the report: (1) the closing agent, (2) the lender who provides new financing, (3) *the seller's broker*, (4) *the buyer's broker*, and (5) the seller. Thus, if there is no nonbroker closing agent for the transaction, and if no new financing is involved, a broker may have to make the report. (Remember, if a broker handles the closing, the broker becomes the "closing agent" for that transaction and *must* make the report.)

The Uniform Settlement Statement

At settlement, both buyer and seller are provided with statements describing all monies received and spent by each of the parties in connection with the settlement of the deal. The Real Estate Settlement Procedures Act (RESPA) requires all residential settlements to use the Uniform Settlement Statement, also called the HUD-1 form, which has been prepared by the U. S. Department of Housing and Urban Development. Such a form is illustrated in Figure 9–2. It has spaces designed for including virtually all information that could possibly be relevant to a real estate settlement; this means that for most transaction a considerable portion of the statement form will be left blank because it does not apply.

The form is divided into several sections. The top third of the first page identifies the buyer, seller, property, lender, settlement agent, and dates used. Section J, the left column, summarizes the borrower's transaction, and Section K, on the right, is for the seller's summary. For the borrower (buyer), lines 101 and 102 describe the price of property bought. Lines 103–105 list settlement charges, which are detailed on the opposite side of the form. Lines 106–112 cover items such as advance payments to taxes, insurance, and other escrows. Line 120 totals all the payments the buyer must make. Line 220 lists the total of all payments that have been made by the buyer or on his behalf by others. This sum is subtracted from line 120 to get line 303: the amount still due from the buyer or due to him and payable at settlement. Items included in lines 201–212 are deposits made by the buyer (earnest money, etc.), loans new and assumed, and prorated items that the seller is required to pay to the buyer.

Section K, describes the seller's side of the transaction. Lines 401–404 describe the payment due to the seller for the propety sold. Lines 405–411 cover

A. U.S. DEPARTMENT OF HOUSING AND URBAN DEVELOPMENT **DISCLOSURE/SETTLEMENT STATEMENT**	**B. TYPE OF LOAN**

B. TYPE OF LOAN

1. ☐ FHA   2. ☐ FMHA   3. ☐ CONV. UNINS.
4. ☐ VA   5. ☐ CONV. INS.

6. FILE NUMBER   7. LOAN NUMBER

8. MORTG. INS. CASE NO.

C. NOTE: This form is furnished to give you a statement of actual settlement costs. Amounts paid to and by the settlement agent are shown. Items marked "(p.o.c.)" were paid outside the closing; they are shown here for informational purposes and are not included in the totals.

Seller's and Purchaser's signature hereon acknowledges his/their approval of tax prorations, and signifies their understanding that prorations were based on figures for preceding year, or estimates for current year, and in event of any change for current year, all necessary adjustments must be made between Seller and Purchaser direct; likewise any DEFICIT in delinquent taxes will be reimbursed to Title Company by the Seller.

We have examined this statement, find it correct and approve the disbursements as shown thereon for our use and benefit. We hereby acknowledge receipt of this statement.

(BORROWER)   (SELLER)

(BORROWER)   (SELLER)   (SETTLEMENT AGENT)

D. NAME OF BORROWER	E. SELLER	F. LENDER

G. PROPERTY LOCATION	H. SETTLEMENT AGENT	DATES
		SETTLEMENT
	PLACE OF SETTLEMENT	DATE OF PRORATIONS IF DIFFERENT FROM SETTLEMENT

J. SUMMARY OF BORROWER'S TRANSACTION	K. SUMMARY OF SELLER'S TRANSACTION

100. GROSS AMOUNT DUE FROM BORROWER:		**400. GROSS AMOUNT DUE TO SELLER:**	
101. Contract sales price		401. Contract sales price	
102. Personal property		402. Personal property	
103. Settlement charges to borrower		403.	
(from line 1400, Section L)		404.	
104.		Adjustments for items paid by seller in advance	
105.		405. City/town taxes to	
Adjustments for items paid by seller in advance		406. County taxes to	
106. City/town taxes to		407. Assessments to	
107. County taxes to		408. to	
108. Assessments to		409. to	
109. to		410. to	
110. to		411. to	
111. to		**420. GROSS AMOUNT DUE TO SELLER**	
112. to			
120. GROSS AMOUNT DUE FROM BORROWER:		**500. REDUCTIONS IN AMOUNT DUE TO SELLER:**	
200. AMOUNTS PAID BY OR IN BEHALF OF BORROWER:		501. Payoff of first mortgage loan	
201. Deposit or earnest money		502. Payoff of second mortgage loan	
202. Principal amount of new loan(s)		503. Settlement charges to seller	
203. Existing loan(s) taken subject to		*(from line 1400, section L)*	
204.		504. Existing loan(s) taken subject to	
205.		505.	
		506.	
Adjustments for items unpaid by seller:		507.	
206. City/town taxes to		508.	
207. County taxes to		509.	
208. Assessments to			
209. to		ADJUSTMENTS FOR ITEMS UNPAID BY SELLER	
210. to		510. City/town taxes to	
211. to		511. County taxes to	
212. to		512. Assessments to	
220. TOTAL PAID BY/FOR BORROWER:		513. to	
		514. to	
300. CASH AT SETTLEMENT FROM/TO BORROWER:		515. to	
		516. to	
301. Gross amount due from borrower		**520. TOTAL REDUCTION AMOUNT DUE SELLER:**	
(from line 120)		**600. CASH AT SETTLEMENT TO/FROM SELLER**	
302. Less amounts paid by or in behalf of borrower		601. Gross amount due seller	
(from line 220)		*(from line 420)*	
	( )	602. Less total reduction in amount due to seller *(from line 520)*	( )
303. CASH (☐ REQUIRED FROM) OR (☐ PAYABLE TO) BORROWER:		603. CASH (☐ TO) (☐ FROM) SELLER	

HUD-1 REV. (5/76)

Figure 9-2. Uniform Settlement Statement.

L. SETTLEMENT CHARGES

	PAID FROM BORROWER'S FUNDS AT SETTLEMENT	PAID FROM SELLER'S FUNDS AT SETTLEMENT
700. SALES/BROKER'S COMMISSION based on price $ @ %		
Division of Commission (line 700) as follows:		
701. $ To		
702. $ To		
703. Commission paid at Settlement		
704.		
800. ITEMS PAYABLE IN CONNECTION WITH LOAN		
801. Loan Origination Fee %		
802. Loan Discount %		
803. Appraisal Fee		
804. Credit Report		
805. Lender's Inspection Fee		
806. Mortgage Insurance Application Fee to		
807. Assumption Fee		
808.		
809.		
810.		
811.		
900. ITEMS REQUIRED BY LENDER TO BE PAID IN ADVANCE		
901. Interest from to @$ /day		
902. Mortgage Insurance Premium for months to		
903. Hazard Insurance Premium for years to		
904. years to		
905.		
1000. RESERVES DEPOSITED WITH LENDER		
1001. Hazard Insurance months @ $ per month		
1002. Mortgage Insurance months @ $ per month		
1003. City property taxes months @ $ per month		
1004. County property taxes months @ $ per month		
1005. Annual Assessments months @ $ per month		
1006. months @ $ per month		
1007. months @ $ per month		
1008. months @ $ per month		
1100. TITLE CHARGES		
1101. Settlement or closing fee to		
1102. Abstract or title search to		
1103. Title examination to		
1104. Title insurance binder to		
1105. Document preparation to		
1106. Notary fees to		
1107. Attorney's fees to		
(includes above items numbers;)		
1108. Title insurance to		
(includes above items numbers;)		
1109. Lender's coverage $		
1110. Owner's coverage $		
1111.		
1112.		
1113.		
1200. GOVERNMENT RECORDING AND TRANSFER CHARGES		
1201. Recording fees: Deed $;Mortgage $ Releases $		
1202. City/county tax/stamps: Deed $;Mortgage $		
1203. State tax/stamps; Deed $;Mortgage $		
1204.		
1300. ADDITIONAL SETTLEMENT CHARGES		
1301. Survey to		
1302. Pest inspection to		
1303.		
1304.		
1305.		
1400. TOTAL SETTLEMENT CHARGES (ENTER ON LINES 103, SECTION J AND 502, SECTION K)		

HUD-1 REV. (5/76)

Figure 9-2. (*Continued*)

payments the seller already has made for items such as taxes, insurance, etc., that the buyer uses after purchase. Line 420 adds these items to get the total gross amount due to the seller. Line 520 describes charges and fees paid by the seller. Lines 501–502 show the amounts necessary to pay off loans on the property that are not being assumed by the buyer. Line 503 shows settlement charges (from the opposite side of the form) that are charged to the seller. Lines 504–509 cover other charges against the seller, including loans assumed by the buyer. Lines 510–516 correspond to lines 206–212 of the buyer's side (lines 405–411 also correspond to lines 106–112), showing the items unpaid by the seller and chargeable to him. Line 603 is the result of subtracting line 520 from line 420, and shows the proceeds due to or from the seller, payable at settlement.

Prorated Items

Charges such as property taxes, interest on assumed loans, insurance, and rents are paid periodically. Usually settlement will occur in the middle of one of those periods, so it is necessary to split the charge for the item between the buyer and the seller. These items are *prorated*, which means that the charges to buyer and seller are split between them depending upon how much of the period covered by the charge will accrue to each. For example, suppose taxes are assessed for the calendar year and have to be paid on June 1 of the year they are assessed. If the property sale is settled on July 31, the seller will have paid the entire year's tax bill, but the buyer will own the property for the last five months of the year. In this case, the buyer will be charged for five-twelfths of the tax bill, and this sum will be entered on line 106 or 107, and on line 405 or 406. This will show that the buyer must be charged for the tax paid in advance for the full year by the seller, and that the seller will be credited with a similar amount.

Suppose, however, that the property changes hands on April 30. This means that on June 1 the buyer will be presented with a tax bill covering the entire year, but the seller will have owned the property for four months of that year. In this case, the seller will owe the buyer four-twelfths of the annual tax bill at settlement. This amount will be entered on line 206 or 207, showing that the item had been unpaid by the seller; on the seller's side it will appear on line 510 or 511. As a general rule for prorated items, if the *seller owes the buyer* for the prorated sum, it will be entered in Sections 200 and 500 of the Uniform Statement. If the *buyer owes the seller* the prorated amount, it will be entered in Sections 100 and 400.

Listing of Settlement Charges

The second page of the form lists settlement charges made to both buyer and seller. Section 700 is of considerable interest to the brokerage firm: it shows the calculation of the commission and provides for splitting it between listing and selling broker, if needed. Section 800 describes the charges associated with the creation of the new loan received by the buyer. Section 900 shows the advance payment items the lender requires; these are interest on the new loan between the settlement date and the beginning of the first regular loan period, mortgage insurance, and other insurance premiums payable at settlement.

Section 1000 is concerned with escrow or reserve accounts required by the lender. Most lenders require their borrowers to pay, in addition to the loan payment itself, a monthly sum that will mount up to enough to pay property taxes and hazard insurance premiums as they come due. Sometimes these are scheduled to come due relatively soon, and the lender requires an intitial deposit so that when the payments have to be made there will be enough money to make them.

Section 1100 lists charges made in connection with guarantees of title that the buyer recieves. These include abstract updates, title insurance, legal fees, document preparation fees, and the like. Section 1200 includes recording fees and taxes, and Section 1300 includes any additional settlement charges that may be made.

The columns down the right hand side of the page provide space for listing the charge for each item to be assessed either to the buyer or seller. Line 1400 shows the totals for each party, and these totals are listed on line 103 (for the buyer) and line 502 (for the seller) on the front page of the form.

DEFAULTS

Default is one of the nightmares of the real estate brokerage business; it happens when a party to a contract refuses to perform. The professional brokerage firm, of course, ought never to default on a contractual obligation, but it has no way of guaranteeing the same high standards in all the buyers and sellers it will deal with. The major sources of default are default by the seller in a listing contract and default by either buyer or seller in a sale contract.

Listing Default by Seller

A seller can default in his obligations to a brokerage firm by trying to terminate the contract before the property is sold; this was discussed in Chapter 8 and is not a serious problem to have to deal with, although it is annoying to the firm. Much more serious is the seller's default on the payment of the commission after the sale has been concluded. If the seller refuses to pay the commission, there is little that can be done at that time. Whoever is in charge of settlement is an escrow or trust agent disposing of monies belonging to either seller or buyer, and he must dispose of those monies as he is instructed by them. This means that if the brokerage firm is handling the settlement itself, and the seller refuses to pay the commission, he must be given *all* his proceeds, and the firm must take legal action to collect the commission.

Suing for the Commission

Taking a dispute to court is inconvenient, costly, and time consuming. Even so, there are times when just that is necessary. Doing so can generate bad publicity and ill will, so a decision to sue for a commission should be very carefully weighed. Certainly, no decision should be made until a competent attorney has been consulted.

Most firms sue only in cases where blatant violation of the listing contract has occurred. Recalling the discussion in Chapter 3, it is technically true that the broker earns his commission as soon as a seller contracts with a buyer for the sale of the listed property. If the buyer should later illegally default on the contract, the seller still is liable for the commission since the risk of default is his once he has accepted the buyer. However, very few brokerage firms would seriously consider suing a seller for a commission under such circumstances. Regardless of the specific legal situation, few sellers would consider such a claim valid or moral, especially since it was the brokerage itself that brought the bad buyer. In these cases, most brokerage firms will join with the seller in an attempt to work things out for both of them.

Default by Buyer

Buyer default is probably the single most dreaded event in the brokerage business; it is the refusal of the buyer to perform under a sales contract. Worst of all is the absolute refusal to buy. This can happen because the buyer decides he does not want the property or because something happens to keep him from going through with the transaction. This is not to be confused with a buyer's withdrawing from a contract *for reasons that the contract allows*. Thus, failure to perform under a contract contingent upon financing when no loan can be found is not default.

Buyer default is usually unexpected and most often occurs at or very close to the scheduled time for closing of the transacation. This only makes matters worse; the seller is financially and emotionally prepared to close the sale, and the broker is ready as well. To have a buyer refuse to deal at this time is very stressful. Some brokerages try to prepare their sellers for such an eventuality, but even this kindness is dangerous. It could cause unwarranted worry during the many transactions in which there is no default or serious problem of any kind.

Little can be done immediately when a buyer defaults. The first thing to do is for both broker and seller to consult an attorney and make sure that a genuine default has occurred. The attorney can contact the buyer, explain the seller's position and the buyer's obligations to him, and try to convince him to go through with the deal and avoid the possibility of litigation. If this does not work, a lawsuit must be considered. Standard sale contracts provide that the buyer's earnest money deposit must be forfeited to the seller at the time of default. Most listing arrangements provide that the seller split the forfeited deposit with the broker in some manner.

When it is obvious that the default is genuine, a decision must be made as to whether or not the property should be put back on the market. Frequently, arrangements may have to be made to enable the seller to go ahead with other real estate transactions he had been planning as a result of the sale that defaulted. For example, he may have obligated himself to buy another property with the proceeds of his sale, and if he is to go ahead with it some kind of temporary financing will have to be arranged.

The seller probably will blame the broker for the default, since he will reason that the buyer was found by the broker. Legally, the brokerage may be blameless, but this is not usually the time to insist on legal niceties. A professional brokerage will make every effort to ease the seller through the situation as painlessly as possible, including finding interim financing, legal assistance, and the like.

If a lawsuit is filed, it can be for *specific performance* or for *damages*. Specific performance would require the buyer to go through with the contract; damages would allow the buyer to default but require him to pay the seller the cost he imposed upon him by defaulting. In neither case would a lawsuit be an immediate solution to the problem unless the act of filing suit is sufficient to encourage the buyer to go ahead with the deal as contracted. Otherwise, it will be months or perhaps years before a court settlement can be reached. This is far too long to resolve the immediate problems caused by default. In a home sale transaction, specific performance may be futile anyway, since many defaults by home buyers are caused by financial inability, and the buyer would be unable to comply with a court order to transact. It may also be that the buyer has no, or few, assets to claim against, rendering even a damage suit a wasted effort. In such cases there is little to do except bear the costs and chalk the event up to experience.

A buyer who does not have the financial resources to transact may be helpless to go ahead with the deal even if he wants to. However, some buyers choose not to transact even though they are capable. Damage judgments against them may eventually pay off, and furthermore, the threat of a damage suit may be enough to goad them into completing the transaction.

Planning Against Buyer Default

In many cases buyer default can be at least in part the responsibility of the brokerage, praticularly if a risky buyer is found. The seller relies on the brokerage to find a suitable buyer; it is up to the firm to make sure that the buyer really does want to buy and is able to do so. For these reasons, it is best to avoid high-pressure selling tactics, since these frequently will lead to offers from people who later will want to reconsider their decisions. In fact, buyers occasionally have sued brokers or complained about them to officials because they had been pressured into buying property they really did not want. It is much better, although perhaps more difficult, to obtain a buyer who wants the property. He will be much more likely to make every effort to go through with the transaction.

Other means of preventing default include requiring relatively high earnest money payments and careful qualification of the potential buyer by the broker. If the buyer has a large deposit at stake he will be more careful not to default, because he has a lot to lose. By qualifying the buyer, the broker makes sure that the property is suitable and that the buyer has the financial capacity to buy. This is done before the property is shown to a prospective buyer.

Qualifying the Buyer

The most effective way to avoid buyer default is to *qualify the buyer*. This is a procedure done by the salesperson or broker at the time the buying prospect first is found. The salesperson tries to find out as much as possible about the prospect—not only the prospect's needs and desires with respect to real estate, but also the financial capability and limitations the prospect has. This includes inquiring about income and its sources, existing obligations, savings, other assets, etc. The objective is to build a financial profile of the prospect in order to determine borrowing needs (and ability), and the ability to meet the necessary initial cash expenses of a purchase.

Buyer qualification informs the professional real estate salesperson about the prospect. This information can be used to steer the prospect toward those listings which best suit his needs and ability to pay. It also helps the salesperson to inform the owner of the listed property when the prospect makes an offer. It can help avoid futile contracts, in which the buyer has little hope of qualifying for needed financing or coming up with necessary cash.

Buyer qualification is an essential duty of the real estate salesperson or broker. The function of brokerage is to bring buyer and seller together; the broker, in effect, brings potential buyers to the seller. Usually the seller does not even meet those who make offers; he sees only a written offer signed by a total stranger. Anyone can write anything on a piece of paper and then have it delivered to someone else. How is the broker's principal to know that the stranger making him an offer can go through with what is written? The principal must rely upon the broker to find out the necessary information and provide it to him.

A properly qualified buyer is much less likely to default. A major reason for buyer default is inability to handle the financial aspects of promises made. Properly qualified buyers encounter such problems infrequently.

If a buyer of questionable capacity makes an offer on a property, the broker should relay that information to the seller. Furthermore, the contract of sale should always be written to allow for all possible contingencies that may arise due to a particular buyer's circumstances. If the buyer has to borrow a small fortune from his Aunt Minnie, the contract should say so and give a reasonable time for him to do so, after which the seller can call off the deal. The same should be done if the buyer has to sell a property before he will have the cash to pay for the one he is making the offer on, or if he will need to secure a mortgage loan. This gives the seller ample warning that the sale is conditional upon certain things happening, and it will avoid default if the conditions cannot be met within the specified time. Also, the seller will have the knowledge to turn down a deal when the conditions are unsatisfactory to him, instead of finding out much later what the true situation is.

DISCUSSION QUESTIONS AND PROJECTS

1. Examine the sale contract forms in common use in your area, analyzing their strengths and weaknesses. Are there any changes you would suggest making? Why or why not?

2. Prepare some examples of improper procedure by a licensee in the process of negotiating offers and counter-offers in a real estate transaction. What would be proper procedure in these situations?

3. Investigate the popularity of franchised realty firms in your area. Which ones are represented? What is the cost of joining? What benefits do members receive?

4. Investigate the use of referral services for out-of-town sources of prospects in your area. Do local brokerage firms find them useful?

5. What are the advantages and disadvantages of realty firm franchises?

6. Determine the current charges for common settlement costs in your area. With this information, fill in the form in Figure 9–2 with simulated information for settlement of a hypothetical transaction devised by you.

7. Determine how taxes are assessed and prorated in your area.

8. Does your area use a multiple listing system? If so, examine it and analyze the charges, fees, regulations, and usefulness of the system.

9. Describe how an offer becomes a contract.

10. Develop a policy for dealing with buyer defaults that could be adopted by a medium sized residential brokerage firm.

11. If a seller refuses to pay a legally earned commission, under what circumstances should the broker sue for the commission? Are there any situations in which it would be better for a brokerage firm just to forget about the commission? Why or why not?

12. Under what circumstances would it be advisable for a real estate sales transaction to involve a land contract?

13. Why is it advantageous for brokerage firms to cooperate with other firms in the sales of their listings?

14. Describe how a competent broker can take steps in the negotiation of a real estate sale transaction to provide assurance that neither buyer nor seller will default.

15. From a closing agent find out exactly what types of transactions have to be reported to the IRS, and how it is done.

16. Interview two or three salespeople and a sales manager. Find out what they do to qualify buyers. Find out also how they get people to reveal the information they need. Are there any suggestions you could make?

17. If there is a multiple listing system in your area, does it have its information on computer? Do member firms have terminals at their offices which can access the MLS computer for information? What kinds of information, sorting and searching capacities are available to member firms? Do you have any suggestions for improvement?

A CASE STUDY

BUYER DEFAULT

Eleanor E. has been in the real estate business for twenty years and has been the principal broker of her own firm for ten. When asked about buyer default, she said:

"I know it sounds bad, but I would guess that in nine out of ten cases of buyer default in a brokered deal, it's the agent's fault. Usually, it's because he or she didn't pay enough attention to qualifying the buyer.

"When an agent high-pressures a person into buying something he can't afford, or doesn't really want, he's asking for trouble. The buyer has several weeks to realize that he's done something unwise and I've seen many cases where they just walk away from the transaction and refuse to close. If they get really mad, they can sue the agent. In a lot of cases like that, I would have to side with the buyer. A good agent has no business forcing people into deals that are not good for them.

"Qualifying is hardly any trouble at all, but even so I spend a lot of time in sales meetings on that point. People usually will tell you practically anything you want to know about their financial affairs. A few minutes' discussion can determine how much they can afford and what their needs are. At this time, the prospect gains the confidence that the agent is sincerely interested in helping him meet his needs in the best possible way. When the prospect sees something he likes, we try to discuss it thoroughly with him and work out a little form that shows what he'll pay, what cash he'll need, what his payments will be—even the moving costs. We don't try to speed him along or rush him into making an offer before he's ready.

"In peculiar deals we try to dig really deep. We had a real stinker last year that shows just what I mean. We had a lovely old seven-bedroom home listed in a downtown area that was well on its way to "coming back" into vogue. We listed it for $75,000. One day an agent with another company brought us an *all-cash* offer for $72,000. It was the cleanest offer I had ever seen: closing in 90 days, no loan, no points, no ifs, ands, or buts at all. The buyers were representing a charity that wanted to use the house for temporary housing for retarded adults who were being trained in vocational programs. When we discovered this, we pointed out to the agent that the house wasn't zoned to permit that. He responded that this wouldn't make any difference; they were willing to buy anyway and then go through the rezoning process. My seller was in heaven! Naturally he grabbed the offer; he had expected three to six months hard work selling and then maybe taking a pretty low offer and paying all sorts of buyer's closing costs and loan fees.

"The day of closing the buyers defaulted. It seems that the charity's board of directors knew nothing at all about the deal! The people we had been dealing with were the executive director and one of the board members. Apparently, the board had discussed the possibility of getting federal funding to buy themselves a new place; when these two talked to the local HEW office they were told that if they qualified they could get the money. So they went right out and signed an offer to buy my seller's place with cash that they did not have and with no authority from their own board to do so. The day before closing they had a board meeting where all this came out, and the board repudiated the whole thing.

"I thought I was mad then, but that was nothing compared to how I felt after I talked to the other agent. He had never asked them where they were going to get the money. When we had mentioned the zoning to him, he answered without ever consulting them. If he'd just asked a couple of simple questions he would have known that they had no idea what they were doing. Instead he brought us this foolish offer from these foolish people, and ended up putting us all through torture. At least the board member who was involved in this paid for his experience: He wrote a personal check for the earnest money, which we kept of course.

"My seller almost went crazy. After we got this contract on his house, we found him a new place, and he was expecting to use his equity to provide the money he needed to buy it. It took us three days of begging and wheedling all over town before we were able to get a bank to lend him the money he needed to close on his new house. It took him six more months before we finally got rid his old place. While we had been waiting to close on the deal that defaulted, the interest rates had risen and the market practically died. He finally sold for $63,500 and paid four points on a VA loan. With the extra six months of loan payments he had to make, he ended up with almost $15,000 less than he would have got from the offer the charity people made.

"His lawyer discovered that the charity didn't have two dimes to rub together. So now he's suing the two people who made the offer to him. Also, they're about to sue the other agent's brokerage firm as well, for incompetence, malpractice—you name it. And frankly, if they call me to testify, I'm going to have to agree that the other agent did not do his duty properly. And you can bet that the next time he brings me an offer on any of my listings, I'm going to go over it with a microscope!"

REFERENCES

ATTEBERRY, WILLIAM L., KARL G. PEARSON, AND MICHAEL P. LITKA, *Real Estate Law*, ch. 11, 14, 16. New York, NY: John Wiley & Sons, 1984.

BROWN, DONALD R., AND WENDELL G. MATTHAU, *Real Estate Advertising Handbook*. Chicago, IL: REALTORS® National Marketing Institute, 1982.

FISHER, FREDERICK J., *Broker Beware: Selling Real Estate Within the Law*, ch. 4, 5. Reston, VA: Reston Publishing Company, Inc., 1981.

FOSTER, RAY, *Sensible Real Estate Selling Skills*. Reston, VA: Reston Publishing Company, Inc., 1981.

GOLDSTEIN, PAUL, *Real Estate Transactions*. St. Paul, MN: Foundation Press, 1985.

HANSOTTE, LOUIS B., "Real Estate Contracts," in *The McGraw-Hill Real Estate Handbook*, ed. Robert Irwin, ch. 22. New York, NY: McGraw-Hill Book Company, 1984.

HULL, DONALD A., "A Complete Guide to Qualifying," *Real Estate Today*, August 1979, pp. 43-52.

KRATOVIL, ROBERT, AND RAYMOND J. WERNER, *Real Estate Law* (8th ed.), ch. 6, 7, 11-13. Englewood Cliffs, NJ: Prentice Hall, 1983.

LEVINE, ARTHUR M., "Dual Agency Trap," *Real Estate Review*, Spring 1985, pp. 109-112.

Handbook on Multiple Listing Policy. Chicago, IL: National Association of REALTORS®, 1975.

Real Estate Office Management: People Functions Systems, ch. 17. Chicago, IL: REALTORS® National Marketing Institute, 1975.

Real Estate Sales Handbook (9th ed.). Chicago, IL: REALTORS® National Marketing Institute, 1983.

RING, ALFRED A., AND JEROME DASSO. *Real Estate Principles and Practices* (10 ed.), ch. 4, 8. Englewood Cliffs, NJ: Prentice Hall, 1985.

SODARO, AUGUSTINE, "How to Market Residential Property," in *The McGraw-Hill Real Estate Handbook*, ed. Robert Irwin, ch. 32. New York, NY: McGraw-Hill Book Company, 1984.

SHENKEL, WILLIAM M. *Marketing Real Estate* (2 ed.), ch. 9. Englewood Cliffs, NJ: Prentice Hall, 1985.

U. S. DEPARTMENT OF HOUSING AND URBAN DEVELOPMENT, *Settlement Costs and You—A HUD Guide for Homebuyers*. Washington, DC: U. S. Government Printing Office, 1984.

TEN

COMPENSATION OF SALESPEOPLE

Commission Sharing

Incentive Plans

Company Listings and Referrals

Nonmoney Compensation

Compensation During Training of New Salespeople

Salespeople in real estate brokerage firms receive their compensation by being given portions of the commissions that they bring into the firm. The exact split depends upon the contracts they have with the firm, but generally they will run from about 40 percent of the total they bring in up to nearly 100 percent. To some extent, the exact split is determined by competition in the market. If a firm offers a split worse than that offered by most others in its area, it will not retain people for long, especially good producers. If it offers a better split, it will be paying more than it should.

COMMISSION SHARING

It would be impossible to spell out rigid rules for commission split arrangements that could apply to all companies in all locations and in all situations. However, we can examine typical plans as a guide to the formulation of those to be used by specific companies in particular situations.

Listing and Selling Commissions

It is normal practice for firms to pay commissions separately for listing property and for selling it. A firm may agree with its salespeople that they will receive 50% of the commissions they bring in. The firm, then, will determine that a certain portion of each *total* commission is received for listing the property and the remainder for selling it. For example, the firm may decide that half of the total commission is payment for listing and half for selling. If a property is listed by salesperson A and sold by salesperson B, each will receive 25% of the total commission with the company receiving 50%. A will have brought in half of the commission by listing the property; his half of this is 25% of the total, and the other 25% goes to the company. B brings in the other 50% of the total commission. His share is 25% of the total (half of what he brought in) and the company gets the other 25%.

In earlier times, and in some rural areas today, the practice was to pay most of the commission for selling and relatively little for listing. This practice may appear to be logical, since one can argue that without a sale there is no point to a listing. However, the result was to encourage salespeople to sell but not to make much effort to list property, unless they were reasonably sure that they could sell it themselves and so get the much larger share of the commission. The modern brokerage firm realizes that unless a very strong buyer's market exists, listings are more valuable than sales because there is always a good chance that a decent listed property will sell, while there is little chance of selling to a good buying prospect if there are few listings to sell.

Adjustments

The exact commission sharing arrangement will be determined by a number of things. Is the commission for a listing, a sale, or both? Was the listing solicited by the salesperson or assigned by the firm's management? Was it a particularly difficult transaction or an easy one? Many firms have incentive programs that offer better commission splits to salespeople who produce well. While the commission split is the primary means of compensation, it is not the only one. Employee salespeople can receive all kinds of fringe benefits. While these cannot be given to independent contractors, other benefits can be. The firm may have particularly pleasant offices to work in or may provide very good support staff service. In the latter case, a salesperson may be satisfied with a smaller split because the support given by the firm enables him to spend more time on his primary activity of soliciting listings and making sales.

Depending upon market conditions, the firm may want to revise its commission payment arrangements. If it is a seller's market, there will be relatively few properties for sale and many people wanting to buy. In such markets it is easier to find buyers than it is to get good listings, so the firm may want to reduce the commissions paid on sales and increase them for listings, to encourage its salespeople to spend more time getting listings. In a buyer's market there are many properties for sale and relatively few buyers. Here a firm might reverse its policy and pay a higher commission split for sales than for listings.

Cooperated Sales

Cooperated sales occur whenever a salesperson at one brokerage firm sells property listed by another. Many firms have adopted policies that give different treatment to commission splits on properties listed by other brokerage firms. Natually, the firm would prefer that its own salespeople sell its listings, since the firm receives a larger amount of the total commission by splitting with its own sales force on both listing and sale. For example, the firm in our previous example may pay its salespeople only 40% of commissions brought in by selling listings of other firms, instead of the 50% that it pays on sales of its own listings. This will encourage greater effort to sell the company's own listings, since the pay is better.

The attractiveness of these arrangements also is affected by the manner in which brokerages split commissions between them on cooperated sales. In some parts of the country, the total commission is split 50–50 between the listing broker and the selling broker. But in other areas the split is uneven, usually with the larger share going to the listing broker. This smaller cooperated selling commission provides an additional incentive for a firm's salespeople to concentrate on its own listings, since there is ample opportunity for the firm to offer a better payment for doing so.

The 100% Commission Arrangement and Variations

In recent years a new manner of employment and compensation has emerged that usually is referred to as the *100% commission* arrangement. Here the salesperson pays the brokerage a flat fee, usually monthly, for the use of the firm's facilities. He then keeps *all* of the commissions he brings in. Some firms vary the program slightly by charging an additional fee to the salesperson for each transaction, but the basic effect is to allow the salesperson to keep virtually all the commission income he produces. This type of arrangement is particularly useful in independent contractor arrangements, since the contractor actually pays the firm a fee for its services, instead of the other way around.

There are several advantages and disadvantages to this type of arrangement. The fees charged by the firm to the salesperson are designed to cover the costs the firm incurs in having the salesperson on its sales force, plus a reasonable profit. The fee charged, if any, for each transaction processed by the firm is designed to cover the firm's costs in that regard. The main advantage to the firm is that almost all of the risk with respect to doing business is borne by the salesperson. He must pay his fees to the brokerage firm whether or not he makes sales and provides himself with income. The firm has a regular source of income from its sales force that will not be affected by conditions in the real estate market. Financial planning is made much easier for the firm and a lot less risky or uncertain. At the same time, the firm will make relatively less money from a very good producer, since it does not share the commissions that he generates, but collects only the agreed upon fees.

From the salesperson's point of view, the arrangement can be either good or bad. If he is good producer he probably will profit; if he is mediocre he probably would be better off under a conventional splitting arrangement. Figure 10–1 illustrates this point.

The 100% commission arrangement has been tried by many firms across the country. Some have found it highly desirable, while others have reverted to a more conventional system. Whether or not it is the right arrangement for a given firm will depend on many factors. It certainly is a way of weeding out poor producers; they will not be able to afford the fees and charges. It is also a way of rewarding very good producers, since they can earn significantly more under most 100% commission plans. As for the large majority of salespeople who are

Figure 10-1 100% Commission or 50-50 Split?

Total Commissions Generated per Year	SALESPERSON'S SHARE	
	50-50 Split	100% Commission
$ 20,000	$10,000	$ 4,800
30,000	15,000	13,200
40,000	20,000	21,600
60,000	30,000	38,400
100,000	50,000	72,000

Depending on the amount of commissions generated, the 100% commission arrangement can be good or bad for the salesperson. The better he is, the better it will be for him. Here we are assuming a 100% commission arrangement that requires the salesperson to pay the firm a fee of $1,000 per month, plus $400 for each transaction. We also are assuming an average commission brought in per transaction of $2,500—either the listing or selling share of a total commission of $5,000.

neither very good nor very bad, the advantages and disadvantages can be quite variable.

Many firms do not go to the 100% plan simply because they find their salespeople don't want to. Often there are other incentive programs that will greatly increase earnings of good producers, and many ways can be found to weed out the poor ones without resorting to a completely different way of calculating compensation. Many salespeople do not like the additional possible burden imposed by the 100% commisssion plan. It is enough, they feel, that they work on commission and have to live with the uncertainty and irregularity of that kind of income pattern. Adding a regular, fairly high fee does not appear to be adequately compensated by the opportunity to keep more of the commissions they generate.

Some 100% commission firms charge relatively small fees to their salespeople and then add in the costs of all the separate services used. An elaborate schedule of fees is set up, including charges for telephone usage, secretary time, message referral, handling of transactions, and the like. The salesperson then has some control over the total fee he pays. He uses the firm's services when he is busy and is generating commission income at the same time. But when his business is slow, he uses relatively few of the services and so pays a smaller regular fee.

Other companies have gone to variations of the 100% commission, such as paying salespeople fairly large splits (75%, 85% or more) of commssions they generate and then leaving them to do their business as they choose. These companies concentrate upon good producers who might prefer to operate independently but do not want the bother of operating their own firms.

In summary, 100% commission plans and their variations require a complete rethinking of the relationship between the brokerage firm and the sales force. Instead of the sales force working "for" the firms, the firm exists as a sort of contractor to the salesperson, providing the conveniences of an office and support personnel in return for fixed payment. In effect, the salesperson can be said to be "renting" the firm's facilities when he needs them and operating virtually independently otherwise. Firms under 100% commission are more difficult to run tightly, since there is less genuine control over the sales force. Assigning open house duty or floor duty becomes more difficult, although it is possible to arrange it so that part of the salesperson's payment to the firm would be in assignable work time instead of cash. However, the effect of this arrangement on the independent contractor relationship is uncertain. Firms might instead have some of the employee support staff acquire sales licenses so that they can take messages, give out information, and otherwise engage in activities that might legally be restricted to licenses.

Practical Considerations

Whatever the commission payment plan chosen, it should accomplish certain objectives. Since it is the source of the salesperson's income, it should be designed so that he feels he is getting a fair share of the total. The firm should make an effort to show that its share is being spent on facilities and work that is of benefit to the salesperson, and that he is getting services from the firm in addition to the money he earns. This means the firm cannot afford to be too generous, because it has its expenses to meet. In areas where a large number of firms exist, competition among then and among salespeople will result in commission sharing arrangements that work well for both the firms and the salespeople. Inefficient firms will be driven out of business along with poorly producing salespeople, and the efficient and productive ones will remain.

INCENTIVE PLANS

While the salesperson may see his compensation as a source of income and sustenance, to the firm it also can be a form of incentive for productive work. Naturally, each successful listing or sale will add to the salesperson's income, and that is indeed an incentive. It pays the brokerage to have a very productive salesperson, because no matter how good he may be, he still uses only one desk and one space in the office. Also, the productive salesperson sets an example for those who are less so, and often he is able to provide hints and even outright instruction to the newer or less able salespeople in the firm.

The best incentive for greater productivity is to offer the salesperson a more generous share of the commission income he generates for the firm, if he generates a lot of it. Several types of plans are in use in the industry today, but they all have the feature of paying the more productive sales force members larger shares of each dollar of commission income they create for the company.

Bonus Plans

The most common form of extra compensation is the bonus plan. These take a variety of forms. A popular one is to set a certain minimum of commission income a salesperson must earn during a particular period. If he earns more than the minimum, he receives the bonus. Many of these plans *graduate* the bonus, so that the greater the excess over the minimum he earns, the larger a proportion of the commission dollar the salesperson is paid.

The bonus plan outlined in the Policy Manual example (Figure 7–1 in Chapter 7) is a program of this nature. Here a minimum of $4,000 per quarter of earned commissions is set. (Note that by earned commissions we mean the total of commission income actually paid to the salesperson, and not the total amount of commission income that was paid to the firm because of his efforts.) If the salesperson earns between $4,000 and $4,500, he will be paid a bonus of 3% of his total commission earnings for the quarter. If, however, he earns $6,000 in one quarter, he will receive a bonus of 8% of his earnings. And if his earnings total $10,000 or more for the quarter, his bonus is 25%. As Figure 10–2 shows, the higher the salesperson's earnings are, the larger percentage bonus he receives, and therefore the larger is his share of each commission dollar he is responsible for bringing into the company.

Figure 10–2 Effect of Bonus Plan on Salesperson's Commission Share (Quarterly Plan)

Commission Receipts Brought In	Salesperson's Share Base + Bonus = Total			Salesperson's Share as a Percentage of Firm's Commission Receipts
$ 8,000	$ 4,000 +	0	$ 4,000	50 %
10,000	5,000 +	250	5,250	52.5
12,000	6,000 +	480	6,480	54
14,000	7,000 +	840	7,840	56
16,000	8,000 +	1,440	9,440	59
18,000	9,000 +	1,620	10,620	59
20,000	10,000 +	2,500	12,500	62.5
22,000	11,000 +	2,750	13,750	62.5
24,000	12,000 +	3,000	15,000	62.5

This figure makes the following assumptions: (a) That the bonus plan is the one described in Figure 7–1, and (b) that the salesperson's base commission averages 50% of the commissions brought in.

The quarterly plan shown in Figure 10–2 was chosen purely as an example. The brokerage firm can base the bonus on any period it feels proper. However, relatively short periods can create some unusual difficulties. For example, if the period is monthly, it is possible that a relatively poor producer may earn a bonus just because an unusual number of his sales closed in one month; if a quarterly, semi-annual, or annual period had been chosen, he might not have received the bonus because several other months of poor production would have been contained in the period. As an extreme example, referring again to Figure 10–2, let us consider a salesperson whose earnings total $15,000 per year. If his earnings are spread perfectly evenly, he will earn $3,750 per quarter and not be eligible for a bonus at all. However, if his earnings are split evenly between only two quarters (and in the other two quarters he earned no income at all) he will receive a bonus of 12% of the $7,500 earned in each productive quarter, for a total bonus of $1,800 for the year. And if he manages to squeeze his entire year's output into a single quarter, he will receive a bonus of $3,750!

Variations in Commission Split

Some firms try to overcome problems such as those mentioned in the preceding paragraph by paying different salespeople different commission splits, depending on the company's evaluation of their performance. A good producer may receive a contract entitling him to, say, 60 or 65% of the commissions he brings in, while new members of the firm or poorer producers will receive contracts entitling them to smaller shares. This method recognizes those who have proved themselves to be superior. Of course, this plan also assumes that good producers will continue to be good at their work and will justify the faith placed in them by the brokerage firm.

At the same time, provision must be made to adjust commission splits of salespeople as their productivity changes. A good producer may lose interest or just burn out, and a newcomer to the business may learn quickly and become a valued professional. If differing commission splits are given to different salespeople, special effort must be made to assure all of them that the variations are fair. The firm should have some sort of formula by which it measures performance, and that formula should be known to the sales force. In this manner, the more advantageous split becomes a kind of bonus, in that the salesperson knows he can earn it by performing to a certain standard.

Delayed Bonuses

Some brokerage firms' bonus plans are designed with a built-in payment delay in them. Our example in Figure 7–1 has one: the bonus is not actually paid until ninety days after the end of the period in which it was earned, and then only if the salesperson is still in the service of the company. The purpose of the delay is to encourage the salesperson to remain with the company, especially if he is a good producer. If he should decide to resign, he will forfeit bonuses that he has earned but not yet had time to collect, so he has an incentive to remain. And, of course, while he is staying on he will continue working and will begin to pile up credit for another bonus, which he can collect only if he remains longer. At the same time, relatively poor producers will be earning little or no bonus, so they will not have the incentive to remain with the company; since they are poor producers, the company will not miss them when they leave.

One drawback to delayed bonuses is that real estate salespeople are a notoriously independent breed; they have to be if they are to function successfully. Many of them feel insulted by delayed bonus plans because they think a brokerage ought to do more to keep them than just holding back part of the money they already have earned. The variable commission split arrangement, although it may have other faults (such as creating poor morale among less able producers), is a solution to this problem, since the salesperson does not actually earn money, but rather the right to earn a higher commission split once he has proved himself. In this manner, instead of having part of his pay held back, which is a negative kind of encouragement, he has the positive goal of an objective he can work for.

Encouraging Specific Activity

The plans discussed thus far encourage greater productivity of all kinds. However, the commission arrangement can be designed to encourage specific activity by the sales force. As we have mentioned, commission shares for listing and selling can be adjusted from time to time depending upon conditions in the real estate market. If buyers are scarce, listing commissions can be reduced and selling commissions increased. The opposite can be done if sellers are hard to find. However, this kind of changing of the commission structure should be undertaken only if there are remarkable departures from the norm in the real estate markets in which the firm operates.

Some firms also institute changing listing commissions that are reduced if the property takes a particularly long time to sell. For example, if a firm normally pays 25% of the total commission to the listing salesperson, it might also stipulate that if the property does not have an offer accepted on it within, say sixty days, the listing salesperson's share of the commission falls to 22½%. The effect of such a program will be to encourage salespeople to bring in *good* listings. These are the kinds that sell fairly quickly. The price is reasonable and the terms under which the seller is willing to transact are not unusually difficult. At the same time, once the listing is in, the listing salesperson has an incentive to "work" the listing vigorously to try to sell it before the high commission period has expired.

COMPANY LISTINGS AND REFERRALS

In a small firm, the managing broker and sales manager may be active members of the sales force as well. In that case, if they secure listings or sell property, they collect the commissions due them. In large firms, management often does not engage directly in selling. However, the management personnel are likely to have contacts or friends who may approach them to list or look for real estate. In these cases, the firm itself secures the listing or finds the prospect. However, for the actual sales work, the listing or prospect is referred to one of the active salespeople.

Buying prospects are referred to a salesperson. Listings are handled in one of two ways: as company listings or as referred listings. A referred listing is a listing prospect given to the salesperson, who then must negotiate the listing contract. A company listing is an actual contracted listing taken by a management member of the firm. Most often these involve multiple properties, such as a company listing with a construction firm that authorizes the company to sell its newly constructed, under construction, and planned properties.

Referred Listing

Probably the most prized possession of a real estate salesperson is a good listing. His name is featured in the advertising of the property. If he holds open house, numerous prospects are likely to come by. His name appears on the For Sale sign on the property. From all of this he will receive calls from people who may be interested in buying real estate. If it turns out that the prospect does not want to negotiate on the listed property, the salesperson still has the opportunity to show him others.

When *management* secures a listing prospect, the very *referral* of that prospect to a salesperson is a bonus of sorts. For this reason, many firms pay smaller listing commissions on *referred listings*; sometimes they pay no commission at all. The idea is that the listing referral itself makes up for the lack of a regular commission, since the salesperson can work the listing and benefit from doing so. He will be able to use it as a source of prospects and, of course, he will have the inside track among the firm's salespeople with respect to selling the listing and earning the selling commission.

The exact amount of commission to be paid, if any, on referred listings must depend on the amount of work that is involved in handling them. Some firms require that the listing salesperson be primarily responsible for "nurse-maiding" the listing through to the final sales and settlement, even if another salesperson produces the buyer. If this is the case, then the listing salesperson is required to do considerable work even though the prospect was referred to him. A portion of the regular listing commission probably would be appropriate here. On the other hand, if the brokerage firm itself, through its support staff and management, handles most of the detail work once the property is under sale contract, the listing salesperson may be adequately compensated just by getting the listing referral. In either case, the listing salesperson handles the property until an offer is accepted, but the other advantages of having a listing in his name are likely to be viewed as sufficient compensation.

The handling of referred listings is a sensitive matter. The company should make them attractive by paying an adequate commission, depending on the work involved in handling them; otherwise the sales staff will view them as a burden to be avoided. It is particularly important that there be no obvious favoritism or unfairness in the manner in which referred listings are distributed among the salespeople. When a manager of a firm gets a call from a friend or business acquaintance and it appears that a referred listing will result, his immediate concern is that the salesperson assigned to the listing will do a good job and make a favorable impression on his friend. This will lead him to refer listings to the better, more accomplished sales force members. It is apparent that if this is done all the time, the less favored salespeople will feel slighted, and the firm will not be doing its part to help them out.

The manager must weigh the goodwill of his friend on the one hand against the overall benefit to the company and the morale of its salespeople. Management may establish certain ground rules for referred listings, such as a minimum level of performance required of salespeople before listings will be referred to them. If this is done, scrupulous care must be taken to assure that referrals are distributed fairly among the qualified people.

As an example, a list may be posted on the bulletin board, with the names of qualifying salespeople drawn at random. As referrals come in, management simply goes down the list in choosing the salesperson to whom it is referred. On occasion it may appear worthwhile to skip over someone on the list because of a special case. Perhaps a referral comes in for a listing in an area in which the next salesperson on the list does not frequently operate; it may be assigned to someone else who does work that area well, and the person skipped over will be assured that the next referral will be his. If this sort of thing is done, it should be kept in the open so that the sales force can be assured that management is committed to fairness. In any case, management should reserve the right to skip around in the list if need be, simply because it is management that is running the company, and it is management that knows what is best for the firm as a whole.

The temptation may exist to refer some listings secretly so as to give them to favored salespeople without the knowledge of the others. That does not work for long. In a brokerage firm where people work with one another every day, it is easy for anyone to find out practically anything. Properly handled referrals are prized commodities among highly competitive people, and management can count on the fact that some sort of "grapevine" will exist among its sales force.

Company Listings

Company listings are those secured and managed by the firm itself, rather than being assigned to a specific salesperson. Even in a firm where management ordinarily does not engage in listing and selling, there may be special cases in which management members will take the listing themselves. Often this occurs when the property involved is of a specialized type that no member of the sales force is capable of handling well. It may be located in an area which no one on the sales force regularly works, or it may belong to a particular friend or other contact of the management person, and the manager wants to be absolutely certain it is handled well.

A frequent source of company listings is new houses. Builders are reluctant to list their new homes for sale under exclusive contracts, but they are willing to sign open listings. In such a case, the firm earns no commission at all unless one of its salespeople makes the sale. Therefore, there is no guarantee that a referred listing will generate any commission to the firm or to the salesperson. Also, the total commission paid on new home sales is traditionally quite a bit lower than that paid on resales. For example, in one area where the normal commission on resales is 7%, the commission on new home sales is 5% "of improvements." The improvements are the building itself and other construction; the cost of the lot is left out of the sales commission calculation. Thus, a new $80,000 house on a $20,000 lot would generate a total commission of $4,000 (5% of the value of the building) on a sale totaling $100,000. If that $100,000 sale had been an existing resale, the commission would have been $7,000 (7% of $100,000).

Generally, open listings on new houses are taken as company listings, in the name of the company. No referral is made, the listing is not "worked," and no salesperson is required to handle the listing end of the transaction. If one of the company's salespeople finds the buyer, the company collects the commission from the builder, and the salesperson is paid an appropriate share. Generally, it will not be as high a percentage share as on other commissions, because the firm will have to handle some of the closing and settlement arrangements, just as it would on any other listing. However, the salesperson does not necessarily come up short. Using our previous example, if he had sold a $100,000 resale and collected 25% of the total commission as the salesperson's share (or 50% of the one-half of the commission allocated to selling), he would have received $1,750. In the case of the new house, the entire $4,000 commission can be viewed as a selling commission. If the salesperson received $1,750 out of it, his share would be only 43.75% instead of 50%. In fact, the actual share can be even lower, because in many markets new homes are relatively easier to sell, since the buyer has the opportunity to specify a number of changes and other alterations to suit his tastes, and because many buyers much prefer new homes to older ones. Therefore, the lower commission rate could reflect the easier sale.

NONMONEY COMPENSATION

While the bulk of compensation will take the form of money, it is possible for the firm to reward salespeople and employees in other ways. Contests can offer prizes to top producers: gifts and prizes can be awarded to all who achieve certain goals. Other types of incentive programs with rewards other than money can also be instituted. These will be discussed more fully in the next chapter.

Advertising

One form of highly valued compensation is advertising of the salesperson himself by the firm. Since it is important to a successful salesperson to be as well known as possible, company-sponsored advertising that features his name is extremely valuable. These advertisements can publicize the firm itself, as well as the salesperson involved. Many firms have a policy of running such an ad in the local newspapers on a regular basis. Some determine the identity of the featured salesperson based upon certain performance criteria; in this manner, being featured in the ad can be a form of "prize." A slight disadvantage of this system is that a few of the firm's salespeople may appear in the ads again and again because they consistently outproduce all the others. Another method is to run a separate ad every so often for each salesperson who achieves a certain level of income, commissions, or other performance measure. Some firms routinely run down their entire list of active salespeople as such ads are prepared, and each salesperson knows that every so often he will be featured.

Because of their interest in their communities, a great many real estate salespeople will be involved in charitable, civic, and sometimes governmental organizations. Many firms have a policy of running a feature ad whenever one of their people achieves some civic honor or is elected to an office in a worthy organization. This rewards the salesperson for his community effort and at the same time presents the firm as one that is interested in the welfare of its community.

Support Service

A very real form of compensation is extensive suppport service provided to the sales force by the firm. Here the compensation is in the form of time rather than money, although it costs the firm cash to supply these services. Examples are excellent secretarial service, reliable message taking, assistance in handling details of settlement and closing, and the like. Also, management assistance in some of the areas of normal sales work sometimes can be of benefit. This usually is most valuable to the newer salesperson who is learning the essentials of the business or the methods of the firm.

When support service is good, the sales force is given more time to devote to actual listing and selling work and spends less time on the other paper work and administrative details. Consequently, it is expected that they will be able to get more listings, show more property, and deal with more prospects, thus generating more commission income both for themselves and for the firm.

Training

Training methods will be discussed in the next chapter. However, training sessions of various kinds can be viewed as compensation, since they improve and sharpen skills and so make the salesperson more effective. Many firms regularly have specialists come in and present lectures and seminars on particular points of real estate selling. Also, the firm can encourage its salespeople to attend courses offered outside the firm. One source of these is the REALTORS'® Graduate REALTORS® Institute, administered by the state REALTORS® associations. In many areas, colleges and universities provide specialized real estate courses. Some firms will go so far as to pay all or part of their salepeoples' tuition fees to attend these sessions.

COMPENSATION DURING TRAINING OF NEW SALESPEOPLE

It can be six months or longer before the new salesperson will be generating enough commission income to cover the bare necessities, and possibly quite a bit longer before he can afford luxuries from his real estate income. Therefore, it is frequent practice to put new salespeople on a *draw*. This is a minimal payment at regular intervals, large enough to prevent starvation and bankruptcy, but not enough to warrant continuing in the business on that basis alone. A draw is really an advance of unearned commissions; the draw payments will be deducted from earned commissions, according to some prearranged schedule, once they begin coming in. The salesperson should be required to acknowledge legally that the draws are against future commissions, and that if he does not earn enough commission income to cover them within a certain length of time, his employment may be terminated and he may be liable to pay back the balance.

Being on draw is inconsistent with the independent contractor relationship!

While it can be done by making the draw payments "loans" that legally must be repaid, the U.S. Internal Revenue Service will look very closely at any situation that combines a draw with an independent contractor relationship.

However, it usually is unwise to treat a new salesperson as an independent contractor, since it is most unlikely that he will be able to perform adequately with the necessary degree of independence. Good practice is to make new salespeople employees; in this manner a draw can be paid, if desired, and the employee can be closely supervised and controlled. This supervision and control is essential during the early stages of acclimatization to the job. If the employer is free to require the employee to perform certain functions at certain times, a much more effective training can be carried out. The new salesperson must learn listing and selling procedures, how the office functions, and how to handle a variety of problems. Many firms have specific training sessions that these people ought to attend and may wish them to spend considerable time on floor duty or at other duties as part of their training. They also can be assigned to experienced salespeople willing to take them along on listing tours, showings, or open houses.

An effective training period, which can only be required of an employee, will enable the new salesperson to learn faster and more quickly become skilled enough to warrant the genuine independence of the independent contractor. It also will enable him to sustain himself without the draw; once he has achieved this expertise, the draw can be ended and he can be put on independent contractor status.

Draw status should be recognized as a temporary situation and one the employee should be able to do without as soon as possible. The draw should never be enough to encourage the employee to stay on for it alone. If he does not begin to earn enough commission to cover the draw and a lot more, it should be expected that he eventually will resign voluntarily, although provisions could be made in his contract that would require termination if commission income did not reach a certain level within a given time period.

DISCUSSION QUESTIONS AND PROJECTS

1. Interview sales managers in your area to determine the typical commission split between brokerage firms and their salespeople.

2. From the same source, collect and evaluate information about any bonus plans these firms use. Could you improve any of them? How?

3. Are there any firms in your area using the 100% commission plan or a similar scheme that allows the salesperson to keep the bulk of the commissions he brings in? How do these plans work? How do the managers of the firms using these plans compare them to the methods they formerly used?

4. What is the typical manner in which buying and selling brokerages split the total commission between them on cooperated transactions? Does this have any effect upon the incentive within a particular firm to encourage the firm's own sales force to sell its listings?

5. How do firms in your area handle company referrals and company listings? Can you make any suggestions for improvement to any of them?

6. How can a commission split plan be structured to give the greatest incentive to the sales force to do the kind of business that is most profitable to the brokerage firm?

7. What use can a firm make of its advertising to reward productive salespeople?

8. How do firms in general handle the training and compensation of new salespeople with little or no real estate selling experience? Can you offer any suggestions for improvements?

9. Contrast the commission splitting system of a firm with little support service to that of a firm with extensive support personnel.

A Case Study

SALESPERSON'S COMMISSIONS

Weldon M. is a successful real estate person. He was approached by a competing firm with the suggestion that he resign from his current firm and become employed with them. In his current position, he earned a 50–50 split on all commissions he brought in. Bonuses and productivity overrides brought his average share to more than 55%. The competing firm offered him a straight 65% share of the commissions he generated for them.

He thought about their offer very seriously. He knew that his own firm wasn't showing unusually high profits; obviously, they spent much of the commission income they retained on something. The sales manager was very well paid, but it was his practice to have himself and his staff work out the details of processing sales once the sales force brought them in. This meant that Weldon had a lot of time freed from "busy work." As he reflected, he realized that this extra time was put to use in generating more business. His firm had, over the years, established very close relationships with a number of lenders. Several times in recent months, it was his firm's management that had been able to work out the critical financing needs that meant the difference between a successfully closed deal (and a commission for Weldon) and one that floundered and died.

The competing firm was smaller, and everyone in management was actively involved in sales work as well. They expected the salesperson to "nursemaid" his own deals as much as possible. Management people naturally used their "connections" to get their own deals through first; only then did they try to work things out for other salespeople.

After analyzing the situation, Weldon decided to turn down the offer. Although they would have paid him a better commission split, he decided that he would have had to work much longer on each deal, and probably would not end up making any more money. His own firm made good use of the larger share of the commission that it kept, and he himself benefited greatly from the extra services his firm provided to him. He appreciated the professional attitude that led his company to handle the work he himself did not do well, and that left him as much time as possible to do what he did best, and what he liked doing the most.

REFERENCES

NATIONAL ASSOCIATION OF REAL ESTATE LICENSE LAW OFFICIALS, *Guide to Examinations and Careers in Real Estate*. Reston, VA: Reston Publishing Company, Inc., 1979, pp. 42–43.

PHILLIPS, BARBARA, "Getting Started in Real Estate," in *The McGraw-Hill Real Estate Handbook*, ed. Robert Irwin, ch. 31. New York, NY: McGraw-Hill Book Company, 1984.

PHILLIPS, BARBARA, "Office Management for Brokers," in *The McGraw-Hill Real Estate Handbook*, ed. Robert Irwin, ch. 33. New York, NY: McGraw-Hill Book Company, 1984.

Real Estate Office Management: People Functions Systems, ch. 22. Chicago, IL: REALTORS® National Marketing Institute, 1975.

SHENKEL, WILLIAM M., *Marketing Real Estate* (2nd ed.) Englewood Cliffs, NJ: Prentice Hall, 1985.

ELEVEN

SALES MANAGEMENT

Sales Meetings

Training

Contests and Incentives

Marketing Procedure

Prospect Management

Property Advertising

Assisting Buyer Financing

Broker Liability

Proper Performance

Although real estate salespeople operate independently, there is a need for the brokerage firm to coordinate their actions, provide training and motivation, and supervise the listing and selling processes. In a large firm, this is the duty of the sales manager; in a small firm the broker-owner may take these duties upon himself or assign them on a part time basis to a salesperson. Whatever the system, it is essential that there be some organization of the sales force and regular, systematic communication with its members.

SALES MEETINGS

The most popular means of communication and management of the sales force is the *sales meeting*. Most firms hold them on a regular basis, usually at a certain time every week or two. At the sales meeting, all matters of importance to the entire sales effort are discussed: listings are updated, information about the latest in financial arrangements is given out. The meeting usually is the forum in which all announcements and news of a general nature are aired.

Although the manager conducts the sales meeting, and although he may have an agenda of matters he wants to discuss, salespeople should be given time to bring up matters of particular concern to them. The meeting can be used for problem solving: a salesperson describes a problem he may be having with a particular listing, sale, or prospect, and others can offer suggestions and solutions. The regular meeting also assures that the members of the sales force get together frequently. This is important because discussion of problems and the various elements of the work gives each one a forum for the exchange of ideas with others who are familiar with the work.

Sales meetings provide an excellent means for the firm to communicate with its sales force. Considerable effort should be made to provide useful talks, interesting speakers, and important information at each meeting, so that the salespeople come to look forward to them. Information that will make them more effective and more knowledgeable in their jobs is what always is needed; these people are professionals and will be interested in anything that will help them. Reports should be timely.

If changes in the laws affecting real estate brokerage have occurred or are being contemplated, these should be presented. If financing markets are in turmoil, the sales manager should present the latest information at every meeting. Mortgage officers at local banks and savings institutions should be encouraged to visit from time to time to answer questions and explain the latest circumstances in the market. Similarly, people representing FHA and VA loan processing offices should be invited occasionally. Whenever new company listings are acquired, they should be described fully. Updates on sales activity of both the firm and individual performances should be presented. Any changes in the firm's policies should be aired in sales meetings. New employees and new salespeople should be introduced.

TRAINING

There are all kinds of training devices the firm can use to sharpen and improve the skills of the sales force. Many of these can be used in the firm's offices, while others such as outside courses are held elsewhere.

Seminars

A frequently used training method is the informal seminar conducted during or after the sales meeting, while everyone is present and has the time. One of the successful salespeople can instruct the others on his methods, or a special instructor can be brought in. Some seminars last only for one session, while others may last for several sessions. A variety of topics can be covered. A firm may offer a seminar on financing methods, listing techniques, or selling procedures, among many topics. The particular topics offered will depend on management's perception of the needs of the firm and its sales force. It should be remembered that regular updating of the conditions of the market and other routine reports made at sales meetings also are a form of training, since they assure that the sales force is operating with the most up-to-date information.

A frequent form of seminar is the "inspirational" session, in which a motivation specialist will provide an uplifting and enthusiastic presentation designed to improve the self-confidence of the listener and to reinforce his self-esteem. These are quite variable in their effects. With disappointing frequency they tend to inspire the listeners for a few days, but in a short while the "inspiration" has worn off and they return to their regular pattern. However, some firms have found that these presentations have long-lasting effect. The important factor seems to be the individual giving the program and, to a lesser extent, the program itself. A firm considering such an effort should do considerable research with other firms that have done so to be sure to select a presentation that will have good effect and will stay with the salespeople for some time.

Role Playing Sessions

A frequently used form of training is *role playing*. Here the salesperson is asked to get up in front of the others and play the role of a participant in some aspect of the business. Another will act as a salesperson and will try to get the first one to agree to buy a property or to overcome his objections as he tries to convince him to list, buy, accept a contract offer, and so on. The other salespeople will observe the scene, and when it is done they will critique it and offer suggestions.

Role-playing sessions can be valuable training devices, but they must be conducted with great care. First, each scene should last only a few minutes. It should be taken seriously by all parties concerned. One player will be the *foil*; the other player will have the goal of convincing the foil to undertake some action or agree with some proposition, in a framework designed to be as close as possible to genuine practice. The foil has to be particularly careful. By playing the role of, say, a property owner who is reluctant to list his real estate, he must not overdo it. Also, he must realize that the average seller does not know as much of the business as he does as a salesperson, so he must take care to make sure that his responses are reasonable given the role he plays.

Frequently the role of the foil will be played by the sales manager, the principal broker, or one of the senior salespeople, on the theory that they have had a lot of experience and are more aware of these kinds of situations. A problem arises, however, because as successful salespeople they often are very forceful, dominant personalities with good powers of persuasion. Thus they might not be good foils, because they are not the typical personality types salespeople will encounter in their work. If they get too involved in their roles, they will dominate the less experienced salespeople, and the value of the experience will be lost.

It is better to have less experienced salespeople play both roles, so that they can see the situation from both sides. The manager, broker, and senior salespeople can critique the session and offer their suggestions and advice in that manner.

Recorded Sessions

For many years various kinds of training courses have been available on cassettes. Even more effective is videotaping. For an investment of $1,000 or so, a firm can purchase a videocamera and player. The actions of a salesperson in a training session can be taped and played back immediately; by viewing himself in action the salesperson can learn a great deal about his performance and can join in the critique himself. Also, it is possible to buy sets of videocassettes with prerecorded training sessions done by professional real estate educators, actors, and others. Many firms use these in their training programs for new salespeople, but they also can be used for brushing up skills or teaching new material to experienced salespeople.

CONTESTS AND INCENTIVES

Many brokerage firms use contests of some kind as an incentive to the sales force. There are three basic kinds of contests:

1. *Each salesperson competes against the others.* Such a contest might offer a trip, a prize of money, extra referred listings, or some other incentive to the salesperson who gets the most listings, sells the most property, or does best in these combined. The disadvantage to this kind of contest is that there is only one winner, and all others are losers even though they may have expended a lot of effort to try to win.
2. *The sales force is divided into teams that compete against one another.* The number of teams depends upon the size of the sales force; the ideal team should have three

to five members. The winning team receives a group prize; losing teams may receive consolation prizes. This kind of contest fosters cooperation among team members and among the sales force. The prizes should not be extraordinarily valuable, since the excitement of the contest itself often is good motivation. Some firms have very good success with a contest in which its sales force is divided into two teams. The winning team is treated to dinner at an elegant restaurant and the losers get a free meal at a fast food chain.

3. *The salesperson competes against himself.* In this kind of contest, everyone can win, since the prizes are awarded on the basis of how much business the individual does. A common contest of this nature is a "points" contest. For example, getting a listing that is subsequently sold is worth 5 points; selling a property is worth 5 points; holding an open house is worth 1 point; a salesperson selling his own listing receives 2 points; and so on. The salesperson's prize depends upon the number of points earned in a given period of time. It is possible for each person in the firm to receive the top prize if all earn the points necessary to get it. One firm regularly holds a contest of this nature every quarter. The prizes range from a portable black and white television (for 20 points earned in the quarter) to a Cadillac automobile (for 300 points earned in one quarter). It might be pointed out that no one ever has earned the Cadillac, but the fact that the firm actually will award it lends excitement to the contest.

The objective of contests is to provide an incentive for more productivity. Since the prizes cost money, offering a lot of contests will reduce the ability of the firm to award cash bonuses. Generally, firms find that a contest or two every year will spark interest and, if they are properly scheduled, will liven up business during normally slack times. At the same time, they will not cost so much money that the firm's bonus program has to be cut back significantly.

MARKETING PROCEDURE

The marketing procedure of the sales force should be kept under constant supervision by the firm. Techniques and methods should be constantly updated. Following is a discussion of some of the common procedures used.

Appraisals

Most firms, as they solicit listings, will present the property owner with a brief appraisal of property, along with a suggestion of the price that it should be listed for. *These are not professional appraisals, and they should not be presented as such!* Generally, a few recent sales should be presented as a basis for determining a reasonable listing price for the property under consideration. Figure 11–1 shows an example of a letter reporting the results of such an appraisal.

Note that the letter makes no mention that an appraisal has been undertaken. The potential seller is presented with bare details about recent sales in his immediate neighborhood of properties similar to his. The summary, which suggests a listing price, is not represented as an estimate of value in the true appraisal sense, but only as a suggestion. If these appraisals are used, the bro-

DOVER REALTY COMPANY

1776 Twelfth Street, Waltham, Xxxxx 12345   (908) 555-4321

September 28, 1988

Jackson Marshall

Vera Marshall

12108 Cedar Road

Waltham, XXXX 12345

Dear Mr. and Mrs. Marshall:

We have examined your home at 12108 Cedar Road and compared it to other similar homes in your area which have recently sold. From this information, we believe that a listing price of $96,500 for your home would be reasonable. This would give "bargaining room" to result in a selling price which we believe would be over $90,000. Please note that this is a survey of available information, and not a professional fee appraisal.

We examined the following recent sales:

(1) 12101 Allison Road. Two bedrooms, two baths, kitchen, great room, dining area. Average lot and landscaping, excellent interior decoration, upgraded carpeting and appliances. 1401 square feet. Contracted 9/16/88, will close within 3 weeks. Listed at $96,000, sold for $93,000, or $66.38/square foot.

(2) 12222 Mallow Lane. Two bedrooms, two baths, kitchen, living room, den. This is the same model as your home. However, landscaping is only average and there is no carpet or appliance upgrade and no special

Figure 11-1. Sample Appraisal Letter.

decor. 1381 square feet. Contracted 9/2/88, closed 9/25/88. Listed at $93,500, sold for $89,900 or $65.00/square foot.

(3) 4335 Toronado Circle. Two bedrooms, kitchen, den, living area. Excellent landscaping, superior appliance upgrade, average decor and carpet, good lot. 1277 square feet. Contracted 8/17/88, closed 9/19/88. Listed at $88,900, sold for $85,500 or $66.95/square foot.

This information suggests to us a base price of about $66 per square foot, or about $91,000. However, the excellent landscaping, appliances and decor of your home could bring as much as $1.50/square foot additional, or up to $93,000 or so, based upon your home's area of 1381 square feet. We suggest listing at $96,500.

I hope that you find this information satisfactory, and I look forward to listing your home with us.

Sincerely,

Joe Chatham
Senior Sales Associate

Figure 11-1. (*Continued*)

kerage should be prepared to defend any information and conclusions presented, and they should not be used to defend unusually low or high prices that the market is not likely to support. If it is difficult to gather such information, the informal appraisal should not be used at all.

Open Houses

The open house is a favorite selling device. Open House signs can be found most Sunday afternoons in neighborhoods where there is frequent real estate activity. The objective of the open house is to attract prospects. It is rare in practice that a prospect who looks at an open house will buy that particular one, but from the salesperson's point of view that does not matter. If he can find prospects, he gets to know who they are and can try to arrange to show them other properties to their liking.

Three kinds of people come to open houses: nosy neighbors, curiosity seekers, and genuine prospects who may be interested in buying a home. The salesperson, of course, is interested in the last. However, he should treat all visitors with friendliness and make sure they receive his card before they leave; while they may only want to look through their neighbor's closets or get in out of the rain right now, they may be buyers some other day, and it does not hurt to make oneself known to them.

The salesperson should get the name and telephone number of each person who visits the open house. If at all possible he should accompany visitors as they look around. The owners and residents of the property should go somewhere else; the salesperson does not want them around, and they will make the lookers uncomfortable. A house is best held open when it is newly listed; if it is held open more than once, later open houses will usually attract fewer genuine prospects.

Showing Property

It is almost impossible to sell property to someone without showing it to him first; property showing is probably the most significant activity of a salesperson in terms of the time spent on it.

A set of general rules for showing property is given in the following box. They should be observed as closely as possible. Showing property means entering someone's home as a stranger with strangers in tow. The privacy and property of the owners must be protected. The salesperson must also protect the right of the listing agent to know that a showing occurs. This is not difficult in the case of a listing made by the salesperson himself or someone in his firm. However, if the listing is held by another firm, the salesperson should contact the other firm's agent and have him arrange for the showing.

Many firms leave keys to listed homes in *lockboxes* attached to the doorknob or fitted over the door itself. These are designed to be opened with a special key; each firm will have its own key pattern to its boxes. The box contains

1. Try to make appointments at least twenty-four hours in advance.

2. Try to see to it that residents of the property are out of the home when it is shown. If this is impossible, make sure that they are in another part of the home as you show it. Better yet, send them outside while you show the inside, and send them in while you show the outside.

3. Call a few minutes before you arrive, if possible. Also, call anytime it is necessary for you to change the schedule or if you are running more than five minutes late.

4. *Do not take children along!* You want the prospect to look at the property, not to watch the children. Children quickly get bored on showing trips and must be watched constantly to make sure that they do not disturb anything in the homes being shown.

5. *Do not take anyone else along who will not be making the decision to buy.* Grandparents like to go along sometimes. Leave them at home, babysitting the kids. You don't need anybody else commenting about how high prices are or how they don't like what they see. Do not allow someone else to intimidate your prospects.

6. Listen a lot more than you talk. You don't have to open the bathroom door and say, "This is the bathroom," or point to an appliance and say, "This is the dishwasher." Answer all questions as best you can. When you make conversation ask if they like what they see, and find out what they like and don't like and WHY. You should use a showing trip to get information about your prospect's needs, so you can find him the home he wants.

7. Research the property before you show it. If at all possible, take a look on your own first. Nothing makes you look more incompetent than wandering around a property without knowing where you are. If you have seen it first,

a key to the listed home; anyone who has a key to the lockbox will be able to get into the home.

While this is a convenient way to make access available to authorized agents, careful security must surround the use of the lockbox and the disposition of the keys to it. In some areas, firms that cooperate with one another regularly will exchange lockbox keys; otherwise an agent desiring to show property listed by another must stop by the other's office to get the lockbox key. Whoever in the brokerage office is in charge of the lockbox keys must keep careful track of them and must be able at any time to give an accurate rundown of who has them. When the property has been shown, the salesperson should return the lockbox key as soon as possible, especially if it was obtained at the office of another firm.

In some localities, the local Board of REALTORS® has instituted a lockbox system for member firms and licensees. The local Board supervises the system, and all lockboxes used by all members can be opened with a single key. Member firms apply, on behalf of each of their salespeople, to the Board for the keys and the Board keeps records of who has keys. Both the salesperson who has the key and the firm are responsible to the local Board for each key issued. A big you can prepare your prospects for what they will see. If you are unable to see the property first, tell your prospects that you haven't seen it yet either. Say something like, "This one was listed so recently that I haven't had time to take a look at it myself." Even in these situations, you should get a lot of information from the listing agent.

8. If the prospects really like what they see, begin talking about writing up an offer, even if it means eliminating other scheduled properties from the showing trip. When people have found what they want, they lose interest in looking.

9. Do not schedule a showing trip to last more than two or three hours. You do not want to exhaust your prospects. If time is precious (they're in for the weekend from out of town), you can violate this rule.

10. If you stop for refreshments, pick up the check. It's only a few dollars and it's a very nice gesture. Avoid alcohol at rest stops, especially for yourself.

11. When you arrive at a property, ring the doorbell two or three times before using the key to enter. When you enter, go first and announce your presence to make sure nobody is at home. If someone answers the door, introduce yourself and the prospects and then try to get the residents to get out of the way. (See #2.)

12. When you leave property, *make sure* that you leave it locked and that you leave it the way you found it. If weather is messy, make sure nobody tracks anything in even if it means removing shoes and walking around in stocking feet.

13. *Always* clear showings through the listing agent. Never show property without the listing agent's knowledge. If no one is at home when you show, leave your card in a conspicuous place. Leave a card with the resident if he is there.

advantage of this type of arrangement is that firms do not have to keep each others' keys on hand. Also, there is rigorous supervision of the use of the keys.

Many firms do not use lockboxes at all, especially in relatively high crime areas or on houses that contain a lot of valuables. In these cases, the keys to the home are kept in the firm's office and must be checked out by salespeople who wish to show the property.

PROSPECT MANAGEMENT

A touchy point in many firms is the manner in which a given salesperson claims a particular prospect. Clearly, if a salesperson has spent a lot of time working with a client, that client should not be fair game for other salespeople in the firm. Most firms have a system that allows a salesperson to "protect" a prospect to whom he has provided a certain minimum of service. Listing prospects can be protected by going so far as to prepare an appraisal for them, as an example. In other firms, a salesperson may "register" any prospects he has found and protect them in that manner; however, in such a system it is good policy to require that the salesperson achieve some result within a certain span of time or else lose the right to protect the prospect against other members of the firm.

On occasion it becomes necessary for one salesperson to offer service to another's protected prospect. The protecting salesperson may be out-of-town, showing property to another, ill, or otherwise unable to provide service. Some firms have elaborate formulas for allocating commissions earned in cases where more than one salesperson is involved. Others allow prospect sharing but insist that the salespeople themselves work out the allocation of the commission. In such cases it is best to get them to agree in a written statement that the sales manager can put in the file for that particular sale.

Protection of prospects among firms is a different matter. There generally is no law regarding that matter, except the provisions in license law that forbid licensees to negotiate directly with property owners who have exclusive listings with other brokers, without the listing broker's permission. The difficulty frequently is compounded by the prospect himself, particularly in the case of a potential buyer. He may contact salespeople from several firms and have each of them show property. A salesperson can guard against this to some extent by assuring a prospect that he can show virtually any listed property and that consultation with another agent is not necessary, but there still is no guarantee that the prospect will not look elsewhere.

Good practice requires that a salesperson not make a frequent practice of soliciting prospects of other firms. Mistakes will be made, but salespeople who appear to make a habit of trying to steal others' prospects soon will find that the others will be reluctant to deal with them or offer them cooperation when they need it. It should be noted that respondents to advertisements or prospects solicited from open houses might be prospects of other firms or salespeople in one's own firm. When dealing with them, an effort should be made to make sure that they are not protected by anyone else or dealing with another firm. However, if a prospect finds the agent he is dealing with unsatisfactory, he should not be prevented from dealing with another.

PROPERTY ADVERTISING

In most areas, advertising in the classified section of the newspaper is the mainstay of residential brokerage advertising. While ads appear every day of the week, a weekend edition of the newspaper usually will carry the bulkiest section of real estate advertising. Some newspapers have special real estate sections featuring syndicated articles concerning real estate matters, and for which real estate brokerage and other advertising is eagerly solicited.

Even where a special real estate section of the newspaper is offered, most residential brokers handling resales will continue to use the classified section, although this section may be integrated into the real estate section to make it look bigger. Classified advertising seems very old fashioned and not very imaginative.

Many brokerage firms have tried advertising in other media, but almost inevitably they discover that use of the classified section reaches the audience they need, and that even if other media do show useful results, they are rarely as effective as classified advertising.

The apparent function of classified advertising is to advertise particular properties the firm has for sale. And indeed it does do that, but it serves many more important purposes for the advertising and promotion of the brokerage itself and of the salespeople. It is rare that someone who responds to an advertisement for a particular home or other property ends up buying the property advertised. However, his response makes him known to the brokerage and salesperson, and therefore makes him a prospect. If the advertised property is unsuitable, perhaps some other will be more attractive. The salesperson gets exposure in the advertising because his name usually is included in advertising for his listings and interested prospects will call him. The brokerage benefits because the advertising features its name as well.

The more homes a firm advertises, the more frequently its name appears. Frequent appearance of the name suggests to a reader of the ads that the firm has lots of listings and therefore can show a wide variety of properties. While the owners of properties advertised may think that they are the major beneficiary of the ads, the fact is that advertising largely benefits the firm and its salespeople. Indirectly, of course, it then will benefit the owners of listed property by helping the firm to accumulate a larger number of prospects.

Column Ads

There are two types of classified advertising: *column ads* and multiple-column ads, which often are nicknamed *tombstones*. The column ad can be categorized into two groups, the single ad and the multiple ad. All column ads fit into a single classified column.

The single ad is the kind most people think of when they consider classified advertisement. It is a few lines long and advertises a single property. The multiple ad is longer; it may advertise several properties. Many firms design their advertisements to feature the name of the brokerage in much larger type than the rest of the ad; it may take up as much as half the space devoted to a single ad. A firm with several properties to advertise may choose to put all of them into a multiple ad, run each of them as a single ad, or do a combination. Some firms feel that the multiple ad is more impressive, since it gives the impression that the firm has a number of properties by listing several in one place. Also, since the firm's name appears only once, less advertising space will be used to advertise a given number of properties, compared to the space required for single ads for each. This will slightly reduce the advertising cost per property, and cost is an important consideration.

Other firms prefer several single ads, especially if they use a large, recognizable symbol or representation of the firm's name in each ad. While the cost per property will be a bit higher, the reasoning is that having the firm's name peppered all over the page, instead of in one place, is an advantage. It will be difficult for anyone looking at the page to miss seeing the name, and it also can give the impression that the firm is very active because the name crops up in several places.

Tombstone Ads

The tombstone ad stretches across two or more columns. These ads usually appear in the classified section on the day of the week on which the largest number of real estate ads are featured. The ad will feature the name of the brokerage in very large print; in ads that are quite long, the name may appear at both top and bottom for more effect. Usually the ads will advertise the open houses being held that day and feature a number of other listings.

Size is important for a good tombstone ad; the larger it is the better, since the very size of the ad and its large concentration of listings impress the viewer. There is a limit to size, of course. While some firms have tried ads as large as two full newspaper pages side by side, a quarter-page ad is effective, also. If the firm wishes to advertise more than that, it may be preferable to take out two or more tombstone ads, perhaps differentiated by the area of town in which the listed properties are located.

Since they involve extra work to typeset, and because they must use larger type size than column ads to be attractive and readable, the cost per property advertised in tombstones is much higher than for column ads. They can be justified on the day that the newspaper traditionally features most real estate advertising because large numbers of people will turn to them. Few firms use them on other days.

Composition of Advertisements

Advertising space costs money. Therefore, great care should be taken to assure that it is used effectively to gain for the firm and its salespeople the maximum exposure per dollar spent. Many firms require that all ads be written by the sales manager or some other person who knows how to write an ad properly. If this is not done, then at the very least the sales manager should review each salesperson's ads before they are submitted for publication.

Ads can be large or small. It is possible, using accepted abbreviations, to compose a two-line ad that transmits the necessary information, but there is doubt that an ad so small will attract the desired attention. On the other hand, it is not advisable to use long, wordy ads, which may discourage people from reading them fully. Generally three to five lines will be plenty. It is not necessary to put in every item of interest about a particular property. Prospective buyers usually will know something about the areas in which they are interested and something about the kinds of property they may expect to find there. Furthermore, it is impossible to describe a property accurately in the relatively few words available in a proper ad.

Brevity and generality in the ad have an additional advantage: Brief descriptions attract potential buyers who may want something similar to the advertised property, but not exactly like it. Once the salesperson has the opportunity to talk to a prospect he can find out what sort of property the prospect is looking for and can review his inventory of listings. However, the more detailed an ad is, the more limited the number of prospects it will draw. An ad that describes a home as a four-bedroom, ranch style colonial at $98,000 will draw more response than if it goes on to describe a lot of minor details; the details will cause a number of prospects to pass the property over (and therefore not call the firm or salesperson) because the ad tells them the property is not suitable.

Even if relatively little detailed information is given, the ad can be made attractive enough and long enough to generate interest. This is done by pointing out features that generally are important to most people. These include such physical features as fireplaces, good landscaping, location on quiet streets, nearby facilities, and the like. Phrases such as "beautifully decorated," "custom deluxe kitchen," "zoned heat and air conditioning," "energy saving," and the like rarely will turn anyone away from inquiring about a propety. Other features such as advantageous financing terms may also be featured. Low down payments, low interest loans or loan assumptions, and the availability of second mortgage financing where large equities are required are sure-fire selling points and should be featured whenever they are available.

It should be remembered that the main function of this type of advertising is to feature the firm and its salespeople, and to bring in prospects. Buyers will respond to advertisements which catch their interest. Potential sellers will also be impressed with a firm that has a large number of listings and appears to be active in the market and capable of selling.

Truth in Advertising

Many states and localities have laws and regulations governing advertising. Blatant misstatement of fact is always a legal violation. However, in some areas more subtle exaggeration and the like may be specifically prohibited.

Usually the legal system will allow advertising and sales effort to use a certain degree of *puffery*. Puffery is not easy to define. It can be ridiculous exaggeration which any reasonably intelligent person would recognize. ("Use our product and your love life will be perfect." "Buy this house and you will be happy forever.") It also includes *euphemism*, where flowery or cute language is used instead of blunt truth. A tiny, cramped house is called a "doll house." A dilapidated home is a "handyman's special," or "needs a little tender loving care." An ad suggesting that the buyer "use your imagination" may mean a peculiar floor plan, an interior that needs considerable rehabilitation, or many other things.

Some other statements, however, may have to be verifiable and true if they are made. Regulation Z (see Chapter 3) requires that any advertisement for real estate mentioning financing terms must also state the annual percentage rate of interest (APR). Stating the size of the home or building (usually in square feet) may be inadvisable in some areas because court decisions have held that advertisers are liable to buyers for damages if there is any discrepancy. (Square footage traditionally is measured around the *outside* of the heated area of the building and does not include porches, garages, balconies, or unfinished attic or basement space. However, the courts may not necessarily agree with this method.)

Value judgments may have to be avoided in advertising. What is a beautiful and stylish home to one person may be gaudy and pretentious to someone else. More importantly, advertising and selling technique should *never* make promises which may not be literally true. A "20-year roof" may leak in five years. "Low utility bills" may not seem so attractive to a buyer moving from an area where costs are even lower. Most important, *no selling technique should ever suggest that a purchase will produce future gain!* It is tempting to suggest to a buyer that a given purchase can be sold at a nice profit sometime in the future, but it is impossible for anyone to predict such a thing.

ASSISTING BUYER FINANCING

Most buyers have to borrow money in order to be able to make real estate purchases. As a result, the mortgage industry is, in dollar volume, one of the largest business segments in our economy. New mortgage commitments amount to hundreds of billions of dollars annually.

Brokers, because they are familiar with the real estate market, often are in a position to assist buyers with their financing arrangements. Often this may mean no more than introducing the buyer to a loan officer. Loan availability and terms will often be the key element in whether or not a potential sale can occur. Interest rates are a key factor in the willingness of buyers to commit themselves to purchases. While the price of the home is very important, nearly every buyer will want to know how much initial cash is needed, and what the monthly payments will be.

Knowing what is happening in the mortgage market is an essential component of a competent real estate professional's knowledge. Usually there is no such thing as *the* interest rate; rates and terms will vary somewhat among lenders. The salesperson or the firm's sales manager ought to know at any given time which mortgage lenders have the best terms, and should try to steer buyers toward them. This saves the buyers money and increases their satisfaction with the firm's performance. Satisfied customers provide good references and good word-of-mouth advertising for the firm.

Professional brokerage firms make it a point to keep up-to-date information about financing rates and terms available in their areas. Mortgage lending officers are frequent visitors to their sales meetings, to keep the sales force current with the latest information. Many multilist systems also survey local lenders and put their rates and terms into the computer files and books where they can be accessed by member firms and their salespeople.

Sometimes real estate brokerage firms will be paid by mortgage lenders for referring borrowers to them. Such "finder's fees" are accepted practice in many areas, and collecting them usually will not violate the broker's agency responsibility to the seller. Certainly, helping the buyer to find financing is no violation, since it facilitates the sale—which is, after all, the whole objective of the agency relationship. This is one area in which the broker's actions on behalf of the buyer also definitely benefit the seller.

BROKER LIABILITY

Throughout this book we have stressed that the real estate brokerage firm operates within a very strict legal environment. License law and agency law are two examples, but there is much more. The industry has been trying for decades to convince the public that real estate brokerage is a profession. These efforts are now bearing fruit. While it is prestigious to be considered a professional person, it also carries its own additional responsibilities. A major aspect of professionalism is that it involves specialized knowledge and/or talent. Again and again the courts have held that the public may expect more from a person recognized as a professional. When professionals do not provide what is thought to be a professional service, they may be sued for *malpractice*. Physicians and lawyers have been sued for centuries; now real estate brokers often are too.

A professional provides advice, guidance, or skills not normally found in ordinary people. The public has a legal right to expect a high standard of performance from professionals, and are entitled to damages if they do not get it. In the past decade or so, real estate professionals have come under increasing scrutiny by the courts. As is often the case in other aspects of the real estate business, this trend originated largely in California.

In the early 1980s several brokerage firms in that state were successfully sued for their performance in arranging "creative financing" among buyers and sellers during the credit crunch of 1979–84. Buyers could not afford the high prevailing interest rates, and so sought purchases in which they could assume a low-interest loan. However, many such situations involved properties in which sellers had large equities (the difference between the value of the property and the amount of the assumable loan). Buyers usually did not have enough cash to buy out such large equities. With the broker's advice, these sellers took some cash and a junior mortgage from the buyer for the remainder of the equity. These mortgages usually had modest payments and were at a relatively low interest rate. However, they were written to come due fairly soon, sometimes in as little as two or three years. The idea was that during that time interest rates probably would fall and the buyer could refinance the entire property, paying off the assumed loan and the junior mortgage to the seller with the proceeds.

Unfortunately, interest rates did not fall as quickly as some of these arrangements anticipated, and some buyers were unable to refinance when the junior mortgage came due. Some sellers foreclosed; some of the buyers sued the brokers who had arranged the transaction. Other sellers reluctantly renegotiated the terms of the junior mortgages, allowing the buyer more time to pay; some of these sellers sued their brokers. In many of these cases the courts ruled that the brokers involved had indeed given bad advice, and found against them.

This is a spectacular example of broker liability, but there are many other pitfalls. Improperly qualifying a buyer can lead to trouble. Assumption of VA and older FHA loans can, too; few sellers realize that when such loans are assumed, the original borrower *may still remain liable to the lender*. If the buyer who assumes the loan later defaults, the seller who originated the loan may then be claimed against. A broker who brings a seller a buyer who later defaults on such a loan assumption may find himself in court over it, especially if he did not advise the seller of this risk.

Sellers expect competent service from brokers, and they deserve it from someone who is going to collect 5%, 7%, or more of their sale proceeds. The broker is expected to give advice, especially to the seller. One advantage of hiring a broker is that a competent one is good at smoothing out potential trouble spots between buyer and seller, and aiding negotiations to a succcessful conclusion. All of these factors contribute to the broker's professionalism, both in fact and in the image the public has of him. But they all also represent areas of possible liability as well. Liability for one's actions is one of the prices of professionalism.

How, then, to deal with these problems? The best way, of course, is to handle things so that if anything goes wrong, no one will think it is the broker's fault. This is not easy to do, especially in tandem with the broker's goal of being thought of as providing good service. The best course of action is to make everyone involved aware of the entire situation, the potential trouble spots as well as the advantages. A good rule to follow, when possible, is this: *explain but do not advise*. What this means is that the broker provides others with the information they need to make decisions *themselves*. Of course, the broker should make sure that the information provided is accurate and reliable.

PROPER PERFORMANCE

In dealings with the general public, the broker must act within the law and the proper ethics of the profession. *Proper performance* is essential not only to avoid legal action, but also to maintain a reputation for honesty and reliability. The brokerage firm's management should insist that all salespeople conduct themselves in this manner.

Some people do not view the real estate brokerage business with great esteem. This is in spite of the fact that just as in any other business the large majority of brokerage professionals act with integrity and pride in their business dealings. In fact, poor practice is not significantly more frequent in the brokerage business than it is in most others, but for various reasons the unsavory or inept activities of a few loom larger in the public mind. One of the reasons is that it is a complicated and difficult business. Still, it is not difficult for people to get into the business; many believe that once they have passed the licensing examination they have accumulated all the necessary knowledge and are perfectly prepared for all aspects of it. In fact, most full time brokerage professionals will tell you that one of the genuine plagues of the profession is the brand-new, ill-prepared, and ignorant licensee who sets out blithely into the business—often only part time—woefully unable to handle even the simplest transaction. Brokerage is a business in which having only a little knowledge can be harmful indeed.

Another factor is that real estate plays such an important role in the lives of most people. We all need a place to live; the businesses we deal with need offices, and we need parking lots, stores, warehouses, and factories. In addition to providing us with the space we need for living, working, and playing, real estate in recent years has become a popular investment vehicle. This interest in real estate often seems to have the effect of making everyone into a self-styled "expert." Only a little knowledge is dangerous to a consumer, too; in spite of the broker's warnings, one may leap into a transaction, find it less attractive than expected, and then search around for someone to blame. At that point the broker becomes a handy outlet for frustrations the individual may have caused entirely by himself.

Buying a home is usually the largest single purchase a family may ever make. Twenty-five to 40% of income may be devoted to making payments and maintenance on a purchase that can amount to three or four years' total income in price. Obviously, where such enormous amounts of a family's resources are involved, there will be a great sensitivity to difficulties that may arise, and once again the broker can be an attractive and convenient target for blame.

DISCUSSION QUESTIONS AND PROJECTS

1. What is the function of the sales meeting?
2. In the class (if this book is being used in a classroom situation), try some role playing situations involving typical brokerage problems.
3. Draft a sample appraisal of a home in your area. You can probably get information about recent sales from a brokerage firm.
4. Write some sample advertisements for a property selected by you.
5. What is the purpose of property advertising?
6. How can contests be used to increase the sales force productivity? What problems should be guarded against?
7. How should property be shown? What rules should be observed?
8. Why is it best not to have property owners or occupants present during open houses or when property is being shown?
9. Try to attend sales meetings of two or three brokerage firms that will let you observe. How are the meetings used? What sorts of things are discussed? Could you suggest any improvements?
10. Are there any limitations on real estate advertising in your area? If so, what are they, and how do they affect the effectiveness of such advertising?

11. Are there any unusual "puffery" terms or euphemisms that are used in real estate advertising in your area? Make a list of them, along with their "real" definitions.

12. Why should real estate salespeople be knowledgeable about terms and requirements in the mortgage market?

13. Investigate the issue of broker liability in your community. Have there been any unusual or ground-breaking cases in your locality or state?

Case Studies

PROPER PERFORMANCE

1. A prospective buyer asks the broker or salesperson whether or not the asking price of a property is reasonable. The broker must remember that he is employed by the seller and not the buyer (except in the unusual case where a buyer has, indeed, employed him, in which case this discussion would not apply). In situations such as this the broker should put himself in the seller's shoes: Would *he* admit that the asking price is unrealistic in a conversation with a potential buyer? No, he wouldn't.

Many prospective buyers assume that the broker works for them and is going to protect their every interest, so they have no compunction about asking him questions they would never consider mentioning to the owner himself. It is best if the broker can let them know just what his legal responsibilities are, so long as he doesn't do it so crassly that he scares them away in the process. Of course, if the broker honestly feels that the asking price is reasonable, he should say so. If he thinks the property is a bargain, he should say so. In either case he is doing his best to convince the buyer he should buy, and that is what he is hired by the seller to do.

However, suppose the broker honestly believes that the property *is* overpriced. He can protect himself from this situation in the first place by not soliciting listings from sellers who wish to price their offerings unreasonably, but that is no help in the case where he is showing an overpriced property listed by another broker. It is a common misconception, even among real estate licensees, that in this case the broker who is showing the prospective buyer around is, somehow, that buyer's agent, and the listing broker is the seller's agent. This is not the case; *both* brokers are agents of the seller. Therefore, the broker cannot say the property is overpriced, at least not directly. The best technique is to get the prospective buyer to make up his own mind, by asking him what *he* thinks. He can consider the asking prices and characteristics of other properties he has looked at, and more properties can be shown to him to get his reaction. If a property is overpriced, he soon will get the idea, by comparing it with others.

2. The prospective buyer asks the broker, "How much should I offer for this property?" This case is similar to the first one; the broker should try to get the prospect to make up his own mind about the amount to be offered, while of course trying to get him to offer as much as possible.

3. The buyer asks the broker to try to talk the seller into accepting his offer. The broker should make it clear that the offer will be submitted promptly, and that the seller will make a decision quickly. The broker should not let the buyer assume that he will act on his behalf in negotiation with the seller. If he does so as a sales ploy, to give the buyer the false impression that he is on his side, he is being unethical at best and probably is breaking the law, depending upon the exact circumstances.

4. The broker refuses to allow another broker to show property listed. This is a very touchy problem. By far the best way of handling it is to make it perfectly clear and *agreeable* with the owner that the broker will not cooperate with other brokers. Some brokers only refuse to cooperate with certain other brokers, and for what they think are legitimate reasons. In such a case the broker should advise his principal that he will not deal with certain other firms because of his previous business experience with them; he need not divulge his reasons (it is not necessary to court a libel or slander suit), but he should make it clear to the owner, writing it into the listing agreement if possible, that the broker will cooperate only with other brokers of his own choosing. Otherwise, the owner might have a case supporting poor performance by the broker, especially in areas where cooperation among brokers is a common practice.

5. The seller tells the broker not to divulge to anyone that the house is infested with termites. If he agrees to this, the broker is becoming a party to fraud or misrepresentation. Legally, he has no choice under these circumstances: either he must convince the seller to allow him to divulge the information, or he must terminate the listing. Otherwise he risks his reputation, his license, and his business, as well as possible suits for damages and criminal prosecution. It is perfectly legal for him to cancel a contract if maintaining it would require him to act illegally.

6. The broker aids (and gets paid for) financing arrangements for a buyer. This is normally all right. Even though he is performing a service for a buyer, by doing so he facilitates a sale for his owner-employer and so serves him too. The broker may do anything he wishes for a client or other parties so long as it does not interfere with his ability to properly represent his employers. It is wise to include in listing agreements language that notifies owners that the broker may receive compensation from other sources in return for such things.

7. The broker shows a prospect several houses. This is reasonable because it enables him to arrange a sale with that buyer. While the sale will not benefit everyone with whom he has listings, it is presumed that the same sort of practice will eventually benefit them all, and showing property in order to determine the genuine wants and needs of the buyer is accepted as normal brokerage practice.

8. A broker refuses to show a house to a prospect he knows cannot afford it. This too is permissible. The broker owes it to his employers not to waste their time or use their homes and properties for unnecessary sightseeing. So long as the broker has every reasonable cause to believe that the prospect is not capable of buying the property, he has nothing to fear by refusing to show it to the client, and indeed, may be doing everyone involved a favor by keeping that prospect's attention elsewhere.

REFERENCES

"Creative Sales Meetings Help Motivate Salespeople," *Real Estate Today*, April 1980, pp. 51-53.

DAY, JOE II, "Farming: the Hydroponic Method," *Real Estate Today*, January, 1986, pp. 49-51.

FISHER, FREDERICK J., *Broker Beware: Selling Real Estate Within the Law*, ch. 2, 5. Reston, VA: Reston Publishing Company, Inc., 1981.

GOLDSTEIN, PAUL, *Real Estate Transactions*. St. Paul, MN: Foundation Press, 1985.

HALL INSTITUTE OF REAL ESTATE, *Managing a Real Estate Team*, ch. 8, 9, appendix J. Hinsdale, IL: The Dryden Press, 1980.

HANSOTTE, LOUIS B., "Real Estate Contracts," in *The McGraw-Hill Real Estate Handbook*, ed. Robert Irwin, ch. 22. New York, NY: McGraw-Hill Book Company, 1984.

HARTER, THOMAS R., "Finance and the Lender's Viewpoint," in *The McGraw-Hill Real Estate Handbook*, ed. Robert Irwin, ch. 4. New York, NY: McGraw-Hill Book Company, 1984.

IRWIN, ROBERT, "The New Mortgages" in *The McGraw-Hill Real Estate Handbook*, ed. Robert Irwin, ch. 2. New York, NY: McGraw-Hill Book Company, 1984.

KRATOVIL, ROBERT, AND RAYMOND J. WERNER, *Real Estate Law* (8th ed.) ch. 20, 21. Englewood Cliffs, NJ: Prentice Hall, 1983.

METTLING, STEPHEN R., *Modern Residential*

Financing Methods: Tools of the Trade. Chicago, IL: Real Estate Education Company, 1984.

MILLER, NORMAN G., AND PAUL R. GOEBEL. *The Buyer, Seller and Broker's Guide to Creative Home Financing.* Englewood Cliffs, NJ: Prentice Hall, 1983.

NATIONAL ASSOCIATION OF REAL ESTATE LICENSE LAW OFFICIALS, *Guide to Examinations and Careers in Real Estate.* Reston, VA: Reston Publishing Company, Inc., 1979, pp. 43-46.

Real Estate Sales Handbook (9th ed.), ch. 7, 8. Chicago, IL: REALTORS® National Marketing Institute, 1983.

SHENKEL, WILLIAM M., *Marketing Real Estate* (2nd ed.), ch. 4, 14. Englewood Cliffs, NJ: Prentice Hall, 1985.

SIROTA, DAVID, *Essentials of Real Estate Finance.* Chicago, IL: Real Estate Education Company, 1986.

SODARO, AUGUSTINE, "How to Market Residential Property," in *The McGraw-Hill Real Estate Handbook,* ed. Robert Irwin, ch.32. New York, NY: McGraw-Hill Book Company, 1984.

TWELVE

FINANCIAL CONTROL

Requirements

Some Basic Financial Concepts

The Company Dollar and Profits

Profit Analysis of the Average Sale

Budgeting

Identifying Financial Problem Areas

Cost Effectiveness of Personnel

Insuring the Business

Using Borrowed Money

Starting Up

Startup Example

Control and management of the financial end of a business is crucial to its continued success. No business can operate indefinitely without earning profits or at least breaking even. Proper financial control requires considerable skill and knowledge, including a grounding in the fundamentals of accounting. In the space we have available here we can only hit the high spots. However, some initial warnings and comments are necessary.

REQUIREMENTS

The brokerage business should have available the services of an accountant who will keep track of the firm's financial records and transactions. Accurate books should be kept, recording each transaction as it occurs. If these books are up to date, it is a simple matter to obtain a brief statement of the operating and financial situation of the business in a short time.

Accurate books serve two purposes. First, they are absolutely necessary in order to file proper income tax and other tax statements and returns. Second, they can provide continuous indications of performance of the business, enabling comparisons with previous periods and analysis of profitability of the firm's various operations.

Particular attention must be given to keeping track of trust monies brokerages hold. These include earnest money payments, escrow monies, undistributed rents, and the like. These records and funds should be handled in exact accordance with the laws and regulations set down by the state in which the firm operates.

SOME BASIC FINANCIAL CONCEPTS

Economists, financial analysts, and accountants have identified a number of financial concepts that are important in the proper analysis of the financial well-being of the company.

Revenue

Revenue is the total of all payments, commissions, fees, and other incoming cash and notes that the firm collects. It also is called *gross income*. It is a good measure of the *volume* of business done by the firm, but not of its *profitability*.

Costs

Costs are the sum total of the money that the firm pays out, except for income taxes and profits. These include all payments to employees and independent contractor salespeople, all commission payments to cooperating and multi-list brokerages, all expenses of operating the business, depreciation on all owned real estate and equipment, all supplies, and all fees paid to others.

Income and Profit

Income is what is left of revenue after all costs have been paid. *Profit*, the bottom line, is what is left of income after the firm has paid all income taxes due on the income that it has earned. Income is sometimes called *gross profit* and profit is sometimes called *net profit, after taxes*. Profit is available for distribution to the firm's owners or stockholders, or for investment in expansion, new equipment, and the like.

Fixed and Variable Costs

Fixed costs are those costs a firm must pay no matter how much or how little business it does: these costs remain constant as the firm's business grows or shrinks. Examples are licensing fees, privilege taxes, rent on office and equipment, and salaries and benefits to people who will be employed no matter how large or small the business volume is.

Variable costs are costs that rise or fall as the firm's business increases or decreases. A good example of a variable cost in the brokerage business is the share of the commission income paid to salespeople. If no sales are made, no payments are made. As business is done, these payments are made on a case by case basis. Other variable cost are property advertising, fees paid to settlement agents, etc. To some extent, other costs can be at least partly variable. Gasoline costs tend to increase as business increases, because more miles are driven. However, depreciation on a company car is a fixed cost, since it will occur even if the car remains parked.

The more variable the costs a firm encounters, the more flexible it is. If many of its costs are variable and a poor market develops, the firm can cut back significantly on its costs as business falls off. Some costs may be fixed in the short run, but are variable over longer periods of time. For example, a firm may sign a one-year lease for office space. During the lease period the rent is a fixed cost, since there is a legal obligation to pay it whether or not the volume of business done justifies the amount of space leased. However, when the lease expires the firm has the option to adjust its space use—and its cost—if necessary. This also points out a possible drawback of *owning* the space that the firm uses. Mortgage and tax costs become fixed for a period of decades, although this is offset by the fact that the property always can be sold.

Cash Flow

Cash flow is another important concept; it refers to the quantity of ready, spendable cash the firm generates. Regardless of the ultimate profitability of an operation, it always must have enough cash on hand, or sources of cash, to pay current bills, costs, and fees. Many a business has gone bankrupt not because it was unprofitable, but because its cash flow structure put it in a cash bind. Consider an unusual but illustrative example: A firm gets a listing on a property with a sale price of $10 million and a 4% selling commission payable upon completion of the sale. The commission will be $400,000, and the firm anticipates that its share, after cooperating with other brokers and paying its salespeople their commissions, will be $100,000. It also figures that it will have to spend $50,000 on advertising and other costs associated with the sale before it can sell the property. In spite of the fact that there is a $50,000 profit due eventually, the firm cannot handle the listing unless it has sources of the $50,000 that it must spend in order to accomplish the sale. Therefore, there must be some sort of cash flow during the selling period to generate that part of the $50,000 cost that it does not already have available.

Company Dollar

The *company dollar* is that part of revenue that ends up belonging to the company, before it deducts its own cost of business. To arrive at the brokerage's company dollar figure, all commissions and fees paid to other brokerage firms (cooperated and multilist transactions) and to its own salespeople are deducted from revenue. While the quantity of company dollar is an indication of the amount of business a firm does, it is not an indication of profitability. That can be derived by analyzing the costs taken out of the company dollar.

THE COMPANY DOLLAR AND PROFITS

Real estate brokerages show a wide variation in the percentage of the company dollar that ends up as profit. Generally, a rule of thumb is that most firms show about 30% of the company dollar as profit, and about 70% as cost. The company dollar itself is about 40% to 50% of total revenues, which means that the average firm distributes about 50% to 60% of its revenues to other firms and to its salespeople, and that profit usually is about 5% to 15% of total revenues.

Following is an example distribution of fees and expenses with respect to the company dollar. These figures are approximations, and there may be considerable variation among firms and geographic areas, depending upon competition and business practice. Generally, larger firms with higher revenues report

REVENUE	100%
less fees and commissions	55% of revenue
equals COMPANY DOLLAR	45% of revenue
COMPANY DOLLAR	100%
less:	
Advertising	20% of company dollar
Telephone	5% of company dollar
Salaries	15% of company dollar
Operation of firm	15% of company dollar
Space and equipment	15% of company dollar
Other	0-20% of company dollar
TOTAL PROFITS	10-30% of company dollar

somewhat higher expenditures as a percentage of the company dollar; however, their larger total sum of company dollars means that their total profits are greater than for small firms.

The "other" category represents differences between smaller and larger firms, mostly in the area of sales management: special incentives, sales manager's salary, office expenses, etc. Once again, these figures are approximate, and are not meant to represent a set of guidelines for all brokerage concerns. Furthermore, they are representative of firms operating in normal markets. Where unusual conditions exist, such as buyers' markets or sellers' markets, a firm may show considerable variation from its normal pattern.

PROFIT ANALYSIS OF THE AVERAGE SALE

A useful measure the firm can employ is the average profitability of a sale. This can be done in many ways. For example, the company may take the total sum of its company costs divided by the number of sales in the period. This will give the *average cost per sale*. Clearly, a sale that does not produce enough company dollars to cover the average cost per sale will appear unprofitable. However, that may not always be the case. In each situation, the company should look at the variable costs associated with the sale to see if it contributes to profit.

A given sale will not add to fixed costs at all, for those will have to be paid whether there are sales or not. Therefore, any given transaction need only cover the variable costs it generates in order for it to be worthwhile. As an example, suppose a firm has a total annual company cost of $100,000. Half, or $50,000, is fixed cost and the other $50,000 is variable cost. If 200 sales occurred during the period, the average cost per sale was $500. The fixed cost per sale was $250 and the variable cost per sale was $250.

Suppose a sale opportunity comes along which will generate a total of $400 in company dollars. If we look at the average cost per sale, we will find that it is $500 and conclude that the sale will cost the firm $100. Actually this is not true, because that sale will not generate any more fixed costs—it can't, because of the way we have defined fixed costs. If the sale is a usual one and generates $250 of variable costs, that will leave an additional $150 of profit from it: the $400 of new company dollars, less the $250 of new variable costs leaves a profit of $150. What has happened is that company dollars have increased by $400, while total costs have increased by only $250. Fixed costs don't increase at all, so they remain at $50,000. Variable costs increase by $250 to $50,250. Total costs, then, increase to $100,250 and not to a larger figure.

BUDGETING

Budgeting is a form of planning, which is done on a periodic basis. Most firms prepare annual budgets, perhaps with quarterly summaries to use as guides as the year proceeds. The function of budgeting is to generate forecasts of income, revenue, and costs and to reconcile them so that the financial comfort of the business is assured. For example, if it is anticipated that total costs of business will exceed projected company dollars for a period, that is a signal that analysis of costs should be undertaken to see if any are excessive. At the same time, analysis of revenue forecasts should be made. The shortfall may be temporary, due to a poor market that is expected to recover; if that is not the case, a signal has been given that some changes have to be made.

If the budget shows that projected costs will be less than the total company dollars, a profit is forecast. Many firms fall into the trap of believing that if profits are anticipated, things must be operating well. A professionally run firm always should be analyzing revenues and costs to find ways of increasing profits either by increasing revenues, decreasing costs, or both. There is nothing wrong with making good profits better.

Budgeting is a preliminary exercise, and it should not be expected that a budget will be met exactly as projected. Budgets are *estimates* of what to expect. If results are different there should be analysis of why, since a good budget is based upon previous experience with the firm's revenues and costs. However, there are traps in budgeting as well. Many firms are satisfied with the performance of various sectors of the company so long as they do not exceed budgeted expenditures or fall short in revenues. This can lead to unwarranted loss of profit because it is not always true that doing something "the way we always have" is the best way.

A recent development in budgeting procedure is the *zero base budget*. Many organizations formulate budgets by inserting items that have traditionally been spent, adding new programs, and then coming up with a final budget. This process does not require justification of expenditure patterns that have been established. Zero base budgeting requires that *all* budgeted expenditures for the period be justified anew every time a new budget is formulated. In this manner, no spending patterns or programs become immune to scrutiny, and each time the budget is formulated all items have to be given careful consideration.

IDENTIFYING FINANCIAL PROBLEM AREAS

One of the most difficult processes in the financial analysis and control of any business is the evaluation of all expenditures a firm makes. If the budget and the relationship among revenues, costs, and profits is not constantly watched, it is easy for cash-draining habits to instill themselves. A number of signs will suggest that review is necessary.

Is the business flexible? Can it adjust quickly to changes in its markets? Recent experience has shown that real estate is a volatile business. A firm that does not have the flexibility to adjust is at a serious disadvantage.

Is the firm using the right amount of space and equipment? While luxurious offices and expensive equipment are nice, they should be *justifiable*.

Each item should be analyzed for the contribution it makes to the profitable operation of the firm in comparison to its cost.

Are all aspects and departments of the firm's business producing profits? It may be that some are bleeding profits from others. If a part of the business is not profitable, or if the business will be more profitable without it, that part should be eliminated.

Are there employees and salespeople in the firm who are not paying their way? This is a very difficult area because if some people are not producing, they must be let go. Particular problems may crop up in the case of people who once were useful but who have been "coasting" for a long time. If there are such people in the firm, they should be let go or convinced to regain their former productivity.

COST EFFECTIVENESS OF PERSONNEL

All personnel in a business cost the business money and should be kept on only if they are worth their cost. For some jobs, it is easy to determine *cost effectiveness*; in others it is more difficult than it might appear. For salaried employees, one can establish the general range of salary that is necessary to hire and keep personnel with certain desired skills; the question then becomes whether or not these services are worth the cost to the firm. If no one is hired to do these things specifically, will they get done by others already employed? If not, are these activities necessary? If others will do them, is that an efficient use of *their* time and skills? As an example, if members of a brokerage's sales force are doing all their own typing and filing and are handling all incoming phone calls and relaying messages on their own, could their time be better spent in sales activity if a secretary-receptionist were hired? These are not necessarily easy questions to answer, but a good manager will be able to get a reasonable idea of what the answer is. Some measure of the value to the firm of secretaries and other support personnel can be developed to determine how many are necessary.

Many firms, especially smaller ones, tend to underestimate the value of support personnel. A secretary's salary, fringe benefits and other costs may drain $15,000 or more per year from the company if it is a full time position. It is not easy to measure how much more listing and selling a particular sales staff may be able to do when a secretary-receptionist is hired. Perhaps the staff will just take more time off or perhaps they will use the freed time for more of the productive work that they do best. It is up to the manager of the brokerage to be familiar enough with the sale staff's capabilities and desire for work that he can evaluate the usefulness of creating and filing a support position.

As a firm grows, it obviously will create more of the kind of work support personnel should be doing. A staff that has too much to do either has to start cutting corners or let backlogged work pile up. Both are inefficient and can be very costly. The function of the support staff is to handle the paperwork and other kinds of busywork that take valuable marketing time away from the sales staff. If they cannot perform this function adequately, they are not serving their purpose, and the firm will suffer.

Desk Cost

One of the least understood financial facts of the real estate brokerage business is that sales staff members cost the firm money as well. At first it may appear that, since they are paid on commission, salespeople pay their own way and no real concern need be given to what it may be costing the company to have them on the staff. Many brokers seem to reflect this view by being willing to hold licenses for as many salespeople as wish to join. They assume that if the salesperson earns no commissions he does not have to be paid and therefore will not cost the firm anything.

This is not true, except possibly in the case of a salesperson who is so ineffective that he never appears at the office, never has any calls, never talks to any of his colleagues, and never asks the sales manager for advice. Brokers who understand the financial nature of their firms realize that for each active member of the sales force, there exists what is called in the business a *desk cost*. This reflects the fact that salespeople do, in fact, make use of support staff, have telephone calls coming in for them, need desk space at which to work, and take up some of the time of colleagues and managers. The space and equipment they use cost money, as do the support staff services. The time they spend talking to colleagues and management is valuable as well. Looked at this way, it should be obvious that the presence of a salesperson on the staff is not free, and that each salesperson should be able to generate at least enough business to pay the cost to the firm of retaining him.

Opportunity Cost

A second factor associated with desk cost is something that economists call *opportunity cost*. In brief, when a given salesperson occupies a slot on the staff, no one else can occupy that particular position. The sales manager should not concern himself only with whether or not a given staff member is covering his basic desk cost; rather, he should make sure that the salesperson is not taking up a space that someone *better* could be occupying instead. While it is nice if every salesperson covers the cost to the firm of keeping him on, the company is in business to make money, and not just to provide space for a collection of people who meet a minimum production standard. The truly successful firm fills its sales staff with people who not only cover their costs, but do far better, making more money not only for themselves but for the company as well.

If a firm has to turn down an opportunity to hire someone productive because there is no space for him, this should be done only because there is no one already on the staff who could profitably be replaced by the potential salesperson. This may sound cold-blooded, but successful business is not a notably sympathetic endeavor. Also, salespeople themselves will be perfectly aware that there are certain standards they must meet if they are to become successful and remain so.

This is not to say that rigid goals, dollar volume of sales or commissions, or other highly specific measures of proper performance should be used. The *total, long-term* value of every salesperson to the firm should always be considered. If they produce very poorly they are likely to leave the business by themselves, because they are unable to make a decent living at it. If they produce enough income for themselves to be satisfied, they probably are worth keeping.

Most problems occur with salespeople who are part time, supplementing other income. They may be less motivated to perform well and set less lofty goals, because their sales work occupies a lower position of importance in their lives than it would if they had to support themselves by it. They may be performing at a level they find satisfactory given the amount of time that they are willing to devote. However, the firm may consider that they are relatively poor producers on balance, compared to those who must earn their livings at sales and therefore are devoting full time to it. Some firms do not hire part-time salespeople at all. Others may tend to give them a second class position within the organization: They share desk space and other facilities with other part-timers and do not receive as much encouragement to take their problems to the managers. In these ways, the desk cost of the part-time salespeople is reduced to make their employment, even though they are less effective producers, feasible for the company.

Many brokerage firms seem to leave out a permanent welcome mat for anyone who has a sales license and is willing to join the firm. As we have seen, that is not necessarily good policy, because holding a salesperson's license is not cost-free to the firm. Further, a firm that *makes* license-holding cost-free, by providing virtually no support to its sales staff and expecting them to train and supervise themselves, is not using its people efficiently and will not attract the genuinely skilled and talented salespeople a firm must have if it is to be a long-term success.

Top salespeople know that they can produce lots of commission revenue, and they expect that if they are to split that revenue with a brokerage firm, they should get something for it. That something is support service, the firm's good reputation, references from firm management, and other advantages of being associated with a professional organization. They will consider an unprofessional organization, which requires them to do everything by themselves, only if the split with the firm leaves the firm only a small token commission share. Even then, they may feel it worthwhile to go with a larger, better firm that will take a larger commission cut, but will do all the paperwork and detail work so that the salesperson can devote most of his time to what he does best: selling and listing.

A professional firm does not fall into the trap of hiring just anybody because holding licenses is cheap. Instead, it wants to assemble a staff of highly productive, competent people who will give the firm a good reputation for professionalism and who will attract business because of demonstrated success.

INSURING THE BUSINESS

Insurance should be part of any financial control system. In return for fixed payments to an insuror, the firm transfers the risk that a large loss or other cost item will occur. Nearly all owned equipment should be insured against theft or loss, and any buildings should be insured against fire, weather, and other casualty damage. Very high coverage should be sought for automobile liability insurance, both on company owned vehicles and those owned and used by salespeople and employees. Insurance against professional liability and covering property owned and used by the firm also should be considered.

Property Insurance

Whether the firm rents or owns its offices, insurance should cover its investment in equipment and furnishings. If the office space is owned, the building should be insured as well. Property insurance covers a variety of perils, and the firm can pick and choose among them. Insurance against theft, vandalism, fire and weather normally is carried. "All-risk" policies cover all forms of damage or loss except for a very few which are specifically listed in the policies. Riders covering even these exceptions can be purchased to include them.

Some special coverages which are not included in standard policies may be worth considering. *Valuable papers and records* coverage reimburses cost of recreating such documents when they are lost or destroyed. Standard policies do not insure against *electrical damage* (except by fire). Data processing equipment is vulnerable to line surges, brownouts, and the like. If the firm owns a lot of such equipment, insurance against this peril should be considered. *Glass and sign* coverage extends insurance to large expanses of glass, and signs which are not part of the building. *Floods and earthquakes* are not usually covered by standard policies, and this extra coverage may be worthwhile in areas prone to these perils. Water damage coverage may not include sprinkler leakage without a special insurance rider.

Consequential losses are those which are not a direct loss to insured property. Firms will encounter expenses beyond replacement or repair cost of damaged property. These would include having to rent or buy other equipment temporarily, or make other expensive arrangements until the lost or damaged property is replaced or repaired. *Extra expenses* coverage will take care of such costs. *Leasehold interest insurance* covers loss when equipment or buildings rented under favorable lease terms are lost and have to be replaced with others having higher rents. If the firm owns a building so large that it rents space to other tenants, *rental value* coverage insures against rent loss if the building is damaged or destroyed.

Liability Insurance

Liability is the potential responsibility for damages due to negligence of one kind or another. Liability insurance pays damage judgments against the insured for covered liability (up to the policy limits), as well as the costs of defending against a suit in court.

One area of liability is that of personal injury. Someone can trip over a carpet, be hurt by malfunctioning equipment, etc. *General liability* policies protect against injury to persons on the firm's premises or otherwise due to the firm's activities. *Owners' and contractors' protective liability* policies insure against injury by contractors or subcontractors working on rental or other owned property. *Comprehensive general liability policies* insure against these injury perils and several others in one single policy. All states impose statutory liability upon employers for injury or death of employees occurring at the place of business. *Workers' compensation* coverage is made mandatory by these laws and is often administered by the state government. (Note, however, that independent contractors usually do not have to be covered by such employers' insurance.)

Automobile liability coverage looms large in the brokerage business because so much automobile use is inherent in the conduct of the business. All automobile users affiliated with the firm should carry high coverage, usually much more than the minimum mandated by state laws. The firm should require continuous reports of coverage from its affiliated licensees, and be informed of any changes. The firm also should purchase its own ancillary automobile liability coverage which will insure the firm itself against auto damage claims that may arise from the business activities of its sales associates.

Professional liability insurance covers against mistakes and negligence of a professional nature. In the real estate business this is usually called *errors and omissions insurance*, and is the same type of coverage that the public calls malpractice insurance as applied to other professionals. This covers claims against the insured due to failure to perform, negligence, error, or lack of knowledge by the broker or salesperson. The firm's insurance covers the firm against any such claims; individual salespersons should consider obtaining personal professional liability insurance to protect themselves as well.

USING BORROWED MONEY

"Neither a borrower nor a lender be!" This is quaint, conservative old saying that is best forgotten. In today's world, properly managed and controlled borrowing is an integral part of good management and business success. A business may rent equipment or office space; borrowing money and paying interest on it simply is "renting" money. Many firms will borrow to purchase expensive equipment that they need but do not have the cash to buy; the income provided by the additional equipment is partly devoted to paying off the loan taken out to acquire it.

Borrowed money has several uses in an ongoing business. Its availability means that the firm need not have substantial cash on hand, since it can borrow when it runs into temporary cash flow problems. Often a business will borrow to cover the expenses of starting up because the people involved do not have enough cash themselves; some of the business's early profits are used to pay off the loan.

Often just as useful as borrowing money is having an arrangement that will allow for a certain level of borrowing on short notice. This is called a *line of credit*. A brokerage firm may arrange with a bank to be able to borrow up to a certain sum anytime it needs it. While it may go some time without using any of its borrowing power, it also knows that there exists a reserve amounting to the unused portion of the line of credit. Immediate availability of borrowed money can be very useful: deals that have to be made immediately can be undertaken and unexpected cash flow problems can be relieved. So long as management uses the line of credit as a resource for temporary and occasional use when needed, it can be very valuable.

STARTING UP

Getting a business underway costs money; a brokerage business in particular will need "seed money" even if it starts out with a bang, because commissions usually are not payable until transactions close, and even if transactions are made very early in the firm's existence, it will be some time before money from them flows into the firm. A more likely situation, however, is one in which the amount of business grows slowly, and several very lean months may have to be weathered before the firm finds the solid financial footing to keep itself going on the income it generates.

Projecting Financial Needs

It is absolutely essential that reasonable financial planning be done before the business actually is set up. Lots of "dry runs" can be played out on paper to examine what might happen if certain assumptions about the immediate success of the firm are made. These imaginary run-throughs cost no more than the time it takes to work them out, but they can prove valuable when the time comes to make serious decisions about starting a business and keeping it going. Probably the worst and most frequent mistakes made by people going into business are that they are too optimistic about how their business will start out, and they start out with too little money. Sensible planning can avoid both problems.

Over-optimism can be thwarted by making every effort to be *reasonable*; if errors enter into the estimates, they should be too conservative rather than too cheerful. In the first case, a broker might find himself with a larger business than expected, and a need for expansion sooner than had been anticipated. But if too much optimism entered the picture, he might instead be faced with mounting debt, rapidly depleting cash reserves, and heavy overhead expenses; this is the road to quick bankruptcy. Clearly, it is better to find more business than expected than less; a firm with too many paying customers is a lot better off than one with too few. Conservative planning allows for the worst and realizes that any business venture entails risks that ought to be anticipated. A certain amount of money is absolutely necessary for the establishment of a business that has reasonable chances for success. However, proper planning can reduce this requirement to the minimum. Probably the most significant aspect of initial financial planning is to allow for a reserve of cash to be used to cover the unknown eventualities that always seem to crop up at the most inconvenient times. A reasonable financial plan, coupled with sensible projections of the rate at which business success will be achieved, will provide a solid foundation upon which decisions can be made.

Projecting Business Activity

Projection of business success should be based upon the record of success of the people to be involved in the firm. How well have they done in the past? Might we expect them to continue to do as well? Normally, a licensee who changes firms is not allowed to take with him the still-active listings he may have with his old firm, so the new firm's listings will have to be generated from scratch. Selling activities can get under way more quickly if the firm is able to arrange cooperation agreements with other firms that already have listings. New firm members can bring their reputations with them, of course, and it is upon these that the initial success of the new brokerage may depend.

There will be a period at the outset during which a lot of work will have to be done and relatively little income will be generated. If the new firm's sales force had managed, among them, ten listings a month on the average for the previous year, a conservative estimate might allow for four new listings the first month, six the second, eight the third, and finally reaching the old average of ten in the fourth month. Projecting sales might be a little more difficult. If the sales staff had generated ten sales a month on the average, a scale of growth similar to that of listings might be anticipated, but some significant questions should still be answered. If a salesperson's record shows that he tends to sell largely his own listings, then it would be unwise to expect rapid sales results from him until he has had time to accumulate a portfolio of his own listings with the new firm. But a salesperson who sold lots of other peoples' listings could be expected to get his successful efforts under way sooner.

Deeper analysis of the outlook of the new firm would focus upon the details of the experience of the sales staff in their previous employment. Some may have been with firms that had provided considerable support service to their sales staff. How well will these people do in a new firm that cannot initially afford to provide all this support? Salespeople who leave their previous firms on good terms may find that they will be able to sell those firms' listings easily and so begin to generate income to the new firm quickly. Others may find it difficult to gain access to their old firm's listings. Some salespeople may have cultivated a considerable group of regular customers whose loyalty will lead them to deal with the new firm; some may not bring this asset with them.

Forecasting Costs and Expenses

Once a reasonable forecast of the business potential of the new firm has been made, it becomes possible to make significant financial analyses. The forecasts of activity will describe the income pattern that may be expected. This should be contrasted with the projected expenses to determine whether or not the new business is financially feasible. For no matter how nice and enjoyable it may be to run one's own business one's own way, if it does not make money it cannot last very long. Expenses and income should be projected on a month-by-month basis for at least a full year; longer, if it is expected that the business will not reach its full potential by that time.

The first important objective in estimating expenses is to determine just what will be needed and will have to be paid for. Offices and equipment are obvious considerations here. Perhaps we should emphasize that an equally important consideration is the elimination of unnecessary expense items. Each anticipated need should be evaluated carefully, and reasonable estimates made of the costs involved. Efforts should be made to avoid heavy initial cost items; these can be difficult to dispose of if the business does not succeed, and they drain away badly needed cash. Many of them can be rented at the outset and purchased when the firm is more financially stable. While planning for growth is necessary, it is not imperative that large suites of offices full of expensive furnishings and equipment be set up at the outset to allow for expansion. Until expansion occurs, the unneeded space and equipment are an unprofitable drain on the company's resources.

Expenses and income should be contrasted on a month-by-month basis. It should be expected that the earlier months will show deficits; that is, expenses will exceed income. However, these deficits should decrease, and within a reasonable length of time monthly profits should show up and become the rule. The startup cash needs of the firm will be the sum of money needed to cover the accumulated deficits that will pile up as the company gets under way. Once the firm is established, the monthly profit level (where income exceeds expenses) should be enough to justify the initial deficits.

Preparedness

One more note of caution is proper here: It is essential to analyze the market as well as the potential brokerage firm itself. Projections of the firm's activity in all cases must be based upon market conditions as well as the history and ability of the firm's participants. If there is reason to believe that the local real estate market is heading into a declining phase, all estimates should reflect this feeling. If the local market appears to be heading for more prosperous times, predictions should still be somewhat restrained just to remain on the safe side. A general rule that is good to follow is that being prepared for the worst that can reasonably be expected is also good preparation for anything better. A conservative approach may result in occasional lost opportunities, but is much less likely to result in the loss of the entire business. It is the long-term success of the firm that should be the ultimate goal of any management.

If a new firm is to be successful it needs all the advance planning and foresight that can be assembled. Financial plans, goals and objectives of business to be done, how and where it is to be done—all are needed. Seed money is essential, along with efficient planning of how it will be spent. Setting up a new and successful firm requires a very large initial expenditure of time, energy, and money, and these costs must be recognized as investment in the future of the business. If these investments are well planned, they should bear considerable fruit as the firm matures. As the firm establishes itself, managers should be aware of the stages of growth, and plan ahead for coping with the problems it will bring, as well as enjoying its rewards. The genuinely successful business enterprise is the one that tries to prepare itself for the future, and to handle whatever it may bring.

STARTUP EXAMPLE

This section presents examples of the steps used to make financial forecasts and plans for a brokerage firm. We are assuming here that our firm is about to get started in business, although these analyses also could be used very effectively for an existing firm.

Figure 12–1 is a breakdown of startup costs. These would not be encountered by an established firm, of course. These figures, as are all those used in this figure, are for presentation purposes only, and should not be taken to be representative costs and revenues for actual firms.

Figure 12–2 analyzes the monthly fixed costs of the firm. This firm is large enough to require a manager, either a sales manager or broker-manager,

Figure 12–1 Startup Costs Example

A. INITIAL ADVERTISING		
Newspaper	$1,440.00	
Radio	750.00	
Television	750.00	
Mailouts	2,350.00	
Open house	750.00	
Marathon sponsorship	1,000.00	
TOTAL INITIAL ADVERTISING	7,040.00	7,040.00
B. OTHER COSTS		
Privilege license	290.50	
Signs and labels	775.00	
Answering machine	185.00	
Furnishings	3,750.00	
Miscellaneous	1,000.00	
TOTAL OTHER COSTS	6,100.50	6,100.50
C. TOTAL STARTUP COSTS		$13,140.50

Figure 12-2   Fixed Costs (Monthly Basis).

Office rental	$ 685.00
Utilities	175,00
Telephone (basic 4-line)	73.50
Salaries:	
Secretary-receptionist	775.00
Manager—base pay	1,000.00
FICA, fringes, taxes	495.00
Advertising contracts	535.00
Equipment rental	
3 typewriters	175.00
Copier	125.00
Little League team sponsorship	125.00
Miscellaneous	250.00
TOTAL FIXED MONTHLY COSTS	$4,413.50

for whom a salary and override are budgeted. The manager's base salary is $1,000 per month; this and the payroll taxes and fringe benefits based upon it are fixed costs. The manager, in our example, also receives an override of 10 percent of the gross company dollar. However, the override is a *variable* cost, since it is based upon company dollar volume, which rises or falls as business increases or decreases. Therefore, the override is shown in Figure 12–3.

Figure 12–3 is an analysis of revenues, fees, company dollars, and profits

Figure 12–3   Sales Analysis.

		COOPERATED SALES	
	In-house Listing & Sale	Company Listing Sold by Another Broker**	Other Broker's Listing Sold by Company**
(1) Gross revenue*	$ 4,480.00	$ 4,480.00	$ 2,016.00
(2) Payment to other firms	—0—	(2,016.00)	—0—
(3) Net revenue	4,480.00	2,464.00	2,016.00
(4) Salesperson's commission***	(2,240.00)	(1,120.00)	(1,120.00)
(5) Company dollar	2,240.00	1,344.00	896.00
(6) Sales manager's 10%	(224.00)	(134.40)	(89.60)
(7) Variable costs****			
(7a) Listing	(350.00)	(350.00)	—0—
(7b) Selling	(220.00)	—0—	(220.00)
(8) Net company receipts	$ 1,446.00	$ 859.60	$ 586.40

Figures in parentheses are negative: they are cost items which must be subtracted from revenues.

*Based upon average sale of $64,000.

**Assuming listing firm receives 55% of total commission and selling firm receives 45%.

***Assuming listing and selling salespeople each receive 25% of total commission.

****Based upon experience.

of sales. There are three kinds of sales: In-house sales occur when the company sells one of its own listings and so does not share the commission with any other brokerage firm. The second kind of sale is the sale of one of the firm's listings by another brokerage firm. The third kind occurs when the firm's sales force sells a listing of another firm. In these last two situations, we are assuming that the two firms split commissions on cooperated sales as follows: 55 percent of the total commission goes to the listing firm and 45 percent goes to the selling firm.

We are also making some other assumptions; a brokerage firm in preparing its own information of this nature will base its assumptions on experience. For our purposes here, we are assuming that: (a) the average value of property sold is $64,000; (b) the salespeople involved in the sale receive 25% of the total commission for listing and 25% for selling; (c) variable costs are $350 for listing and $220 for selling; and (d) the sales manager receives a 10% share of the company dollar.

A firm should make forecasts of the number of each of the kinds of sales it expects to make. In Figure 12–4 we are assuming that the firm is new; its objective is to sell three in-house listings, sell three listings of other brokers, and have three of its own listings sold by other firms, each month. However, it expects to start slowly. It will be relatively easy to sell listings of other firms, since they already exist; listings acquired by the new firm will take longer to accumulate, so these kinds of sales will grow more slowly. Note that in the forecast we assume it will take seven months for the firm to achieve the goals it wants as an established firm.

Figure 12–4   Sales Forecasts for New Firm (First 7 Months).

MONTH	IN-HOUSE LISTING AND SALE	COMPANY LISTING SOLD BY OTHER BROKERS	OTHER BROKERS' LISTINGS SOLD BY COMPANY
1	0	0	2
2	0	1	3
3	1	1	3
4	1	2	3
5	2	2	3
6	2	3	3
7 and later	3	3	3

The elaborate Figure 12–5 combines all the information we have assembled in Figures 12–1 through 12–4 into one single financial forecast, spread over a period of ten months. It is assumed that sales made in each month correspond to those shown in Figure 12–4. Month 0 represents the very beginning, as the firm gets underway. Here we have included all the initial startup costs shown in Figure 12–1.

For each of the remaining months we give several figures. Column 1 is total revenues, calculated from Line 1 in Figure 12–3 applied to the appropriate kinds and numbers of sales shown for each month in Figure 12–4. Column 2 is

Figure 12–5 Firm's Business Forecast

Analysis of first ten months' operations—revenue, costs, deficits, and profits based upon data in Figures 12–1 through 12–4.

Month	(1) Total Revenue	(2) Company Dollars	(3) Fixed Costs	(4) Variable Costs	(5) Manager's Override	(6) Profit (Deficit)	(7) Cumulative Profit (Deficit)
0	INITIAL STARTUP EXPENSES					($13,140.50)	($13,140.50)
1	$ 4,032.00	$ 1,792.00	$4,413.50	$ 440.00	$ 179.20	(2,792.70)	(15,933.20)
2	10,528.00	4,032.00	4,413.50	1,010.00	403.20	(1,794.70)	(17,727.90)
3	15,008.00	6,272.00	4,413.50	1,580.00	627.70	(348.70)	(18,076.60)
4	19,488.00	7,616.00	4,413.50	1,930.00	761.60	510.90	(17,565.70)
5	23,968.00	9,856.00	4,413.50	2,500.00	985.60	1,956.90	(14,978.80)
6	28,488.00	11,200.00	4,413.50	2,850.00	1,120.00	2,861.50	(12,792.30)
7	32,928.00	13,440.00	4,413.50	3,420.00	1,344.00	4,262.50	(8,529.80)
8	32,928.00	13,440.00	4,413.50	3,420.00	1,344.00	4,262.50	(4,267.30)
9	32,928.00	13,440.00	4,413.50	3,420.00	1,344.00	4,262.50	(4.80)
10	32,928.00	13,440.00	4,413.50	3,420.00	1,344.00	4,262.50	4,257.70

the company dollar remaining after commission payments to other firms and to salespeople have been paid: this corresponds to Line 5 in Figure 12–3. Column 3 is monthly fixed costs, from Figure 12–2. This figure is the same for all months, since fixed costs do not vary. Column 4 shows variable costs, once again taken from Figure 12–3, this time using Lines 7a and/or 7b. Column 5 is the manager's 10% override on the company dollar, from Line 6 in Figure 12–3.

Column 6 shows the monthly profit or deficit. Deficit figures are given in parentheses. The monthly figure is derived by taking the company dollar figure in column 2 and subtracting from it fixed costs, variable costs, and the manager's override: columns 3, 4, and 5, added together.

In early months (1, 2 and 3) the monthly figures show deficits because costs exceed company dollars. However, these deficits are getting smaller, as more sales are being made each month. Beginning with month 4, the company shows monthly profits; they increase each month until month 7, at which time the firm's goals are achieved, and it is assumed that business steadies at the month 7 rate, and figures for columns 1 through 6 stabilize.

Column 7 shows the firm's *cumulative* deficit. This is found by adding up the figures for column 6 for all the months up to and including the current month. Note that the firm starts out with a deficit of over $13,000 before it ever gets underway; these are the startup costs. The accumulated deficit will *rise* in any month that a deficit is registered, and will *fall* in any month that shows a profit. Therefore, the deficit in our example will rise in months 1, 2, and 3, since deficits are run in each of these months. At the end of month 3, the accumulated deficit reaches a bit over $18,000 and then begins to fall as subsequent months show profits. By the end of month 9, the accumulated profits from months 4 through 9 have been enough to virtually wipe out the deficit, and in month 10— and from then on—the firm shows accumulated profits.

This information, then, will tell us that the owners of the firm will need at least $18,000 on hand or available as they start the firm in order to have the cash they will need to see the business through the formative period. Actually, to be safe, the firm should have more funds than that, to have a reserve for *contingency*: unplanned expenditures or deficits. If, for example a fund of $25,000 is budgeted as *seed money*, an extra $7,000 will be available to cover unforeseen problems. If business develops more slowly than expected, or unexpected expenses are encountered, this extra money will come in handy. The actual $25,000 need not be held in cash; the firm can arrange a line of credit for some or all of it, and use these borrowed funds when necessary. Of course, if borrowed money is expected to be used, an additional cost must be accounted for: interest on the borrowed funds.

DISCUSSION QUESTIONS AND PROJECTS

1. Analyze the concept of the *company dollar* and explain its usefulness.
2. Discuss the concept of *desk cost* and *opportunity cost* with respect to the retention of salespeople.
3. Survey two or three firms in your area to determine how much of revenue becomes company dollars.
4. From these firms determine what the average expenses (in terms of percentage of the company dollar) are in the categories defined in the text.
5. Based upon the information you gathered in 3 and 4, determine what percentage of the company dollar in your area is retained as gross company profit.
6. Interview a manager of a relatively new firm. Find out what kinds of costs were sustained to get the business under way and how long it took to recoup these costs. How long did it take before the business considered itself established? What kinds of problems were encountered?
7. Based upon information you can gather about the operations of the brokerage firms in your area, develop a profile of the "typical" firm, showing volume of sales activity, revenue, company dollars, costs, and profits.
8. Develop a budget for the next twelve months of the firm you profiled.
9. From a typical brokerage firm in your area, determine the variety and extent of insurance coverage that it carries. Explain anything unusual. Do you have suggestions for improvement?

A Case Study

TIME MANAGEMENT

In a recent interview, the principal broker of a respected residential firm had the following to say about the efficient use of time.

"I always try to tell my people to evaluate everything they do on the basis of the time it will take. I use the example of listings. Before they accept a listing, they should consider the time and effort that it will take to get the property sold. They should 'work' every listing they get: I don't want our firm to get the reputation of accepting listings and then just letting them sit until they sell themselves.This means that if a particular property is going to be hard to sell, they will have to invest a lot of time and effort into it.

"If the listing is going to be a dog, I tell them to consider if they might be better off turning it down, and spending the time it would have taken by getting other listings that will be easier sales. Naturally they expect that they will have to work on all their listings, and that they don't earn their commissions by just sitting around doing nothing. But I've seen too many cases where a salesperson spent enormous amounts of time trying to sell a bad listing, when he could have handled two or three others at the same time.

"For some reason this example really hits home. Once it does, I go on to suggest other ways of budgeting their time. I suggest that they plan an afternoon of showings to a prospect so that they waste as little time as possible driving from one home to another. I suggest that they do their listing negotiations in the evenings when people are at home and when it's too late to do showings anyway. When they're on floor duty, doing open houses, or otherwise have some moments of free time, I suggest that they do some cold calling or check up on recent clients just to say hello.

"And finally, I tell them that if they organize their time they can accomplish an awful lot without wearing themselves out."

REFERENCES

CARTER, JERRY T., C.R.B., "The Company Dollar: a Vital Budgeting Tool," *Real Estate Today*, January 1976, pp. 32–35.

HALL INSTITUTE OF REAL ESTATE, *Managing a Real Estate Team*, ch. 6. Hinsdale, IL: The Dryden Press, 1980.

KOTLER, PHILLIP, *Marketing Management: Analysis, Planning, and Control* (5th ed.). Englewood Cliffs, NJ: Prentice Hall, 1984.

LITKA, MICHEAL P., AND KARL A. SHILLIFF, *Contemporary Real Estate Incidents*. Columbus, OH: Grid, Inc., 1980, pp. 73–79.

PHILIPPATOS, GEORGE C., AND WILLIAM W. SIHLER, *Financial Management: Text and Cases*, ch. 12. Boston, MA: Allyn & Bacon, Inc., 1987.

PHILLIPS, BARBARA, "Getting Started in Real Estate," *The McGraw-Hill Real Estate Handbook*, ed. Robert Irwin, ch. 31. New York, NY: McGraw-Hill Book Company, 1984.

SHENKEL, WILLIAM M., *Marketing Real Estate* (2nd ed), ch. 19. Englewood Cliffs, NJ: Prentice Hall, 1985.

"Staying Small," "Growing Large," *Real Estate Today*, May-June, 1976, pp. 22-40.

THIRTEEN

THE WORKING ENVIRONMENT

Locating the Office

Office Layout

Furnishings and Equipment

Computer Facilities

Outside the Office

The real estate brokerage firm's offices are the most important single tool it has. If they are well located, properly designed and staffed, and well equipped, they will contribute greatly to the overall efficiency and profitability of the organization.

It might seem that the offices themselves are not very important, because the sales force will spend most of its time outside them. However, the office is an important home base, as well as a symbol to the general public of the firm's efficiency and professionalism. Much of the work done by a brokerage must take place in the office, including everything done by those who are not active salespeople. Even sales personnel will need a place to keep their records, meet people, and do much of their work that does not involve direct contact with the public.

The office should have a convenient and visible location and a proper design and layout that makes the available space as useful as possible. It should be staffed with permanent support personnel that will be available to the salespeople. It also serves as a central place where much important information is kept available for the use of the firm's personnel.

LOCATING THE OFFICE

Newly licensed brokers, especially if they intend to work alone, are tempted to get by with as little office space as possible: usually a room or a corner in the home. Such a location is most disadvantageous: it is difficult for customers to find, and it is awkward for receiving them when they do come to the office. It also does little to establish any sort of public confidence that the broker's business is indeed a full time and professional one. Furthermore, many localities have zoning ordinances that prohibit housing a business such as a real estate brokerage in residentially zoned districts. It would be awkward, to say the least, if a real estate broker of all people were to be found in violation of zoning ordinances.

Any broker intending to establish a permanent and successful business ought to have a genuine office. Particularly when he begins to take on salespeople, the office in the home becomes an unwise and inconvenient choice. Very small but comfortable offices can be found in even the most prestigious buildings. Shared facility offices have recently been developed, wherein the occupant rents a single office in a large, well-arranged suite and shares a receptionist and other facilities provided by the building management. These arrangements are relatively inexpensive, while offering many useful office services whenever the tenant may need them. They also provide a serious, businesslike environment that enhances the credibility and appearance of even the smallest enterprise.

Site Selection

Given that a general district for location has been chosen, it still is necessary to pick a specific site for the business. The firm has many options, but upon closer examination many of them can be eliminated. For example, the firm could build a structure to house its offices; it could buy an existing building; or it could rent available space. Usually the new firm ought to limit itself to renting, because it involves the lowest immediate cost. Furthermore, as the business grows it will need larger and larger quarters. Changing to more commodious offices is much easier when this space is rented than when it is owned.

Most new firms do not have a lot of cash; buying space requires substantial allocation of funds for down payments and closing costs, even if much of the purchase price is borrowed. Unless money is readily available for starting the new business, it ought to be conserved to meet more immediate needs. Once the firm is established and well under way, purchase of space can be considered more seriously.

Small Towns

In a small town, the firm generally will locate in the major business district, since it will be convenient to most parts of town and will be close to other firms and businesses with which the real estate brokerage deals. In many towns, however, the older central business district is being replaced as a center of business activity by a more modern, newer district usually located on the fringe of town in the direction of the most intensive growth. This is particularly true of towns that are near interchanges with the interstate highway system: The growth of businesses servicing travelers on the new road attracts additional growth of the town in that direction.

In such cases the new brokerage firm has to make a choice as to whether it will locate in the older, downtown area or cast its lot with the newer development (see Figure 13–1). Various considerations enter here. If other, similar service-oriented businesses have located successfully in the newer area, that is a good sign that the location should be there. Also, if the areas of specialization of the firm are in the newer area, a natural choice of that section is dictated.

Location in Larger Towns

In larger towns, the general area of location has already been specified by the interests of the firm's sales force. Still, a specific location must be chosen. Here, the types of properties dealt in by the firm takes command. A firm oriented toward home sales should locate in the area it intends to serve, and preferably somewhere along a well-known street, highway, or road that potential customers are familiar with and can find easily (see Figure 13–1). However, this kind of real estate brokerage business does not depend heavily upon walk-in customer traffic; rather, the sales force finds its customers by going to *their* home ground via canvassing, references, telephone inquiries and the like.

Attraction

It is relatively infrequent that a potential customer just walks in the door unannounced and with no appointment. For this business, too much walk-in

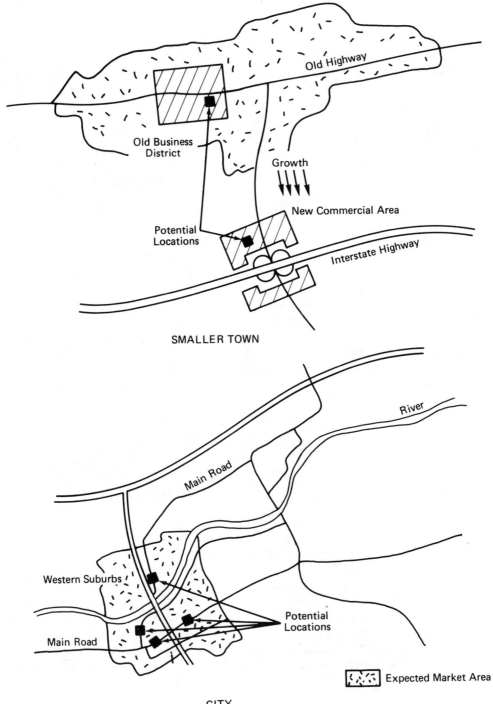

Figure 13-1. Location Choices.

traffic can be a distinct drawback, as the sales force will have to spend considerable time at the office to humor walk-in traffic composed mostly of curiosity seekers. For this reason, residential real estate offices usually are not located, say, in the middle of large regional mall shopping centers. Businesses in such centers cater to browsing, but it is rare that someone who is just looking around will suddenly evolve on the spur of the moment into a customer willing to spend several years' income for a house.

This is not to say that specific location is meaningless, but rather that it is not essential to locate specifically with an eye toward walk-in traffic. Still, an attractive location should be chosen, and one with easily available parking. The main road location provides not only a recognizable address, but an opportunity to erect an eye-catching sign that a lot of motorists will see. While they will not turn into the business on the spur of the moment as they drive along, they will know that the brokerage is there and may remember it when it is time for them to buy or sell a home.

Site Features

The office itself should be on a site that does not detract from the image the company wishes to project. This means that rundown, unattractive locations should be avoided; but it is not necessary to rent the Taj Mahal, either. The office should be in a clean, well-run building with good parking facilities and an attractive, businesslike appearance. It should be easy to find and easy to get to. Addresses along limited access roads or roads with center dividers can pose access problems. (See Figure 13–2 for advantages and disadvantages of various locations.) If there are no ordinances prohibiting signs, there should be some provision for identifying the location of the business in a way that will make a good and *memorable* impression upon passers-by.

Commercial and Investment Firms

A firm specializing in commercial or investment sales or property management has different locational needs. Usually it should locate in the central business district of the city, close to the financial institutions, investment firms, attorneys, and others with whom it will deal. Furthermore, in this area of brokerage there is little or no geographical discrimination; a firm would be expected to deal with properties in any part of the metropolitan area in which it is located, and it would not be unusual to find it dealing on a statewide, regional, or even national basis. The location should be at a reasonably prestigious address, not necessarily in the most expensive or impressive building in town, but in the kind of building that would help customers used to dealing in very large sums of money to feel secure.

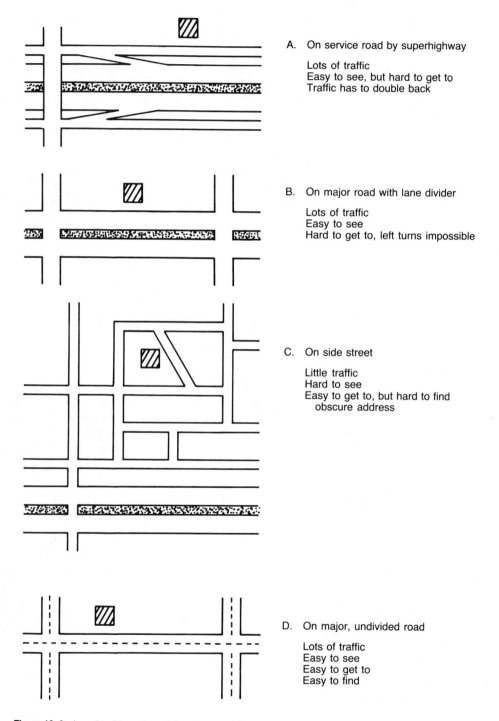

A. On service road by superhighway

   Lots of traffic
   Easy to see, but hard to get to
   Traffic has to double back

B. On major road with lane divider

   Lots of traffic
   Easy to see
   Hard to get to, left turns impossible

C. On side street

   Little traffic
   Hard to see
   Easy to get to, but hard to find
      obscure address

D. On major, undivided road

   Lots of traffic
   Easy to see
   Easy to get to
   Easy to find

Figure 13–2 Location Alternatives, Advantages and Disadvantages.

OFFICE LAYOUT

It is not necessary that a large, impressive (and very expensive) office be established at the outset; it is only important that there be enough room for the necessary work to be accomplished comfortably and efficiently. When the firm grows, adjacent space can be added; or it can move to a new, larger location. However, if it is at all possible, some forethought should be given to the likelihood that more space will be needed, and it should be planned for accordingly. A location that offers the opportunity to expand directly into connecting space at some time in the future would be ideal; almost as good would be the opportunity for future expansion to larger quarters elsewhere in the same building or center. In either case, growth could be accomplished without having to educate the public about new addresses.

Room Arrangement

The office space must meet certain needs. There must be some kind of reception area at the front through which all traffic—walk-in and invited—must pass. The area should be large enough to accommodate a receptionist's desk and equipment, and there should be enough seating space for people who are waiting to see brokerage staff. Usually the licenses of the sales force are required by state law to be displayed in this area; if enough wall display space is available, some can also be devoted to displays featuring current listings, accomplishments of the staff members, and certainly any awards and certificates of a professional or community service nature.

Conference Room and Sales Work Areas

A fairly large conference room can be very useful. This space can be multipurpose: it can be used for sales meetings, closings, and any other meetings that involve groups of people too large to be accommodated in other office space. Generally, there also will be an office for the broker-owner. The sales staff themselves can have individual offices, or there can be a large space (called a "bullpen") in which the salespeople's desks are arranged.

While individual offices give the salespeople a sense of importance and a certain degree of privacy that may occasionally be needed, they also offer the opportunity to be reclusive and to separate themselves from the rest of the staff. The bullpen arrangement sees to it that the sales staff are accessible to one another, and provides a convenient and comfortable arrangement for sales meetings and other large gatherings of the firm's members. However, it does eliminate most opportunities for privacy, and can be a problem when dealing with customers who are not particularly fond of discussing matters they feel are very personal in such an obviously public environment.

The actual choice of offices or bullpen has to be left to the broker-owner's particular vision of the firm's needs, but the prime objective should be to obtain the arrangement that contributes most to the firm's efficiency and productivity. A compromise could be the arrangement of cubicles: small office-like spaces separated by partial walls, sometimes glassed, which create the feeling of some privacy and personal space without closing the entire office into small, separated spaces.

Broker's and Manager's Offices

The broker and the sales manager, if there is one, should have separate offices near the salespeople's work area. In a bullpen arrangement, the sales manager's office can have glass walls, but there must be some way of assuring the broker's office of privacy (curtains across glass areas, for example), because he will need it frequently. Often he will discuss matters with individual staff members that are their business alone; also, as a manager, there will be occasions when he needs a disturbance-free environment in which to do the planning and decision making necessary to run the firm properly. Figure 13–3 shows two possible arrangements of a typical 1800 square foot (30 × 60 feet) office area.

Careful attention should be paid to sound control, especially in bullpen arrangements. Carpeting and acoustical ceiling absorb a lot of noise, but wall paneling and other flat surfaces reflect it. The use of draperies, tapestry-type wall decoration, and the like will cut down considerably on reflected noise. It should be noted that a quiet environment is an impressive one, and that the relatively small cost of sound control can pay big dividends with respect to earning the admiration of customers for the brokerage's surroundings.

The Reception Area

The arrangement of the reception area is of great importance, as it is the first part of the office space that potential and actual customers will see. It should be decorated conservatively and comfortably, and people should feel at ease when they enter it. Lavish surroundings are not necessary, but care should be taken to assure that the appearance and comfort of the area do not detract from the firm's image objective. A typical reception area arrangement is shown in Figure 13–4. The receptionist's work area is arranged to allow for typing, answering telephones, and greeting customers. The desk space should be large, but not imposing, allowing for proper work space without crowding, and identifying the receptionist as the person that a customer should speak to upon entering. A small, comfortable seating area is located within easy view of the receptionist but far enough away that waiting customers can converse without feeling that they are disturbing anyone.

The arrangement provides a large wall area for display, if desired, and a clear path from the main door to the doorways leading to the offices. However, this path goes directly past the receptionist, thus providing control over entry into the office area. Usually the receptionist will call whomever the visitor wants to see; the desired party then will come to the reception area to escort the

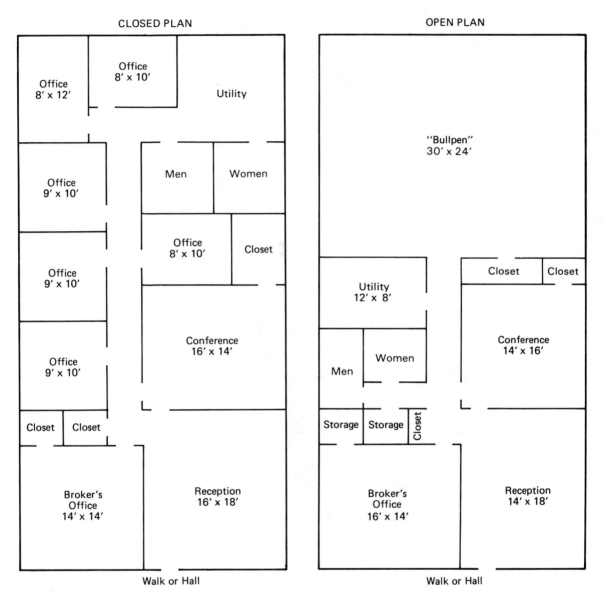

Figure 13-3. Office Plans - Typical 1800 Square Foot Office (60′ × 30′).

customer to his office or desk. The receptionist can escort back into the office area also, but this will mean leaving the reception area unattended.

The reception area should have separate doors leading into the office area and to the conference room, especially if that room is used for closings and other frequent meetings with customers. If the office area is of the bullpen type and the door from the reception room opens directly into it, it is advisable to

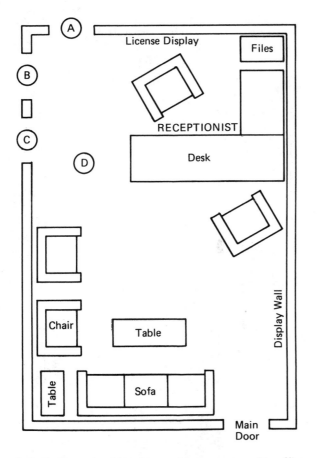

Figure 13-4. Typical Reception Area - 14' × 18'.

A, B, C: Doors should lead to conference room and to offices. If office area door leads directly into bullpen-type area, a third door should lead into broker's private office.

D: Location of doors gives receptionist control over passage to them.

provide another door, if possible, between the reception area and the broker's private office.

Storage

The brokerage firm will require a large amount of storage space. Considerable recordkeeping is required, and space for the necessary files must be provided. Supplies, unused signs, copying machines, and numerous other items must be stored as well. Much of this space could be incorporated into a utility room, which could also contain coffee machines, a small refrigerator, a hotplate, and other necessary items for the use of the staff. The conference room ought to have a storage closet, especially if it is used for staff meetings: items and exhibits used in these meetings could be kept there. A bullpen arrangement might include a handy supply closet in which contract forms, stationery, and the like might be stored; if separate offices are chosen, these items could be kept in a hall closet. And, of course, the office will have a bathroom. Larger ones might require separate ladies' and men's rooms.

FURNISHINGS AND EQUIPMENT

Office equipment and furnishings should be chosen for comfort and efficiency. Luxury for its own sake should be avoided because it wastes a lot of money and because comfortable surroundings are more important to good business performance than expensive trappings. This is not to say that the office should be stark and bare, but rather that money spent on furnishing and equipping the office should return value in the form of better performance by the firm and its personnel.

The Salesperson's Station

Salespeople spend much of their time outside the offices of the firm itself, so they will usually equip their automobiles and homes with some of the things they need. Still, they will need places to work in the office as well. Ideally, each should have a desk (or "station") and seating area that they can use exclusively. The desk can be any type, so long as it is comfortable to use. Most salespeople will appreciate one with two file drawers, instead of a row of smaller drawers, since they will have to keep many records, contracts, and papers in a place where they can be well organized for easy reference. If smaller desks with little drawer space are provided, then there must be access to filing cabinet space for each salesperson.

A salesperson's desk should be equipped with a telephone; if possible it should have a very soft ring, since blaring telephones are disturbing. This is most important if the bullpen arrangement is used. While it may seem extravagant to put a telephone on each desk, it must be remembered that real estate sales people make extensive use of the telephone, and assigning more than one to a telephone can create difficult conflicts and considerable inconvenience.

Access to typewriters will depend upon the availability of secretarial service in the firm. If the sales staff does most of its own letter writing and other typing, then several typewriters should be provided, although it is not necessary for each salesperson's station to have one. An efficient system is to have two or three typewriters arranged along the wall of the bullpen for use by all salespeople. Typewriters should be electric, preferably with carbon film ribbons. These make clean, clear copy and also strike hard enough to make several clear copies at once. Since contracts often require multiple copies, the need for clarity and the ability to strike through several sheets at once is obvious.

Some firms have salespeople who do a lot of work with the public at their desks. If this is the case, a somewhat larger area is required, to allow for several people to gather comfortably around a desk at the same time. While the salesperson's own chair obviously should be comfortable, if additional seating is required, it too should be comfortable and handy. Large, heavy chairs should not be used since they are hard to move about when people wish to draw up to the desk to read contracts or sign them. In this type of situation, a desk with an oversized top that projects several inches beyond the base is very useful. These are convenient for other people to use at the same time that the salesperson is in his own place. Such a desk is almost mandatory for the broker's own station, since he is the most likely to have dealings with others in his office. The same can be said for the sales manager's facilities.

Secretarial Stations

Secretarial desk space should be devoted to the work that is to be done. If the secretary is not a receptionist or does not take messages, a telephone is not required. However, proper access to all the supplies and materials needed in the job is necessary. The secretarial station should be convenient to the personnel who will use it, but if possible it should be located where any noise will not interfere with other activities.

Office Equipment

Office equipment is required for word processing and information storage. Some kind of copying machine is a necessity, but only the largest firms will require sophisticated copiers capable of rapid copying and with extra features. The broker's office should be equipped with a fireproof safe in which essential documents and valuables may be kept. Brokerage firms must keep large numbers of records, so filing space and cabinetry are essential. The broker should have such facilities in his office and the sales staff should have access to such space either in their desks or in easily available storage units. It probably will be necessary eventually to keep several filing units in some part of the office to keep the papers and documents that the law and sensible practice require.

The telephone system is very important. It should have several lines coming into the office, with access to as many lines as possible at each telephone. It also can be used as a means of communication within the office, a convenience if the firm is large enough to occupy a considerable space.

Reference Materials

Brokerage firms have to keep a lot of information on hand for reference by various personnel. The firm should make a significant effort to maintain up-to-date records of all sales activity that takes place in its areas of interest. This is the most effective way to keep abreast of its markets. A small library of useful reference books ought to be kept. These should include a dictionary, a law dictionary, one or two books of real estate principles, books dealing with sales and listing techniques, and other materials of interest. A property law book should be available as well.

Special reference materials also are necessary. Highly detailed maps of the firm's geographical area of interest ought to be kept, and they should be frequently replaced with new ones showing the latest development that has occurred. Most firms will keep plat books. These are large volumes of maps that show the division of the area into lots and often give measurements and ownership. City directories are assembled by business groups or firms specializing in them. These try to list as many of the population as possible, by address, giving as much information on them (income, profession, age, family size, etc.) as possible. Address-first telephone books are very convenient; instead of listing telephones by the user's name, they list them by address. Those can be used to obtain names of occupants of properties and for making groups of calls to specific areas.

COMPUTER FACILITIES

Not only is this the age of the computer, it is now the age of the *cheap* computer. A small desktop computer, with monitor and rudimentary printer, costs less than electric typewriters did in the 1970s, and will do much more. Most brokerage firms as a matter of course will have at least one of these machines, used for some filing and recordkeeping, word processing, and mailing list generation. Properly used, computer facilities greatly increase the efficiency and output of the sales force and support staff alike. Improperly used, they can be a terrible cash drain.

The computer equipment and attached devices are called *hardware*. The programming that makes the hardware useful is called *software*. Now that small computers have been in use for a decade or more, there has been plenty of time for imaginative programmers and software companies to develop software for virtually any application. Included is software for the real estate office. Some of this is very specialized, and some is general.

Problems with Computers

The great danger in using the computer is buying too much equipment, and using the wrong software. Perhaps the greatest problem for the businessperson who is not a computer expert is finding the necessary information needed to make reasonable decisions about computer equipment and software use. While there are computer stores almost everywhere, the level of knowledge of the sales force of many of them is deplorable. Even if a computer salesperson is knowledgeable about what he sells, he probably does not know the ins and outs of the real estate business and so can impart only general information.

Usefulness of Computers

Computers are good at high-speed calculation and storage and retrieval of information. From these capacities, a wide variety of software applications have been derived. The most popular groups of these are *word processing, spreadsheet analysis, database analysis,* and *accounting.* Word processing is the production of documents—anything from letters to novels and more. Though word processors can be used simply as expensive typewriters, where such software shines is in its editing capacity. A document can be written and then changed, edited, and rearranged at will, quickly and easily. Many word processing programs also have *mailing list* features that can be of great use to the real estate brokerage. These features allow the production of a "boilerplate" document, such as a letter. From a list of names and addresses, and possibly other information, the computer can generate printed letters based upon the boilerplate version, but with the recipient's address and possibly other "personalizing" features added in.

Spreadsheet analysis develops tables of data, usually financial in nature. This software features the ability to alter an entire sheet if changes are made in parts of it. This would be of most use to the accounting arm of a brokerage firm. A firm which does a lot of commercial real estate dealing may find such software useful for making income and return projections on properties. Also, many such programs also can generate mortgage amortization schedules.

Database analysis is generalized, systematic filing with the computer. The database can be anything of interest: invoices, salespeople's records, listings, comparable sales. The database program keeps this data stored and can sort and rearrange the information to present all or part of it in a variety of useful ways.

Accounting software does what the name implies: It keeps the necessary accounting books for the firm. Most applications have a general module and then allow the user to purchase other modules as needed (general ledger, invoice, payroll). Many sophisticated software systems combine features of all of these into very powerful applications. In addition, a huge variety of specialized software performs certain limited functions.

Perhaps the most significant advantage of computers is that they can store information for future use. This is done with *disks*. The *floppy* disk is a piece of magnetic material in a stiff envelope. When inserted into the computer's drive, it can be "read" and "written to" by the computer. The disk becomes a permanent copy of the information on it, available for use on the computer at any time. Depending on the computer being used, the floppy will hold 300,000 to over a million characters of information. (The manuscript for this entire book fits on two 360,000 character floppy disks with room left over.) A *hard* disk is a sophisticated extension of the same principle, able to hold tens of millions of characters of information and to access them much more rapidly. Hard disks usually are installed within the computer itself.

A real estate brokerage firm might use accounting software for its own books and payroll. Database software could handle listings, salesperson data, comparable closed sales, etc. Word processing software could generate all written information for the firm, and could store it as well. For documents such as policy manuals, boilerplate letters, contract forms, and the like, information stored on disks can always be accessed and easily edited to allow for incorporation of changes as they become necessary.

Choosing Computer Equipment

A minimal desktop computer, monitor and rudimentary printer can cost less than $1,000. Also, one can spend tens of thousands for state of the art equipment. The differences have largely to do with data storage capacity, computer memory (RAM), and speed of execution. Computer power is relatively cheap, and it is easy to buy more than one could ever need and still not seem to be spending all that much money.

Two important features seem to be the norm of the computer world: Things are changing all the time, and everything is getting cheaper. Today's state of the art is tomorrow's relic. Your author's own brief history as a computer user is an example. The first edition of this book was typed on an electric typewriter in 1980. In 1981 the author bought his first desktop computer. It had 64K of memory and two 180K disk drives, a black and white display, and cost $2,700. ("K" in computer lingo means 1,000: the 64K memory could hold 64,000 characters of information at one time.)

New and better computers were bought in 1984, early 1986, and late 1986. Each represented a two- to fourfold increase in memory and speed. The manuscript for this second edition of this book was typed, in 1987, on a system with 10 times the memory and 16 times the speed of the first one. Its disk drives are 360K capacity, and it includes a hard disk that holds over 20 million characters. The display is high-tech color. The system cost $3,200 in late 1986. This system would be adequate for most small or medium sized real estate brokerage firms.

Usually whatever is "previous generation" equipment is the best buy. It has been around a while, has had the bugs worked out, and has a lot of software applications. It usually is much less expensive than the very latest developments, and yet has very elegant and powerful sophistication. "Brand name" equipment should be bought, because one of the worst problems in the computer world is the fly-by-night nature of many manufacturers. It is true that "clone" machines can be bought for less, but many manufacturers of such equipment go bankrupt or otherwise disappear, and often the quality of their wares is inferior. Besides, most well-known brands can be bought from discount suppliers or mail-order houses; "list price" usually can be considered a fiction.

Serviceability of equipment is important. If a service center for a particular brand is not conveniently nearby, that brand should be ignored unless the purchaser is willing to run the risk of time-consuming and possibly damaging shipping of the unit back and forth when necessary.

A basic unit should have the maximum available RAM memory, at least one floppy disk drive, and a hard disk. Color displays are nice, but monochrome displays cost hundreds less and, for the real estate brokerage, show everything necessary. Some larger firms may wish to consider a *local area network*. With this arrangement, a powerful central computer is connected to one or more terminals or smaller computers located throughout the office. The central unit contains the data storage system, and may even do the "computing" for the remote units. Such systems are expensive, and may not offer any real advantages to smaller firms.

Choosing Software

Two important questions must be asked when any software purchase is being considered: (1) Is it useful to the business? (2) How difficult is it to learn and use? Usefulness to the business can be a very deceptive thing. While it is nice to know that a given software package will perform this or that function, are those functions really needed? And if they are, is this particular package the best of its kind for the needs of the firm?

A very important consideration is the degree to which the firm itself will have to be discommoded in order to use the software. Some software is fairly rigid, and permits only limited flexibility of use. An accounting package, for example, may do a lot of useful things, but if its required format means that the firm will have to change its accounting records around and alter the ways in which it has been summarizing information, will it really be such a useful tool after all? A key factor will be the degree to which the business itself will have to adjust to fit the software it uses. Ideally, the software should be adjustable to suit the firm's way of doing things.

Some software is very sophisticated, and learning to use it takes a lot of time. If this is the case, then only a few people in the firm actually will use it. For some software that may be all right, but it certainly will not do for software which is intended to be used by the entire sales force. Great strides are being made in this *user interface* problem with software, and as time passes we will see more and more very powerful applications that can be easily learned and used.

OUTSIDE THE OFFICE

Salespeople do much of their work outside the office. In fact, the average salesperson may spend more time in his automobile than he does in the firm's offices. Thus, it is important to give some consideration to the equipment and environment for these out-of-office times.

Of course, some of the environment is beyond control. When a salesperson visits a prospect's home or office, he can do nothing about the surroundings he finds. When he shows property he can have some control, especially if it is his own listing. Then he can instruct the owner how to prepare the property to show well. However, for the current discussion, these are minor considerations.

Work Space at Home

The salespeople and the managers of the firm should set aside some space in their homes for a work area. Even if it is only a desk in a corner of a room, it will be a valuable asset to the job. A lot of the desk work that does not need supervision can be done here, with the comfort of home nearby. It usually is advantageous to have a telephone with a separate line; the salesperson will sometimes spend hours on the telephone, and without the separate line the rest of the family will have no use of the telephone at all. Also, a separate line will mean that the salesperson will use that number as his home number for business calls, and it will be easy to tell whether a call coming in is business-oriented by observing which line is ringing. The salesperson can install an answering device on his line to avoid the problem of having other family members take messages when he is not there and, especially when children would answer, getting the messages garbled or confused.

The Salesperson's Automobile

The salesperson spends much of his time in his automobile. He uses it to carry buying prospects to and from properties that he shows. Often it doubles as his office. It should be chosen and equipped carefully so that it will be the useful tool it is capable of being. It may seem odd to discuss the choice of an automobile in a book that concerns real estate brokerage, but for many of the firm's customers the salesperson and his automobile are the only evidence of the firm they see until they arrive at the offices for the signing of settlement documents. Some customers never see anything else.

The automobile must double both as a temporary office of sorts for the salesperson and as a carrier of passengers. It should be chosen to do both well. Unfortunately, most automobiles are wretchedly designed for the first purpose. Since the salesperson will usually be driving, he needs space in the front seat to store the materials he will use. Glove compartments are notoriously deficient for that purpose. A few cars are available with parcel shelves under the dashboard, but most of these are unsuitable for a real estate salesperson for other reasons. Usually there is nothing to do with the forms, listing books, and other materials except to pile them in the front seat. Salespeople also carry around For Sale signs, stakes, and the like; these, of course, go in the trunk.

The salesperson's car should provide a comfortable place for passengers. The most frequent passengers a salesperson carries are a husband and wife to whom he is showing property, but often he will carry only one person. It is fairly rare that more than two or three people will accompany the salesperson to see property, so there is little need to provide for more.

Given all these requirements, the specific nature of the automobile can be stated with reasonable precision. It should be a four-door sedan. Passengers—especially married couples—will tend to ride together in the back and will not appreciate having to crawl over and past the front seats to squirm in and out of the front doors of a two-door car. It should be a fairly large car; regardless of the number of doors, the back seats of many smaller cars are very uncomfortable. The car should be air-conditioned, except perhaps in the coldest climates. It should run quietly, because there is likely to be considerable conversation going on among the occupants.

What we have described is, essentially, a full-sized, four-door sedan. Unfortunately, these aren't being made much anymore, and few modern smaller cars, even with four doors, can be said to be particularly spacious. One alternative is a van. Large ones are available, but several manufacturers produce minivans. These are relatively small and fuel-efficient, but due to their design can be extremely roomy inside.

DISCUSSION QUESTIONS AND PROJECTS

1. How should the location of a real estate office be selected?
2. How should a real estate office be arranged?
3. Compare and contrast the advantages and disadvantages of the bullpen sales area and the plan of giving individual offices to salespeople.
4. Take a small survey of successful real estate salespeople in your area. What kinds of cars do they use? What equipment do they keep with them and at their homes?
5. Examine the reference area of a local successful brokerage firm. What kinds of materials does it keep on hand? What purposes do they serve?
6. Do any brokerage firms in your area make extensive use of in-house computer systems (i.e., systems owned and used by the firm itself for its own purposes)? Why do they do so?
7. From a survey of one or more brokerage firms, determine the kinds of computer equipment and software which are most useful to a typical real estate brokerage firm. Do you have any suggestions as to improvements which could be made?
8. Survey some of the computer stores in your area to determine how helpful they could be to a real estate brokerage firm looking to make use of computer equipment.

REFERENCES

DOOLEY, THOMAS W., "The Real Estate Office of Tomorrow", in *The McGraw-Hill Real Estate Handbook*, ed. Robert Irwin, ch. 36. New York, NY: McGraw-Hill Book Company, 1984.

MESSNER, STEPHEN D., BYRL N. BOYCE, HAROLD G. TRIMBLE, AND ROBERT L. WARD, *Analyzing Real Estate Opportunities: Market and Feasibility Studies*. Chicago, IL:REALTORS® National Marketing Institute, 1977.

O'MARA, W. PAUL, *Office Development Handbook*. Washington, DC: Urban Land Institute, 1982.

PHILLIPS, BARBARA, "Getting Started in Real Estate," in *The McGraw-Hill Real Estate Handbook*, ed. Robert Irwin, ch. 31. New York, NY: McGraw-Hill Book Company, 1984.

PHILLIPS, BARBARA, "Office Management for Brokers," in *The McGraw-Hill Real Estate Handbook*, ed. Robert Irwin, ch. 33. New York, NY: McGraw-Hill Book Company, 1984.

Real Estate Office Management: People Functions Systems, ch. 19. Chicago, IL: REALTORS® National Marketing Institute, 1975.

FOURTEEN

ESTABLISHING AND MARKETING THE SUCCESSFUL REAL ESTATE BROKERAGE

Establishing a New Brokerage Firm

Choosing the Market Area and Segment

Marketing the New Brokerage

Publicity

Advertising in Media

Brokerage Office Open Houses

Mailouts

Advertising Cost: The New and the Established Firm

Identification of the Firm

A Final Word: Philosophy and Policy

A real estate brokerage firm is in the business of selling. Not only does it sell real estate, but it also must be able to sell *itself*, by convincing people to use its services. Much of the sales and marketing effort, of course, is provided by the salesmanship skills of the sales force and is not directly a management operation, although there is much that management can do to improve and refine the abilities of its salespeople to do the job well.

However, the firm must have its own marketing policy and program in addition to the efforts made by the sales force. A generalized publicity and advertising program will help the company to establish and maintain an image as a professional firm, and there also is much the firm can do to advertise and market the individual properties that are listed and sold by its salespeople. While individual salespeople can and do establish their own reputations, the firm should make the same effort to establish its own image as a successful competitor in its field. The good reputations of the firm and the salespeople will complement each other; both firm and sales force will benefit.

Our discussion begins with consideration of establishing and publicizing the new firm, for this will cover most methods of general publicity. Then we will consider more specific aspects of publicity and advertising as they apply to the established firm, and the support of its sales force.

ESTABLISHING A NEW BROKERAGE FIRM

Once one has obtained a broker's license, one has the legal right to set up an independent real estate brokerage business. A great many potential broker-owners stop at that point: They set up shop in their own homes and languish from then on. They have invested time and money in the preparation and fees necessary to obtain the required licenses, but do not follow up with the even greater investment necessary to get their businesses off the ground and heading for possible career success. They set up offices in a spare room, in the corner of the recreation room, or even in the glove compartments of their cars! They may handle a listing here or there for friends or acquaintances, and may on occasion show a buyer around to listings held by other, better-established firms, but since they do not really exert the effort to establish themselves as recognizable, credible businesses with genuine, working operations, their chances for long-term success are very limited.

Broker Qualifications

In a few states it is possible to obtain a broker's license without ever having been licensed as a salesperson, and so without having had any genuine experience in the real estate field at all. In most other states, however, the requirement that a broker license applicant have been a licensed salesperson for a certain length of time does not guarantee that new brokers are genuinely experienced, since they could have had their licenses held active for the required period of time without actually participating to any significant extent in the business. While such poorly prepared new broker licensees face a tremendous uphill battle, they can achieve success by diligence and hard work, although many of them will find they know so little of the true nature of the business that they will become disheartened and give up.

A great many new brokers, however, have had extensive experience in the real estate sales field, and seek to establish their own businesses as a logical continuation of their career pattern. While they may have the talent and expertise to handle sales, they must become aware of the requirements and responsibilities of actually running a business for themselves. They know where and how to find the customers that they need and are familiar with the real estate markets they will operate in. They may even have regular customers they cultivated previously and who will continue to deal with them once they set out on their own. Even so, the actual running of a business entails much more than they have been used to doing, and in any case the manner in which a business is established and the amount and suitability of the effort undertaken to get it underway are essential to future success.

Permanent Business

In order to establish a successful business, a real estate broker needs more than listings or potential buyers. These will only last a short time, and must continually be replaced with new listings and new buyers. A new broker may experience an initial flush of success as he makes deals involving his friends and family, but soon they will run out. They cannot be expected to be frequent repeat customers, because very few people engage in real estate transactions more than once every few years. Occasionally, the new broker may find a buyer or two who is interested in accumulating properties, and so may be a frequent customer, but unless these people deal in large, expensive purchases, it is unlikely that they can sustain the broker with their commissions alone. Furthermore, investors and large-scale buyers rarely find the services of a new broker satisfactory when they just as easily can use the services of established and experienced firms. It is even less likely that a new broker will find a seller with many properties to sell, and so many listings for him. A large-scale owner seeking to sell holdings is almost certain to employ an experienced firm with a good track record.

Long-Range Plan for Success

If the new firm is to succeed, it must be planned for sensibly. A simple idea that it would be nice to run a business or organize with certain people is not enough. The firm must be viewed as a business enterprise. A vision of what the firm should be and will be is necessary, and it must include all aspects of the business. Plans, even at the very beginning, should anticipate *reasonably* what the new firm can expect to encounter, how to cope with the problems that will arise, and what goals and objectives to strive for. Plans should be made for every step of the process of making a successful, permanent business out of a new one.

The following considerations all play an important part in the proper establishment of a new real estate brokerage business:

1. The firm must select the geographic market area and the types of properties it will specialize in initially.
2. An office must be set up, with proper consideration given to location and physical layout.
3. An initial publicity and advertising plan should be designed to familiarize the public with the firm and the services it offers, and to create a public view of the firm as a successful business offering reliable and desirable service.
4. From the very beginning, the firm should have a management plan that establishes the philosophy and goals of the business and considers future growth and development. The firm's management should be aware of the proper management and organizational techniques to assure success in the achievement of the firm's goals.

Some aspects of (2) and (4) already have been discussed in previous chapters.

CHOOSING THE MARKET AREA AND SEGMENT

Quite often the type of geographic and property market the brokerage will concentrate on already is decided by the experience and knowledge of the participants in the new firm. Obviously, it makes sense for them to continue, at least initially, in the same market areas in which they have achieved their success. Nonetheless, it is necessary to point out some possible pitfalls.

First, it appears from experience that a great many brokers starting new firms pick that time to try to enter new markets as well. Thus the time and effort they should be spending getting their new businesses going is cut into by the equally demanding task of expansion of their business horizons. Each of these efforts is important and deserves the kind of attention that it can get only when there are no other serious considerations (including each other) to be handled. The new broker who has achieved success as a salesperson already has a certain degree of knowledge and expertise concerning his own specialized niche in the market; while he concentrates upon establishing his business, he should limit his market penetration to those areas he already knows. Once his new firm is on a solid footing and running smoothly, he can begin to concentrate upon well-planned and conducted expansion.

Experience of the Sales Force

It should be emphasized that we are considering the market experience of all participants in the new firm, and it is not always the case that all of them have been specializing in exactly the same types of property and geographical areas. Thus, any individual in a new firm may find that the firm as a whole can consider a larger market than he can individually. Indeed, a diversity of background among the sales force of the new firm will make for much more efficient expansion, in that the experience and knowledge of each member becomes easily available to all the others.

Still, it is not advisable for a new firm's sales force to be so widely divergent that the firm's *own* market penetration, which is essentially the sum of that of all its participants, is too widespread. The reason is that the firm itself will establish a market identity, and it is advisable that this identity be something that appears concrete and well thought out. A firm that covers the map in all types of real estate may appear to be spread too thin. It may seem to offer only the services of an *individual* who is associated with the firm, instead of the services of the total sales force of a *business*. Very large firms can offer a wide diversity of services because they have depth in all of them; the small firm just starting out is better off to give the impression that while its services are limited to particular areas, in those areas it can offer depth and considerable knowledge, talent, and expertise.

Geographical Areas

In a small city or town the geographical area of specialization may not be particulary important, since most brokerage firms in such places are expected to cover it entirely. However, in cities of 75,000 or larger populations it becomes more important to consider only a part of the metropolitan area as the prime district in which the firm will specialize. Too large a geographical area can lead to a number of problems. First, there will be great distances between some of the properties being listed and shown and the firm's offices; this will lead to a lot of time spent traveling to and from appointments and consequent loss of valuable direct contact time.

More important, the market itself will be accustomed to firms that specialize geographically. This means that a firm located some distance from a particular neighborhood may be at a competitive disadvantage with those firms that more obviously specialize in that area. Furthermore, in larger cities there is much more significant diversity among large sections and neighborhoods. This can mean that a firm located in one area will be viewed as specializing in that area only, and in the types of properties predominating in that area. Firms with different locations will have to work harder to establish confidence in their ability to compete head to head with more local firms. Larger firms can overcome this problem by setting up branches in each district in which they do business; they can capitalize on the prestige and impressiveness of their overall size as well as offering the specialization associated with each branch.

A multiple branch business usually is well beyond the capability of a new firm, and is not advisable for it in any case. There is little point in exposure to more problems than are absolutely necessary. Therefore, the new firm should make a very careful assessment of the location it will occupy. The knowledge and experience of the members of the firm should be taken into consideration. If it appears that the total area of possible coverage is too large for a single firm to handle properly, certain compromises have to be made. It is not necessary to prohibit sales force members from dealing in certain market areas, so long as it is within their capabilities, but the choice of location can create a public image suggesting certain areas of specialty, and the firm must consider just what this image will be. It will tend to force a certain amount of specialization upon the firm, and therefore a location should be chosen with an eye to promoting the forms of business the firm is most likely to perform well.

Market Segment

Only the largest firms are equipped to handle comfortably all kinds of real estate sales; the new firm generally must specialize in a particular *market segment*, and depend on growth and experience to allow it to expand its offerings. Usually the types of property that will be handled by a firm are determined by the experience of the sales force that is assembled. Most new firms specialize in houses, since this is where the experience of most salespeople lies. Of course, experienced commercial or land salespeople may decide to start their own firms, and when they do they are best advised to continue in the areas that they have experience in. Also, an occasional new broker may establish his own firm for the specific reason that it allows him to branch out into new types of properties that were forbidden to him during his employment with other firms. In these cases, the new broker will be taking some extra risk: not only is he setting up a new firm, but he also is trying to establish himself in a new market.

It generally is easiest for new brokerage firms to establish themselves as residential sales specialists at first. The market for homes is by far the largest and broadest real estate market, and one in which new firms are familiar sights. Homeowners and buyers are large in number and are not nearly so likely to have built up loyalty or confidence in particular firms or salespeople; therefore they will be more receptive to employing a new firm. Buyers and sellers of investment property are much more discriminating in their choices of real estate firms to use, and are more difficult to convince that a new firm can provide the services that they need—unless, of course, the new firm includes personnel with whom they are familiar and comfortable.

MARKETING THE NEW BROKERAGE

The main objective of a new brokerage firm is to get its business going as quickly as possible. Advance organizational planning prepares the new firm to operate efficiently as soon as it is established. However, in order for it to be successful and efficient, it must have some business to do. An initial advertising and publicity campaign should be undertaken, designed to make both the public and the rest of the local brokerage industry aware of the new brokerage, its personnel, and what it can do. This kind of advertising may initially be considerably wider in scope and more expensive than the ongoing advertising and publicity efforts that will be maintained once the firm is established.

The new firm usually lacks listings, since it is generally impossible (and in most states illegal) for a salesperson or broker to take his listings with him when he transfers to a different firm. Since a major source of listings is activity with buyers (once they have bought, they may have to list currently owned property for sale that they no longer need) and, more generally, activity in the market of any kind, it is important for the new firm to establish good relations with other firms, which then will allow the new firm to cooperate on the sales of their listings. In return, of course, the new firm agrees to allow the existing cooperative firms access to its own listings once they begin to accumulate.

The new brokerage should make a sustained effort to contact the existing firms with which it expects to do business. The reputations of the members of the new firm will be very helpful here, and in many cases they will find that it will not be difficult to make cooperative arrangements with the firms that they have departed. Membership in local brokerage industry professional organizations and groups is essential, because they provide an efficient means of contact with others in the field. If the local area has a multiple listing arrangement, the new firm should try to join it, since it will immediately supply a good source of other companies' listings with which to engage in initial efforts.

A good effort should also be made to make the firm known to the general public, because reputation and a high profile also provide a good source of listings as well as potential buyers. Mailout campaigns, neighborhood canvassing, and similar activities can be effective. While intensive activity of this kind may not be economically possible all the time for an established company, a short-term, intensive campaign of this nature can be an effective way of building rapid public identification and recognition of the new company.

Careful attention should be given the legal situation of a new firm when these initial contacts are made. Generally, the new firm does not exist until a license has been issued to the principal broker (or the firm itself, in states that allow companies to be licensed), and all public announcements of any kind should be delayed until the license has been issued. Individual salespeople should not communicate their new association to the public until their licenses are issued to and held by the new brokerage. This requirement can mean that active publicity cannot begin until the company is actually ready to start business, unless it has been decided that there will be some delay between the time the licenses are issued and the time the new brokerage opens for business. Whatever the scheduling, it is usually advisable that active publicity, advertising, and similar efforts not occur until the firm's existence has been recognized by the issuance of a license, and that no individual salesperson engage in such activity until his license is issued to and held by the new firm.

PUBLICITY

A firm's success depends upon its ability to attract customers; if customers are to patronize a business, they must know that it is there and what services it offers. A firm that has been in existence a long time can rely upon its reputation, repeat business from satisfied customers, referrals, and other sources of customers, while a new firm must cultivate these, in the meantime establishing its identity in the markets in which it competes.

Even before the firm opens its doors for business, planning must be under way and introduction of the firm to the public can begin. When the business actually gets under way, additional introductory steps should be taken, and all during the time the firm is striving to gain the acceptance it desires these efforts must continue. Once the firm is established, it should have a continuing program of advertising and other means of publicity to keep its name before the public and to make the public aware of the quality of its services. Several means of introducing the firm and continuing publicity and advertising efforts can be employed.

Previous Customers of the Sales Force

The brokerage's experienced sales personnel will have built up their own reputations in their earlier activities, and these reputations should be traded on vigorously. Periodically, each salesperson should contact all customers for whom he has provided satisfactory service within the previous year or two, so as to maintain their acquaintance. This is usually accomplished by letter, although telephone and other, more direct contact should not be ruled out.

If the salesperson has joined a new firm, the message should emphasize the salesperson's enthusiasm concerning his new association, and should point out the advantages to his customers of his new firm and the new people he will be working with. A brief but informative description of the new brokerage should be included, as well as special mention of any particular emphases the new firm plans to add to its services that would be of interest to potential customers. Particular qualifications of the salesperson's new associates should be mentioned, as well as indication of how his new association will enable the salesperson to improve his service.

The same kinds of communication should be directed at other people who might be a future source of business to the salesperson; this would include members of organizations he belongs to, friends, acquaintances, and others whom he has met in the course of business. Former customers and friends and associates are valuable sources of referral business; they should be cultivated continuously all during a salesperson's career. Informing them of his change of position and the new firm he has joined will have the double effect of putting both himself and his new firm into their thoughts.

Other Brokerage Firms

A real estate salesperson quickly establishes relationships and connections among other agents and firms in his business, even though they are also his competitors. Since so much real estate selling involves more than one firm, these relationships are important. The new firm should communicate its existence to all other firms with which it may do business in the future. It should outline its objectives, so far as its cooperative services are concerned, and the terms under which it will engage in cooperative deals. It should also describe any special services that it intends to offer. The new firm's sales force should also inform the salespeople and firms with which they have dealt of their new situations. If the local brokerage industry is aware of the new firm's existence, the possibility that referrals and cooperative deals with other firms will materialize is greatly enhanced.

An existing firm ought to maintain contact with other firms through its day to day business activity, so the need for formal communications of a purely publicity nature is reduced. Other firms will be able to evaluate the brokerage by its performance and the ease (or difficulty) of dealing with it, and these are far more important and impressive than specific publicity efforts can be.

Personal Contacts

Each salesperson knows a large number of people who ought to be kept informed about him. These include people with whom he regularly deals, friends, associates, members of organizations he belongs to, and others who can be classified as important contacts because of their influence or ability to give the salesperson useful leads and information. These people should be contacted individually, as many as possible by telephone or face-to-face meeting, when a new firm has been organized.

At the very least they should be sent letters—not the same letter used in cold canvassing, but one that is more personal and less of a form letter. Each of these contacts offers the opportunity to publicize a new firm and to give the salesperson's own reasons for choosing the new association.

Community Activity

Individual salespeople and brokers can generate considerable positive public response for themselves and their firms by becoming involved in community activity. Fraternal and charitable organizations always need volunteers for fund drives and other community work. Firms themselves sometimes may be able to act as corporate sponsors for civic and charitable events. The list of possibilities is long. However, certain ones should be avoided, especially if they are controversial or are intended to advocate certain policies. A high profile in these activities can alienate those who hold the opposite view. For example, visibly working to promote the United Way drive will likely produce only desirable and beneficial responses from the public. On the other hand, demonstrating in favor of anti-abortion or pro-choice positions may alienate people who disagree. For the same reasons, partisan political activity should be kept quiet unless it is likely that most members of the public whom the salesperson or firm wants to impress hold the same views.

ADVERTISING IN MEDIA

While advertising through the media is not as effective an attention-getter as individual contact, it is valuable because it reaches a lot of people at a relatively low cost per contact. Newspaper advertising should be done in series, rather than as a single explosion of one or two large ads, even though this may mean that smaller ads must be used.

Traditionally, placement of such advertisements is in the classified section or homes section of the newspaper where real estate advertising predominates, and in the financial section. The former location aims at the market itself, while the latter usually impresses only those most economically important citizens who may have a reason to read the business section of the paper on a regular basis. The ads should, over time, tell quite a lot about the firm, but it is unwise to try to squeeze too much information into a single ad, especially if it leads to a cluttered look. The actual layout and composition of these advertisements is very important, and they should be designed by professionals in the field, unless the new firm happens to have someone on hand who is genuinely effective in producing good advertising copy.

Radio and Television

Radio and television advertising can be effective, but expensive. While popular newspapers tend to get into the hands of practically everyone in a given area, radio and TV are much more selective. Therefore it is essential that some information be gained before launching a radio or TV campaign to assure that the right people will be contacted by the advertising. Spot ads (ten seconds or less) are effective and relatively inexpensive, but they cannot relay much information, and are most useful in establishing name recognition. Longer ads require more elaborate production, particularly in television, where visual interest is so important and so expensive to obtain.

Different times of day are priced differently for ads, and the advertiser should make a careful analysis of the composition of the audience he will reach compared to the cost he will entail. One analytical technique used in the radio and television business is the *cost-per-thousand* measure, in which the cost of the advertisement is compared to the number of thousands of people whom the ad reaches. But the composition of the people hearing the ad is important as well; a cheap cost per thousand is not much use if the people being reached are mostly children or other people who will not be likely to use the services of a real estate brokerage.

Audience

One drawback to most media advertising is that the ad reaches an audience considerably larger than the one the brokerage firm is aiming for. In some states a given television station's signal may be shunted to an enormous geographical area, most of whose inhabitants will have no use at all for the advertising brokerage's service. It is not much consolation to a brokerage to discover that its television advertising has made it the most recognized name in areas where it does no business, while its competitors' more locally oriented advertising has given them the edge in the areas in which the firm actually operates. Even in larger cities where radio and television audiences are largely local, the individual brokerage will find that its message gets all over town, including into many local areas in which it does not operate. Therefore, it is essential that the advertising firm get as much information as possible with respect to a particular medium's reach into its own market area so that the effectiveness of the advertising can be accurately measured against its cost.

BROKERAGE OFFICE OPEN HOUSES

An effective way to introduce a new business is the open house, at which members of the public are invited to the new office to see and learn about the operation first hand. A single event can be held, but it often is more effective to have a series of open houses. This will make it more convenient for people to come when they can, and will create a continuing hospitable atmosphere. Open houses should be informal gatherings; most of the salespeople should be present, but relatively little hard selling should take place. The objective of the open house is to introduce the business to the neighborhood, but it also is an excellent source of prospects for present and future business. Visitors should be encouraged to leave their names and addresses; since they were interested enough to show up it is likely that they may become customers in the future.

At the open house brochures can be distributed, and attractive displays that emphasize the firm's services can be employed. Salespeople should circulate among the guests and find out all they can about them; if any of them express interest in doing business they should be cultivated, but even curiosity seekers should be made to feel welcome. If visitors leave with a positive impression of the business, they probably will relay that feeling to others.

The established firm also can make good use of the open house. Instead of introducing itself as a new firm, it can reintroduce itself to the community from time to time. Open houses can be combined with picnics or other community functions the firm sponsors; in fact, many firms prefer to sponsor some activity away from the office just to avoid the disruption.

The open house should be well publicized in advance; newspaper advertising is effective, as is mention of the open house in any mailings that are made. If the brokerage has decided not to send out cold letters, then it ought to consider sending open house invitations to residents of the neighborhoods in which it will operate. Invitations and envelopes can be made up at relatively modest cost, sometimes in the form of postcards, which greatly reduces the cost and complexity of envelope stuffing and mailing.

MAILOUTS

Mailouts are letters, brochures, or other information mailed to individual members of the general public who are unknown to the person or firm doing the canvassing. A brokerage can send a mailing to every address in the geographical area in which it expects to concentrate. In this letter the new firm is described, its services promoted, and one or more of its agents profiled. The objective, of course, is to make the firm known to a large population in a manner somewhat more personal and direct than media advertising. The direct contact, it is hoped, will make a more significant impression and so will help the firm and its services to be remembered. It is likely that such a mailing will reach people who actually are considering buying or selling real estate, so the enclosures should solicit them to contact the new firm for a future discussion of its services.

Attractiveness

A key factor in a mail campaign is assuring that the letters will be opened and read by the addressees. The firm's own letterhead should be used, and the design and appearance of the letterhead, paper, and firm's logo (the identifying symbol that it uses on its signs, advertising, and forms) should encourage the proper degree of curiosity. A frequently effective ploy is to use stamps, at the first class rate, on the envelopes; people are more likely to open a letter from an apparent stranger if it appears that he took the effort to affix a stamp. Such letters also appear more important to the sender than letters with bulk mail imprints or obviously cut-rate stamps on them. The recipient does not know what the letter contains, and if he is given the impression that the sender made a special effort to send it to him, he is much more likely to open it. A great many people ignore mail that is obviously of an advertising nature, so other steps may have to be taken to assure that at least at first glance the letter appears interesting enough to open. Address labels pasted to the envelope are a giveaway, as is cheap paper or printing.

Letter

The enclosure and its purpose cannot be disguised, but it can be made attractive. A salutation that begins "Dear Sir . . ." or "Dear Occupant . . . ," makes a very poor impression. Best of all is genuine typewritten name and address of the recipient, followed by "Dear Mr. _____." This becomes a personal letter, and as such will rarely be ignored. Even if the recipient is not immediately interested in the brokerage's services, he cannot but be impressed by the obvious care and effort devoted to gaining his personal attention, and this favorable impression will remain with him. Once again, the letter should be on good-quality letterhead paper with the firm's name, address, and telephone number attractively and prominently displayed.

The letter should cover no more than one page and should be brief and to the point, without crowding the page. Some firms consider mailing attractive brochures in which a great deal more can be said about the firm, but the brochure is much more impersonal and less likely to be read. It is not necessary to tell everything at first contact; a better strategy is to say enough to get the person interested in the firm, but not so much that he becomes bored with the details or chooses not to read anything at all because it looks too imposing or time consuming. Therefore, for mail canvassing, the letter is preferable.

Figure 14–1 shows such a letter. Note its attractive appearance and the fact that it is not wordy. Still, a lot of information is contained: (a) the fact that the firm is new; (b) that the firm was organized to improve the opportunity for the sales staff to give good service; (c) that the salesperson writing the letter is experienced and professional; (d) that by implication his associates are too; and (e) that the firm intends to offer a high standard of service. In this case, the firm has decided to hold an open house at its offices, and the letter leads off with an invitation to attend. This kind of opening is effective, because at the very beginning a hospitable offer creates a positive mood.

Costs

Sending such individual letters is not cheap, but the extra expense is usually worth it. The main objective of the new firm is to make itself known as quickly as possible to as many people as possible; the established firm wants to keep itself known. The mailout can provide wide immediate contact and, properly handled, can get the message to most of the people contacted. Considerable labor is involved in typing the addresses individually on the envelope and affixing the stamps. If the letters themselves are individually typed, the time expended can become prodigious. It is here that computer equipment with word processing software can be very useful. With the proper mailing list features, the computer can print the letters individually. It can even address the envelopes, since envelopes affixed to a punched liner for continuous feed into a printer are available. Furthermore, most of this work can be done while the computer equipment is unattended, and at times when it is not needed for something else.

Mailing lists should not be difficult to come by. City directories or some other compilation of names and addresses in relevant market areas should be in the reference collection of every real estate brokerage firm. Mailouts should be confined to the firm's perceived market area so that the expense involved in them has the most effective results.

DOVER REALTY COMPANY

1776 Twelfth Street, Waltham, Xxxxx 12345   (908) 555-4321

Mr. James R. Patton
3318 Martin Avenue
Waltham, XXXXX 12345

Dear Mr. Patton:

    I and my associates have joined together to found Dover Realty, Inc.
We will be having an open house at our new offices on Saturday, April 18
from 3PM to 9PM and I would like to extend to you and your family my invitation to visit us at that time.

    Dover Realty is the result of our philosophy that a real estate company
should offer dedicated, sincere service to the people whom it represents.
I and all my new associates understand how important buying or selling a home
is to a family such as yours and we believe that a real estate professional's
best measure of success is the satisfaction and confidence of everyone he works
with.

    I have been listing and selling homes in the Marlowe Hills area for over
five years, and our other sales associates, Ken Marlowe, Nancy MacConnell,
Rupert DePlane and Margaret Sayers bring the same kind of experience to our
new firm. We offer every service that a buyer or seller may need. We constantly monitor and evaluate all information available concerning the markets in
which we specialize, and pride ourselves on our up-to-date knowledge. We intend
to offer the highest possible standard of professional service.

    If you are considering buying or selling a home, please consider our
service. If not, then we hope that you will remember us when the need arises
in the future. In any event, I hope that it will be possible for you to visit
with us at our open house on the 18th.

    Very Sincerely,

    George Reich
    Senior Sales Associate

Figure 14-1. Sample Cold Mailing—New Firm

ADVERTISING COST: THE NEW AND THE ESTABLISHED FIRM

The established firm points to its record and the results it has achieved. The new firm cannot do this, except by referring to the past performances of its members during their earlier associations with other firms. Since the established firm has a certain amount of recognition and reputation that it has earned, its advertising strategy will differ from that of the new brokerage.

A particular consideration for the established firm is budget. For a short while, the new firm can invest in a fairly large advertising program. The established firm must do its advertising and marketing on a pay-as-you-go basis; in the long run, the advertising expenditures must pay for themselves in business, because they must be financed out of the revenues that business brings in. Unduly expensive types of advertising must be avoided, no matter how glamorous they are. Any firm must consider the effectiveness of every dollar spent and make sure that the limited funds available for marketing and advertising are used to the best possible advantage.

As part of its startup costs, the new firm should budget an effective publicity and advertising effort to help make it known to the public. An established firm budgets and chooses its advertising based upon a continuing program of evaluation of its needs. While adjustments are made from time to time, its advertising will follow a fairly well-established pattern. The new firm will switch into this pattern as it becomes established.

IDENTIFICATION OF THE FIRM

The firm should adopt a symbol that it can use on all its advertising, letterhead paper, and signs. Such a symbol is called a logotype, or *logo*. All of us are familiar with several of these, and when we see one we immediately think of the company that uses it, and its products. Familiar examples are the Coca-Cola red and white circle, the arches of McDonald's restaurants, and any of a large number of filling station signs.

The objective of any business is to create a symbol as easily recognized as these. Except for a participant in a franchise program, a real estate firm does not need a nationally known symbol, since it does not do business nationwide. But it does have the opportunity to have a symbol well known in its locality.

Logo Symbol

A good symbol should be simple and easy to recognize. It also must be versatile: it must look good on letterhead, on business cards, in advertising, and on For Sale signs. Throughout this text, we have used a fictitious brokerage firm for our examples, the Dover Realty Company. Its logo can be seen in several of the figures in the book, including the two in this chapter. Note that it is quite simple: little more than a large capital "D," with the name of the company next to it. Simplicity is a virtue in the design of a logo. Simple design means instant recognition, provided that the design is memorable enough.

For Sale Sign

While our illustrations do not show color, it can be used in the logo and in the firm's For Sale sign. One consideration, however, is that the color reproduction costs more and in any case it cannot be used in newspaper advertising because of prohibitive cost. If the company's sign uses color, certain warnings are necessary. The purpose of the For Sale sign is to attract attention and to be easily visible as a means of identifying not only the real estate for sale, but also the firm holding the listing and the salesperson who secured it. Colors that blend into the background on which the sign will be placed should be avoided. These include many shades of green and brown, which are close to the tones of grass and earth and will not stand out satisfactorily from them. Signs that feature a lot of red ought to be avoided as well; for various reasons red, while it stands out well, is an offensive or annoying color to many people.

A great many firms use signs that feature white as the background with lettering and logo of a suitable color, usually with a border of the same color around the edge of the sign. This allows for one-color printing or painting of the signs, since most stock that is used is white to begin with. While it might be thought that a white sign will not stand out against the snow, the lettering on the sign will, and that is what the passers-by are supposed to notice. Against other natural backgrounds, white stands out very well.

The sign shown in Figure 14–2 is a good one. The large logo D is an immediate eyecatcher. The rest of the sign includes only the absolutely necessary information: a For Sale notice at the top, where it usually is placed, the name of the firm and its telephone number in large letters, and space at the bottom of the sign for the placement of the salesperson's name and telephone. No additional elaboration is necessary or desirable. There is room for all the information to be presented clearly. It is essential that the letters be large enough for someone to read at a distance of up to 30 feet or so; the sign usually is placed close to the front of the lot, and many people walking or driving by may want to stop and take down the names and numbers on it.

Construction of Sign

For Sale signs used to be made of metal, designed to be reused again and again. Holes were drilled at top and bottom to allow for the salesperson's placard and the SOLD notice to be bolted on when necessary. The main problem with metal signs is that they deteriorate after a time; they begin to acquire rust or get scratched and otherwise messy and unattractive.

A recent trend has been for brokerage firms to have signs made of tough fiberboard, prepared by a printing specialist rather than a painting shop. These are much less expensive than metal signs, although they are also less durable.

Figure 14-2. Examples of For Sale Sign, SOLD Sign, and Business Card.

Many firms will use a sign only once; when the property is sold the sign is discarded. With the fiberboard sign, the salesman's information placard (his name and telephone number) is printed on self-stick paper or plastic just like the familiar bumper sticker. When he posts a sign, he attaches his information sticker to each side in the appropriate place; on most signs this should be across the bottom, and the sign should be designed to allow for this space. When the property is sold, another sticker with the SOLD label is placed on the sign. It should be located where it will not obliterate the firm's or salesperson's name or telephone number. SOLD indicators should be of a contrasting color to the sign so that they will stand out; white lettering on a red background is suitable for most; however, if the background of the sign itself is a fairly dark color, red lettering on a white background will stand out better.

SOLD signs are one of the most effective forms of advertisement available to the firm and the listing salesperson; they are clear evidence that they operate successfully. Therefore, it is wise to arrange for the SOLD sign to remain up as long as possible.

Vandalism and Damage

The worst plague affecting For Sale and SOLD signs is vandalism; people remove them, knock them down, mark them up, or otherwise damage them. An advantage of the cheap fiberboard sign is that a vandalized one can be replaced at minimal expense, while a more expensive sign has to be written off at a much higher cost. If the sign is not vandalized, and weathers well, many salespeople will save it for use later on another property as a means of saving money. Some salespeople carry extra used signs with SOLD stickers on them; when the property is sold, they simply switch signs and then have a sign available to reuse on a new listing before it too is sold.

Cost, wear and tear, vandalism, and other damage argue against the use of other types of expensive signs. Some firms (particularly those affiliated with franchises) use very large wooden signs set on heavy posts. These are expensive, and may not be worth the extra cost even though they stand out well. Many of them are so large that they cannot be carried in the trunk of a normal automobile, so transportation to the site by truck is necessary. A large hole must be dug to accommodate them. Smaller signs on wooden or metal stakes can be driven into the ground by one person with a household hammer. When the large sign is removed, it leaves an ugly hole that the firm must pay to fill and even replant with grass; the smaller sign can be lifted out of the ground and the hole pressed down with a foot. If the large, elaborate sign is damaged or destroyed it will cost up to several hundred dollars to replace it or to repair it.

A FINAL WORD: PHILOSOPHY AND POLICY

This book has described the business philosophy and policies the successful real estate brokerage firm uses. Brokerage is a business, and must be treated as one if it is to be a successful enterprise. In our economic system, competition and the ups and downs of the real estate and money markets are continuous features of the industry.

Within our system, there is ample opportunity for both success and failure. Both will be due to the abilities and skills of the businesspeople operating the firms. Real estate brokerage can be an intensely rewarding business when the people involved are willing to work to make it so. Professional attitudes are essential. Honest, ethical, and skillful service at a fair price is the keystone to success in this business as it is in so many others. We hope that this book has given an indication of the needs and prospects that will lead to success for its readers.

DISCUSSION QUESTIONS AND PROJECTS

1. How should a new firm go about choosing the geographical area in which it will specialize?
2. How should a new firm go about selecting the type of property in which it will specialize?
3. Devise a program of long range (three years or more) goals and objectives that a new brokerage firm might establish. Be sure to include strategy for achieving them.

4. Compare the advertising needs and costs of a new firm and an established one.

5. What are the advantages and disadvantages of advertising on radio or television, from the point of view of a real estate brokerage firm?

6. Secure a sample of a cold mailing piece recently used by a firm in your area. Find out from the firm what the response to it was, and whether they feel it was worthwhile. Could you have made any suggestions for improvement?

7. Assume you are a real estate licensee (if you are not already). Make a list of all the people you think you should keep reminded of your work and availability. How would you accomplish this? Why are these people useful to you?

8. Collect pictures of the logos and sign designs for as many of the firms in your area as you can. Carefully critique them, making suggestions for improvement (with reasons given) for each one.

REFERENCES

HALL INSTITUTE OF REAL ESTATE, *Managing a Real Estate Team*, ch. 2. Hinsdale, IL: The Dryden Press, 1980.

MARCUS, BRUCE W., *Marketing Professional Services in Real Estate*. Chicago, IL: National Association of REALTORS®, 1981.

Profile of Real Estate Firms. Chicago, IL: Nationa' Association of REALTORS®, 1983.

PHILLIPS, BARBARA, "Getting Started in Real Estate," in *The McGraw-Hill Real Estate Handbook*, ed. Robert Irwin, ch. 31. New York, NY: McGraw-Hill Book Company, 1984.

PHILLIPS, BARBARA, "Office Management for Brokers," in *McGraw-Hill Real Estate Handbook*, ed. Robert Irwin, ch. 33. New York, NY: McGraw-Hill Book Company, 1984.

Real Estate Office Management: People Functions Systems, ch. 18, 19. Chicago, IL: REALTORS® National Marketing Institute, 1975.

SHENKEL, WILLIAM M., *Marketing Real Estate* (2nd ed.) ch. 18, 20. Englewood Cliffs, NJ: Prentice Hall, 1985.

Code of Ethics and Standards of Practice

of the
NATIONAL ASSOCIATION OF REALTORS®

Where the word REALTOR® is used in this Code and Preamble, it shall be deemed to include REALTOR-ASSOCIATE®. Pronouns shall be considered to include REALTORS® and REALTOR-ASSOCIATE®s of both genders.

Preamble...

Under all is the land. Upon its wise utilization and widely allocated ownership depend the survival and growth of free institutions and of our civilization. The REALTOR® should recognize that the interests of the nation and its citizens require the highest and best use of the land and the widest distribution of land ownership. They require the creation of adequate housing, the building of functioning cities, the development of productive industries and farms, and the preservation of a healthful environment.

Such interests impose obligations beyond those of ordinary commerce. They impose grave social responsibility and a patriotic duty to which the REALTOR® should dedicate himself, and for which he should be diligent in preparing himself. The REALTOR®, therefore, is zealous to maintain and improve the standards of his calling and shares with his fellow REALTORS® a common responsibility for its integrity and honor. The term REALTOR® has come to connote competency, fairness, and high integrity resulting from adherence to a lofty ideal of moral conduct in business relations. No inducement of profit and no instruction from clients ever can justify departure from this ideal.

In the interpretation of this obligation, a REALTOR® can take no safer guide than that which has been handed down through the centuries, embodied in the Golden Rule, "Whatsoever ye would that men should do to you, do ye even so to them."

Accepting this standard as his own, every REALTOR® pledges himself to observe its spirit in all of his activities and to conduct his business in accordance with the tenets set forth below.

Articles 1 through 5 are aspirational and establish ideals the REALTOR® should strive to attain.

ARTICLE 1

The REALTOR® should keep himself informed on matters affecting real estate in his community, the state, and nation so that he may be able to contribute responsibly to public thinking on such matters.

ARTICLE 2

In justice to those who place their interests in his care, the REALTOR® should endeavor always to be informed regarding laws, proposed legislation, governmental regulations, public policies, and current market conditions in order to be in a position to advise his clients properly.

ARTICLE 3

The REALTOR® should endeavor to eliminate in his community any practices which could be damaging to the public or bring discredit to the real estate profession. The REALTOR® should assist the governmental agency charged with regulating the practices of brokers and salesmen in his state. (Revised 11/87)

ARTICLE 4

To prevent dissension and misunderstanding and to assure better service to the owner, the REALTOR® should urge the exclusive listing of property unless contrary to the best interest of the owner. (Revised 11/87)

ARTICLE 5

In the best interests of society, of his associates, and his own business, the REALTOR® should willingly share with other REALTORS® the lessons of his experience and study for the benefit of the public, and should be loyal to the Board of REALTORS® of his community and active in its work.

Articles 6 through 23 establish specific obligations. Failure to observe these requirements subjects the REALTOR® to disciplinary action.

ARTICLE 6

The REALTOR® shall seek no unfair advantage over other REALTORS® and shall conduct his business so as to avoid controversies with other REALTORS®. (Revised 11/87)

- **Standard of Practice 6-1**

   "The REALTOR® shall not misrepresent the availability of access to show or inspect a listed property. (Cross-reference Article 22.)" (Revised 11/87)

ARTICLE 7

In accepting employment as an agent, the REALTOR® pledges himself to protect and promote the interests of the client. This obligation of absolute fidelity to the client's interests is primary, but it does not relieve the REALTOR® of the obligation to treat fairly all parties to the transaction.

- **Standard of Practice 7-1**

   "Unless precluded by law, government rule or regulation, or agreed otherwise in writing, the REALTOR® shall submit to the seller all offers until closing. Unless the REALTOR® and the seller agree otherwise, the REALTOR® shall not be obligated to continue to market the property after an offer has been accepted. Unless the subsequent offer is contingent upon the termination of an existing contract, the REALTOR® shall recommend that the seller obtain the advice of legal counsel prior to acceptance. (Cross-reference Article 17.)"

- **Standard of Practice 7-2**

   "The REALTOR®, acting as listing broker, shall submit all offers to the seller as quickly as possible."

- **Standard of Practice 7-3**

   "The REALTOR®, in attempting to secure a listing, shall not deliberately mislead the owner as to market value."

- **Standard of Practice 7-4**

   (Refer to Standard of Practice 22-1, which also relates to Article 7, Code of Ethics.)

- **Standard of Practice 7-5**

   (Refer to Standard of Practice 22-2, which also relates to Article 7, Code of Ethics.)

- **Standard of Practice 7-6**

   "The REALTOR®, when acting as a principal in a real estate transaction, cannot avoid his responsibilities under the Code of Ethics."

ARTICLE 8

The REALTOR® shall not accept compensation from more than one party, even if permitted by law, without the full knowledge of all parties to the transaction.

ARTICLE 9

The REALTOR® shall avoid exaggeration, misrepresentation, or concealment of pertinent facts relating to the property or the transaction. The REALTOR® shall not, however, be obligated to discover latent defects in the property or to advise on matters outside the scope of his real estate license.

• Standard of Practice 9-1

"The REALTOR® shall not be a party to the naming of a false consideration in any document, unless it be the naming of an obviously nominal consideration."

• Standard of Practice 9-2

(Refer to Standard of Practice 21-3, which also relates to Article 9, Code of Ethics.)

• Standard of Practice 9-3

(Refer to Standard of Practice 7-3, which also relates to Article 9, Code of Ethics.)

• Standard of Practice 9-4

"The REALTOR® shall not offer a service described as 'free of charge' when the rendering of a service is contingent on the obtaining of a benefit such as a listing or commission."

• Standard of Practice 9-5

"The REALTOR® shall, with respect to the subagency of another REALTOR®, timely communicate any change of compensation for subagency services to the other REALTOR® prior to the time such REALTOR® produces a prospective buyer who has signed an offer to purchase the property for which the subagency has been offered through MLS or otherwise by the listing agency."

• Standard of Practice 9-6

"REALTORS® shall disclose their REALTOR® status when seeking information from another REALTOR® concerning real property for which the other REALTOR® is an agent or subagent."

• Standard of Practice 9-7

"The offering of premiums, prizes, merchandise discounts or other inducements to list or sell is not, in itself, unethical even if receipt of the benefit is contingent on listing or purchasing through the REALTOR® making the offer. However, the REALTOR® must exercise care and candor in any such advertising or other public or private representations so that any party interested in receiving or otherwise benefiting from the REALTOR®'s offer will have clear, thorough, advance understanding of all the terms and conditions of the offer. The offering of any inducements to do business is subject to the limitations and restrictions of state law and the ethical obligations established by Article 9, as interpreted by any applicable Standard of Practice."

• Standard of Practice 9-8

"The REALTOR® shall be obligated to discover and disclose adverse factors reasonably apparent to someone with expertise in only those areas required by their real estate licensing authority. Article 9 does not impose upon the REALTOR® the obligation of expertise in other professional or technical disciplines. (Cross-reference Article 11.)"

ARTICLE 10

The REALTOR® shall not deny equal professional services to any person for reasons of race, creed, sex, or country of national origin. The REALTOR® shall not be party to any plan or agreement to discriminate against a person or persons on the basis of race, creed, sex, or country of national origin.

ARTICLE 11

A REALTOR® is expected to provide a level of competent service in keeping with the standards of practice in those fields in which the REALTOR® customarily engages.

The REALTOR® shall not undertake to provide specialized professional services concerning a type of property or service that is outside his field of competence unless he engages the assistance of one who is competent on such types of property or service, or unless the facts are fully disclosed to the client. Any person engaged to provide such assistance shall be so identified to the client and his contribution to the assignment should be set forth.

The REALTOR® shall refer to the Standards of Practice of the National Association as to the degree of competence that a client has a right to expect the REALTOR® to possess, taking into consideration the complexity of the problem, the availability of expert assistance, and the opportunities for experience available to the REALTOR®.

• Standard of Practice 11-1

"Whenever a REALTOR® submits an oral or written opinion of the value of real property for a fee, his opinion shall be supported by a memorandum in his file or an appraisal report, either of which shall include as a minimum the following:

1. Limiting conditions
2. Any existing or contemplated interest
3. Defined value
4. Date applicable
5. The estate appraised
6. A description of the property
7. The basis of the reasoning including applicable market data and/or capitalization computation

"This report or memorandum shall be available to the Professional Standards Committee for a period of at least two years (beginning subsequent to final determination of the court if the appraisal is involved in litigation) to ensure compliance with Article 11 of the Code of Ethics of the NATIONAL ASSOCIATION OF REALTORS®."

• Standard of Practice 11-2

"The REALTOR® shall not undertake to make an appraisal when his employment or fee is contingent upon the amount of appraisal."

• Standard of Practice 11-3

"REALTORS® engaged in real estate securities and syndications transactions are engaged in an activity subject to regulations beyond those governing real estate transactions generally, and therefore have the affirmative obligation to be informed of applicable federal and state laws, and rules and regulations regarding these types of transactions."

ARTICLE 12

The REALTOR® shall not undertake to provide professional services concerning a property or its value where he has a present or contemplated interest unless such interest is specifically disclosed to all affected parties.

• Standard of Practice 12-1

(Refer to Standards of Practice 9-4 ad 16-1, which also relate to Article 12, Code of Ethics.)

ARTICLE 13

The REALTOR® shall not acquire an interest in or buy for himself, any member of his immediate family, his firm or any member thereof, or any entity in which he has a substantial ownership interest, property listed with him, without making the true position known to the listing owner. In selling property owned by himself, or in which he has any interest, the REALTOR® shall reveal the facts of his ownership or interest to the purchaser.

• Standard of Practice 13-1

"For the protection of all parties, the disclosures required by Article 13 shall be in writing and provided by the REALTOR® prior to the signing of any contract."

ARTICLE 14

In the event of a controversy between REALTORS® associated with different firms, arising out of their relationship as REALTORS®, the REALTORS® shall submit the dispute to arbitration in accordance with the regulations of their Board or Boards rather than litigate the matter.

• Standard of Practice 14-1

"The filing of litigation and refusal to withdraw from it by a REALTOR® in an arbitrable matter constitutes a refusal to arbitrate."

• Standard of Practice 14-2

"The obligation to arbitrate mandated by Article 14 includes arbitration requests initiated by the REALTOR®'s client."

ARTICLE 15

If a REALTOR® is charged with unethical practice or is asked to present evidence in any disciplinary proceeding or investigation, he shall place all pertinent facts before the proper tribunal of the Member Board or affiliated institute, society, or council of which he is a member.

• Standard of Practice 15-1

"The REALTOR® shall not be subject to disciplinary proceedings in more than one Board of REALTORS® with respect to alleged violations of the Code of Ethics relating to the same transaction."

• Standard of Practice 15-2

"The REALTOR® shall not make any unauthorized disclosure or dissemination of the allegations, findings, or decision developed in connection with an ethics hearing or appeal."

• Standard of Practice 15-3

"The REALTOR® shall not obstruct the Board's investigative or disciplinary proceedings by instituting or threatening to institute actions for libel, slander or defamation against any party to a professional standards proceeding or their witnesses." (Approved 11/87).

ARTICLE 16

When acting as agent, the REALTOR® shall not accept any commission, rebate, or profit on expenditures made for his principal-owner, without the principal's knowledge and consent.

• Standard of Practice 16-1

"The REALTOR® shall not recommend or suggest to a principal or a customer the use of services of another organization or business entity in which he has a direct interest without disclosing such interest at the time of the recommendation or suggestion."

ARTICLE 17

The REALTOR® shall not engage in activities that constitute the unauthorized practice of law and shall recommend that legal counsel be obtained when the interest of any party to the transaction requires it.

ARTICLE 18

The REALTOR® shall keep in a special account in an appropriate financial institution, separated from his own funds, monies coming into his possession in trust for other persons, such as escrows, trust funds, clients' monies, and other like items.

ARTICLE 19

The REALTOR® shall be careful at all times to present a true picture in his advertising and representations to the public. The REALTOR® shall also ensure that his status as a broker or a REALTOR® is clearly identifiable in any such advertising.

• Standard of Practice 19-1

"The REALTOR® shall not submit or advertise property without authority, and in any offering, the price quoted shall not be other than that agreed upon with the owners."

• Standard of Practice 19-2

(Refer to Standard of Practice 9-4, which also relates to Article 19, Code of Ethics.)

• Standard of Practice 19-3

"The REALTOR®, when advertising unlisted real property for sale in which he has an ownership interest, shall disclose his status as both an owner and as a REALTOR® or real estate licensee."

• Standard of Practice 19-4

"The REALTOR® shall not advertise nor permit any person employed by or affiliated with him to advertise listed property without disclosing the name of the firm."

• Standard of Practice 19-5

"The REALTOR®, when acting as listing broker, retains the exclusive right to represent that he has 'sold' the property, even if the sale resulted through the cooperative efforts of another broker. However, after the transaction has been consummated, the listing broker may not prohibit a successful cooperating broker from advertising his 'participation' or 'assistance' in the transaction, or from making similar representations provided that any such representation does not create the impression that the cooperating broker had listed or sold the property. (Cross-reference Article 21.)"

ARTICLE 20

The REALTOR®, for the protection of all parties, shall see that financial obligations and commitments regarding real estate transactions are in writing, expressing the exact agreement of the parties. A copy of each agreement shall be furnished to each party upon his signing such agreement.

• Standard of Practice 20-1

"At the time of signing or initialing, the REALTOR® shall furnish to the party a copy of any document signed or initialed."

• Standard of Practice 20-2

"For the protection of all parties, the REALTOR® shall use reasonable care to ensure that documents pertaining to the purchase and sale of real estate are kept current through the use of written extensions or amendments."

ARTICLE 21

The REALTOR® shall not engage in any practice or take any action inconsistent with the agency of another REALTOR®.

• Standard of Practice 21-1

"Signs giving notice of property for sale, rent, lease, or exchange shall not be placed on property without the consent of the owner."

• Standard of Practice 21-2

"The REALTOR® obtaining information from a listing broker about a specific property shall not convey this information to, nor invite the cooperation of a third party broker without the consent of the listing broker."

• Standard of Practice 21-3

"The REALTOR® shall not solicit a listing which is currently listed exclusively with another broker. However, if the listing broker, when asked by the REALTOR®, refuses to disclose the expiration date and nature of such listing; i.e., an exclusive right to sell, an exclusive agency, open listing, or other form of contractual agreement between the listing broker and his client, the REALTOR®, unless precluded by law, may contact the owner to secure such information and may discuss the terms upon which he might take a future listing or, alternatively, may take a listing to become effective upon expiration of any existing exclusive listing."

• Standard of Practice 21-4

"The REALTOR® shall not use information obtained by him from the listing broker, through offers to cooperate received through Multiple Listing Services or other sources authorized by the listing broker, for the purpose of creating a referral prospect to a third broker, or for creating a buyer prospect unless such use is authorized by the listing broker."

• Standard of Practice 21-5

"The fact that a property has been listed exclusively with a REALTOR® shall not preclude or inhibit any other REALTOR® from soliciting such listing after its expiration."

• Standard of Practice 21-6

"The fact that a property owner has retained a REALTOR® as his exclusive agent in respect of one or more past transactions creates no interest or agency which precludes or inhibits other REALTORS® from seeking such owner's future business."

• Standard of Practice 21-7

"The REALTOR® shall be free to list property which is 'open listed' at any time, but shall not knowingly obligate the seller to pay more than one commission except with the seller's knowledgeable consent." (Revised 11/87)

• Standard of Practice 21-8

"When a REALTOR® is contacted by an owner regarding the sale of property that is exclusively listed with another broker, and the REALTOR® has not directly or indirectly initiated the discussion, unless precluded by law, the REALTOR® may discuss the terms upon which he might take a future listing or, alternatively, may take a listing to become effective upon expiration of any existing exclusive listing."

• Standard of Practice 21-9

"In cooperative transactions a REALTOR® shall compensate the co-operating REALTOR® (principal broker) and shall not compensate nor offer to compensate, directly or indirectly, any of the sales licensees employed by or affiliated with another REALTOR® without the prior express knowledge and consent of the cooperating broker."

• Standard of Practice 21-10

"Article 21 does not preclude REALTORS® from making general announcements to property owners describing their services and the terms of their availability even though some recipients may have exclusively listed their property for sale or lease with another REALTOR®. A general telephone canvass, general mailing or distribution addressed to all property owners in a given geographical area or in a given profession, business, club, or organization, or other classification or group is deemed 'general' for purposes of this standard.

Article 21 is intended to recognize as unethical two basic types of solicitation:

First, telephone or personal solicitations of property owners who have been identified by a real estate sign, multiple listing compilation, or other information service as having exclusively listed their property with another REALTOR®; and

Second, mail or other forms of written solicitations of property owners whose properties are exclusively listed with another REALTOR® when such solicitations are not part of a general mailing but are directed specifically to property owners identified through compilations of current listings, 'for sale' signs, or other sources of information required by Article 22 and Multiple Listing Service rules to be made available to other REALTORS® under offers of subagency or cooperation."

• Standard of Practice 21-11

"The REALTOR®, prior to accepting a listing, has an affirmative obligation to make reasonable efforts to determine whether the property is subject to a current, valid exclusive listing agreement."

ARTICLE 22

In the sale of property which is exclusively listed with a REALTOR®, the REALTOR® shall utilize the services of other brokers upon mutually agreed upon terms when it is in the best interests of the client.

Negotiations concerning property which is listed exclusively shall be carried on with the listing broker, not with the owner, except with the consent of the listing broker.

• Standard of Practice 22-1

"It is the obligation of the selling broker as subagent of the listing broker to disclose immediately all pertinent facts to the listing broker prior to as well as after the contract is executed."

• Standard of Practice 22-2

"The REALTOR®, when submitting offers to the seller, shall present each in an objective and unbiased manner."

• Standard of Practice 22-3

"The REALTOR® shall disclose the existence of an accepted offer to any broker seeking cooperation."

ARTICLE 23

The REALTOR® shall not publicly disparage the business practice of a competitor nor volunteer an opinion of a competitor's transaction. If his opinion is sought and if the REALTOR® deems it appropriate to respond, such opinion shall be rendered with strict professional integrity and courtesy.

The Code of Ethics was adopted in 1913. Amended at the Annual Convention in 1924, 1928, 1950, 1951, 1952, 1955, 1956, 1961, 1962, 1974, 1982, 1986, and 1987.

EXPLANATORY NOTE CONCERNING THE STANDARDS OF PRACTICE

The reader should be aware of the following policy which has been approved by the Board of Directors of the National Association:

"In filing a charge of an alleged violation of the Code of Ethics by a REALTOR®, the charge shall read as an alleged violation of one or more Articles of the Code. A Standard of Practice may only be cited in support of the charge."

The Standards of Practice are not an integral part of the Code but rather serve to clarify the ethical obligations imposed by the various Articles. The Standards of Practice supplement, and do not substitute for, the Case Interpretations in *Interpretations of the Code of Ethics.*

Modifications to existing Standards of Practice and additional new Standards of Practice are approved from time to time. The reader is cautioned to ensure that the most recent publications are utilized.

INDEX*

Abstract company, 163
Advertising, 161-62,
    200-204, 258-68
  of brokerage firm, 260-68
  classified, 200-202
  composition, 202-3
  costs, 258-59, 261
  mailouts, 260-62
  office open house, 259-60
  radio-tv, 258-59
  tombstone, 202
  truth in advertising, 203-4
  types, 200-202
Agency law, 42-44, 134-35,
    206-9, 268-71
  agent defined, 42-43
  duties, 43-44
  general agent, 42
  special agent, 42
Application, 100-111
  application form, 104-5,
    106-7
Appraisals, 194-97
Annual percentage rate
    (APR), 23-24, 203-4
Automobile, 246-48

Bonuses, 100-101, 180-82
  delayed, 182

Borrowing, 221-22
Branch office, 253-54
Breach of contract, 51-53,
    86-93, 168-72
Broker, 3-11, 13-27, 37 (see
    also relationship or
    aspect desired)
Brokerage, 3-11, 13-27 (see
    also relationship or
    aspect desired)
Budgeting, 215-16
Building codes, 21
"Bullpen," 237, 239

Cash flow, 144, 213-14
Caveat emptor, 31
Classified advertising,
    200-202
Closing, see Settlement
Commingling funds, 38-40
Commision payments,
    141-46, 158-60,
    176-80
  antitrust, 141
  100%, 171-79
  split: between brokers, 38,
    158-60, 177
  split: broker-salesperson,
    176-80, 181-82, 189

suing for, 135-38, 169
  when earned, 38, 135-38
Commission rates, 141-46,
    148
  flat fee, 145
  setting rate, 141-43
  7-5-3, 144
  varying, 143-44
Communication, 66, 191-93
Company dollar, 160,
    214-15
Company listing, 183-86
Compensation, 82-83,
    112-13, 143, 176-89,
    226-27 (see also
    Bonuses, Commission
    payments, Incentive)
  during training, 85, 93,
    187-88
  of independent
    contractor, 82-83,
    176-78
  nonmoney, 183-87,
  of support personnel,
    112-13
Competent parties, 48-49,
    56-57
Computer, 243-46
Conference room, 237-39
Consideration, 46-47

*The terms *broker, brokerage, management* and *salesperson* appear so frequently in this book that a listing of the pages upon which they are used would be so long as to be virtually useless. Therefore, for other than general references, the reader should consult the specific terms for which a relationship to, or aspect of, these four terms is sought.

Contests, 193-94
Contracts, 44-54, 55-56,
    62-63, 86-94, 113-14,
    131-35, 151-56,
    168-74
  breach of, 51-53, 86-93,
    168-72
  competence, 48-49, 56-57
  consideration, 46-47
  discharge, 51-52
  employment, 86-94
  enforcement, 45-46
  forms, 89-92, 132, 154-55
  independent contractor,
    87-93
  injustice, 52-53
  lawful purpose, 49-50
  legal form, 50
  listing, *see* Listing contract
  mutual agreement, 46
  nature, 44-45
  preparation, 131-33,
    151-52
  requirements, 46-50
  sales, *see* Sales contract
  termination, 62-63,
    113-14, 133-35,
    146-49, 168-72
Control, 84-85, 191-97 (*see
    also* Compensation,
    Training)
  of independent
    contractor, 84-85
Cooperation among brokers,
    6, 14, 133-34, 158-60,
    177 (*see also* Multiple
    listing)
Cost-effectiveness, 217-19
Costs, 212-15, 217-19,
    222-29
  desk cost, 214
  fixed costs, 213, 216,
    223-27
  opportunity costs, 219-21
  startup, 222-29
  variable costs, 213, 216,
    224-27

Damages (in lawsuit), 170

Default, 52-53, 55-56,
    169-72, 173-74
  by buyer, 169-72, 173-74
  by seller, 168-69
Desk cost, 214
Discrimination, 108
Draws against commissions,
    82-83, 187-88
Duress, 50-51

Earnest money, 138, 170,
    173
Education, 28-29, 31-32
Employee, 79-85 (*see also*
    Independent
    contractor, Support
    personnel)
Employment contract, 87-92
Errors and omissions,
    220-21
Escrow account, 38-40
Establishing new firm,
    222-29, 250-58,
    258-67
Exclusive agency listing, 133,
    138-39
Exclusive right-to-sell listing,
    133, 138-39, 159

Fair housing, 23
Favoritism, 73-74, 183-84
Federal legislation, 23-25,
    79-86, 163-64
Financial concepts, 160,
    204-5, 212-14, 217-19,
    222-29 (*see also*
    Company dollar)
Financial planning, 215-16,
    222-29
Financing, 23, 204-5
Firing, *see* Termination
Fixed costs, 213, 216, 223,
    227
Floor time, 85, 96
Forecasting costs and
    expenses, 222-29
For sale by owner (FSBO),
    139-40

For Sale signs, *see* Signs
Franchising, 28-29, 161-62,
    265, 267
Fraud, 40, 50-51, 208-9

Goals and objectives, 60,
    67-71, 118-20

HUD-1 form, *see* Uniform
    Settlement Statement

Image of firm, 256-58
Incentive, 100-101, 180-84,
    191-94
  bonuses, 100-101, 180-82
  contests, 193-94
Income, 213, 227-29
Incompetency, 48-49, 56-57
Independent contractor,
    79-94, 176-89
  advantages, 79-80, 84
  compensation, 79-80,
    176-79
  contract, 86-94
  contract example, 87-92
  control, 84-85
  definition, 79-82
  draws against
    commissions, 83
  expenses, 79, 83
  floor time, 85, 96
  fringe benefits, 79, 83
  and IRS, 79-83, 85-86
  and 100% commission,
    177-79
  problems, 84-85
Information card, 131, 142
Information services, 162-63
Insurance, 220-21
IRS, *see* US Internal
    Revenue Service

Job description, 69-71, 101,
    117-18

Land contract, 152-53
Land sales regulations, 25
Land use regulation, 21-22, 232
Law:
  agency, 42-44, 55-56, 86-94
  contract, 44-54, 131-35, 146-49, 151-57, 168-72
  federal, 23-25
  license, 32-42, 51-52, 55-56
Lawsuit, 135-38, 169-70
Leasing, 3
Legal action, broker's vulnerability, 31-32, 205-6
Legal person, 48
Liability of broker, 205-7
License law, 1, 32-42, 55-56, 136
  administration, 34-35
  commission payments, 38
  education requirements, 28-29, 31-32,
  examination, 32-33
  exemption, 34
  handling money, 38-40, 55-56
  infractions, 40-42, 55-56
  licensee liability, 31-32, 55-56
  penalties, 35-36, 55-56
Line functions, 61, 64-66
Line personnel, 61, 64-66, 79-85
Listing activity, 5, 16-18, 131-41, 183-86
  company listing, 183, 185-86
  referred listing, 185-86
Listing contract, 130-35, 137, 146-49
  cancellation, 133-35, 146-49
  dissolving, 146-49
  example, 130-32

exclusive agency, 133, 138-39
exclusive right-to-sell, 133-34, 138-39
expiration, 133
information for, 131, 141-42
net listing, 134
new homes, 139
open listing, 133, 139
termination, 134-35, 146-49, 168-69
Listing policy, 138-40, 181-83
Lockbox, 197-98
Logo symbol, 263-64

Mailouts, 260-62
Management, 60-77 (*see also* specific relationship or aspect desired)
Market area, 233, 252-54
Market segment, 252-54
Marketing, 17-19, 131-33, 141, 151-74, 194-204, 254-66 (*see also* Advertising)
  of brokerage firm, 254-66
Misrepresentation, 41, 50-51, 208-9
Mortgage financing, 204-5
Multiple listing (multilist), 6, 14, 159-60

National Association of REALTORS®, 26-27, 118, 130, 187, 198, 268-71
Net listing, 134
New properties, 181-84

Offer and acceptance, *see* Sale contract
Offers, 153, 156-57
  acceptance, 153
  alterations, 153, 156

counter-offer, 153, 156
  nonbinding nature, 156-57
  notification, 157
  transmitting, 152-53
Office, 232-46
  broker-manager, 239
  computer facilities, 243-46
  conference room, 237-39
  furnishings and equipment, 241-43
  in home, 232, 247-48
  layout, 237-41
  location, 232-36
  reception area, 238-40
  salesperson's station, 237-39
  shared facility, 232
  storage, 240-41
100% commission plan, 177-79
Open house, 197, 259-60
Open listing, 133, 139-40
Opportunity cost, 219-21
Organization, 60-66
  charts, 63
  patterns, 62-66

Personnel, 61, 64-66, 72-76, 97-114, 157-63
  application, 101-5, 109
  interview, 102-3, 108, 110-11
  investigations, 108-10
  line personnel, 61, 64-66, 111-13
  qualifications, 102-3, 108
  selection, 100-113
  sources, 97-100
  support personnel, 61, 64-66, 111-13
  termination, 183-84
  testing, 108, 112
Planning, 10-11, 67-68, 170-71, 222-29, 251-54
Policy manual, 86, 116-28

arrangement, 118
example, 120-27
and independent
    contractor, 119
purpose, 117
revision, 119
Principal, 42, 133
Principles of Real Estate
    requirement, 10
references, 10
Professionalism, 25-27, 117,
    119-28, 131, 206-9,
    268-71
Profit, 212, 214-15, 216-17,
    222-29
Profit analysis, 222-29
Proper practice, 32-42,
    42-44, 206-9, 268-71
Prospects, 199-200, 203

Qualifying buyers, 171-72

Real Estate Commission,
    34-35
Real Estate Recovery Fund,
    35
Real Estate Settlement
    Procedures Act
    (RESPA), 25, 164
REALTOR®, 26-27, 118,
    130, 187, 268-71
REALTORS® Code of
    Ethics, 26, 118,
    268-71
Reception area, 238-40
Receptionist, 238, 240
Recruitment, 97-100
Reference materials, 242-43
Referral service, 162-63
Referred listing, 185-86
Regulation Z, 23-24
RESPA, see Real Estate
    Settlement Procedures
    Act

Revenue, 212, 214-16,
    226-29
Role-playing, 192-93
Room arrangement (office),
    237-41

Sale contract, 6, 19-20,
    151-55
form, 152, 154-55
land contract, 152-53
use as offer, 153, 156-57
Sales contests, 193-94
Sales force, see Sales
    personnel
Sales management, 64-66,
    69-71, 117-27, 140,
    147-48, 191-209
Sales manager, 64-66, 69-71,
    79-85, 93, 95-96, 101,
    140, 147-48, 198-209,
    228-30
Sales meetings, 97, 191
Salesperson, 37-38, 79-85,
    229-30 (see also
    specific relationship
    or aspect desired)
Salesperson's office station,
    237-39, 241-42,
    246-48
Sales personnel, 33-39,
    72-75, 79-83, 85-86,
    100-14, 116-28,
    135-36, 141-43,
    176-89, 226, 229-30,
    237-39, 246-48
application, 101-3, 104-5,
    109
commission split, 176-82,
    189
compensation, 83, 86, 101,
    112-13, 143, 176-89,
    217-18, 226
desk cost, 218
employment contract,
    86-94
favoritism, 73-74, 182-84
floor time, 85, 96

independent contractor,
    79-86, 95-96
licensing, 32-42
office station, 237-39,
    241-42, 246-48
100% commission, 177-79
policy manual, 86, 116-28
qualifications, 102-4
selection, 97-101,
sources, 97-100
termination, 113-14
testing, 108
training, 94, 117-18, 177,
    187-88
Secretarial station, 239, 242
Secretary, 75-76, 101
Seed money, 229
Seller's market, 177
Seminars, 187-88, 192
Settlement, 163-68
agent, 163-64
proration, 167
reporting to IRS, 163-64
Uniform Settlement
    Statement, 164-68
7-5-3 commission, 144
Showing property, 197-99,
    208-9
Signs, 22, 138-39, 161-62,
    264-67
construction, 264-66
costs, 264-67
For Sale, 22, 138-39,
    161-62, 264-67
ordinances, 22
Sold, 22, 139, 264-67
vandalism and damage,
    265-66
Site selection, 232-33
Specialization, 250-54
Specific performance, 170
Software, 246
Startup, 222-29, 250-67
Statute of Frauds, 50
Statute of Limitations, 52
Supervision, 116-17, 180-83
Support functions, 61-62,
    65-66, 183, 187

Support personnel, 61-62, 65-66, 75-76, 93-94, 101, 111-13, 183, 187
  compensation, 112-13
  selection, 111-13
  testing, 112
  termination, 113-14

Telephone, 239-41
Termination, 113-14
Time management, 229-30
Title company, 163
Tombstone ad, 202
Training, 99, 117-18, 177, 187-88, 192-94

Trust account, 38-40, 55-56, 211
Trustee, 136
Trust money, 38-40, 55-56, 136, 211
Truth in advertising, 203-4
Truth in lending, 23-24, 203-4

Uniform Settlement Statement, 164-68
US Internal Revenue Service, 80-82, 84-85, 163-64

Unsold listing, 146

Variable costs, 213, 216, 224, 227
Videotaping, 192-93

Women in real estate brokerage, 108

Zero-base budgeting, 216
Zoning, 21-22, 232